Type This URL in Your Browser → **https://bit.ly/Guess_What_This**

Robin McRaven..Words Count: **81,615**
United States, Nashua, NH, 03063.............................Number of Pages: **328**
Documented Publishing LLC...................................Book Size: **5*8 Inches**
documented.publishing@gmail.com

The Untold Story Behind <u>Satoshi Nakamoto</u> and Bitcoin

Digital Currencies, Ethereum, Crypto Tokens, and Blockchains Revolution.

Robin McRaven

Robin McRaven

Type This URL in Your Browser → **https://bit.ly/Guess_What_This**

As a huge thanks for landing on this page, you can enjoy these ***100% FREE Bonuses today!***

• **Bonus 1**

Join Our Exclusive Mastermind
"MEMBERS ONLY"
Group ***for FREE*** Where We Discuss
More About the Book, Share Our Opinions,
and Support Each Other.
Go to: https://bit.ly/Exclusive_Freebies

• **Bonus 2**

Love Audiobooks? Get Instant Access
to The ***Audio Version*** Once Available
For a Limited Time…
Secure Your FREE Copy
Here: bit.ly/Exclusive_Freebies

• **Bonus 3**

Get All Future Updates, Freebies and Offers
Directly with ***NO Extra Charges!***

Robin McRaven

Type This URL in Your Browser → **https://bit.ly/Guess_What_This**

© Copyright [2024] [Robin McRaven] All rights reserved.

- No part of this book may be reproduced, stored in a retrieval system, or transmitted in any form or by any means, electronic, mechanical, photocopying, recording, or otherwise, without prior written permission of the publisher, except for brief quotations in a review or scholarly article.

- This is an original work of fiction [or non-fiction] by [Robin McRaven]. Any resemblance to actual persons, living or dead, or actual events is purely coincidental.

Legal Notice:
The reader is <u>solely responsible for any actions</u> taken based on the information contained in this book. The author and publisher expressly disclaim any responsibility or liability for any damages or losses incurred by the reader as a result of such actions.

Disclaimer:
This book is intended for <u>educational purposes only.</u> The information contained within is not intended as, and should not be construed as medical, legal, or professional advice. The content is provided as general information and is not a substitute for professional advice or treatment.

Robin McRaven

Table of content

Introduction	10
Chapter 1: Origins of Satoshi Nakamoto	12
Chapter 2: The Enigma of Satoshi's Identity	15
Chapter 3: Early Influences on Satoshi's Thinking	18
Chapter 4: A Vision Takes Shape	21
Chapter 5: The Birth of Bitcoin	24
Chapter 6: The Genesis Block	27
Chapter 7: Mining the First Bitcoins	30
Chapter 8: The Cypherpunk Connection	33
Chapter 9: The Mysterious Forum Posts	36
Chapter 10: Satoshi's Early Collaborators	39
Chapter 11: The White Paper Revealed	42
Chapter 12: Initial Reactions to Bitcoin	45
Chapter 13: The First Transactions	48
Chapter 14: The Creation of BitcoinTalk	51
Chapter 15: Satoshi's Growing Influence	54
Chapter 16: The Rise of Alternative Cryptocurrencies	57
Chapter 17: Satoshi's Disappearance	60
Chapter 18: Satoshi's Last Correspondence	63
Chapter 19: Satoshi's Legacy in the Crypto Community	66
Chapter 20: The Hunt for Satoshi Nakamoto	69
Chapter 21: The Satoshi Nakamoto Controversies	72
Chapter 22: Theories on Satoshi's True Identity	75
Chapter 23: Satoshi's Possible Motivations	78
Chapter 24: Satoshi's Economic Philosophy	81
Chapter 25: The Evolution of Bitcoin's Technology	84
Chapter 26: Scaling Challenges and Solutions	87
Chapter 27: Bitcoin's Adoption by Merchants	90
Chapter 28: The Silk Road and Bitcoin's Dark Side	93
Chapter 29: Government and Regulatory Responses	96
Chapter 30: Satoshi's Influence on Blockchain Technology	99
Chapter 31: Bitcoin's Price Volatility	102
Chapter 32: The Mt. Gox Scandal	105
Chapter 33: Satoshi's Reemergence?	108

Chapter 34: The Bitcoin Halving Events	110
Chapter 35: Bitcoin's Impact on Remittances	113
Chapter 36: Satoshi's Vision for a Decentralized Future	116
Chapter 37: Forks and the Creation of Bitcoin Cash	119
Chapter 38: The Lightning Network and Scalability	122
Chapter 39: Institutional Adoption of Bitcoin	125
Chapter 40: Satoshi's Intellectual Contributions	128
Chapter 41: Bitcoin's Role in Financial Inclusion	131
Chapter 42: Bitcoin and Energy Consumption Concerns	134
Chapter 43: The Rise of Bitcoin Exchanges	137
Chapter 44: Satoshi's Unspent Bitcoin	140
Chapter 45: Government Seizures of Bitcoin	143
Chapter 46: Satoshi's Influence on Privacy and Security	146
Chapter 47: Bitcoin's Impact on Global Politics	149
Chapter 48: The Evolution of Bitcoin Wallets	152
Chapter 49: Satoshi's Absence and the Bitcoin Community	155
Chapter 50: The Emergence of Bitcoin ATMs	158
Chapter 51: Bitcoin and the Gig Economy	161
Chapter 52: Satoshi's Potential Wealth	164
Chapter 53: Bitcoin's Role in Humanitarian Aid	167
Chapter 54: The Bitcoin Mining Industry	170
Chapter 55: Satoshi's Technical Prowess	174
Chapter 56: Bitcoin's Impact on Financial Institutions	177
Chapter 57: The Cryptocurrency Market Volatility	181
Chapter 58: Satoshi's Influence on Privacy Coins	185
Chapter 59: The Future of Bitcoin Governance	188
Chapter 60: The Rise of Central Bank Digital Currencies	191
Chapter 61: Satoshi's Cultural Impact	194
Chapter 62: Bitcoin's Relationship with Traditional Banking	197
Chapter 63: Satoshi's Ideals and Libertarian Philosophy	200
Chapter 64: The Decentralized Finance (DeFi) Movement	203
Chapter 65: The Ethereum and Bitcoin Connection	206
Chapter 66: Satoshi's Stance on Smart Contracts	210
Chapter 67: Bitcoin and the Internet of Things (IoT)	213
Chapter 68: The Global Reach of Bitcoin	217
Chapter 69: Satoshi's Influence on Cryptocurrency Regulations	220

Type This URL in Your Browser → **https://bit.ly/Guess_What_This**

Chapter 70: Bitcoin's Role in Wealth Inequality	*224*
Chapter 71: Satoshi's Educational Contributions	*228*
Chapter 72: The Psychology of Bitcoin Adoption	*232*
Chapter 73: Bitcoin's Impact on Developing Economies	*236*
Chapter 74: Satoshi's Potential Identity Revealed?	*240*
Chapter 75: The Role of Whales in Bitcoin's Ecosystem	*243*
Chapter 76: The Environmental Debate Surrounding Bitcoin	*247*
Chapter 77: Satoshi's View on Digital Privacy	*251*
Chapter 78: Bitcoin's Influence on Traditional Investments	*254*
Chapter 79: The Quest for Satoshi's Lost Bitcoins	*258*
Chapter 80: Bitcoin's Integration with Social Media	*261*
Chapter 81: Satoshi's Influence on Cryptocurrency Exchanges	*264*
Chapter 82: Bitcoin's Use Cases Beyond Currency	*268*
Chapter 83: Satoshi's Intellectual Legacy	*271*
Chapter 84: The Role of Bitcoin in Political Campaigns	*275*
Chapter 85: The Battle for Bitcoin's Soul	*278*
Chapter 86: Satoshi's Impact on Online Fundraising	*281*
Chapter 87: The Connection Between Bitcoin and Cybercrime	*285*
Chapter 88: The Rise of Stablecoins and Satoshi's Perspective	*288*
Chapter 89: The Socioeconomic Implications of Bitcoin	*291*
Chapter 90: Satoshi's Philosophy on Financial Empowerment	*294*
Chapter 91: Bitcoin's Intersection with Artificial Intelligence	*297*
Chapter 92: The Bitcoin Community's Response to Satoshi's Absence	*300*
Chapter 93: Satoshi's Influence on Cryptocurrency Education	*303*
Chapter 94: The Dark Web and Bitcoin's Role	*306*
Chapter 95: Bitcoin's Influence on Microtransactions	*309*
Chapter 96: Satoshi's Vision for a Cashless Society	*312*
Chapter 97: The Bitcoin Patent Controversy	*315*
Chapter 98: The Cultural Impact of "Satoshi Nakamoto"	*318*
Chapter 99: Bitcoin's Potential in Peer-to-Peer Lending	*321*
Chapter 100: The Enduring Mystery of Satoshi Nakamoto	*324*
So,	*327*

Introduction

Welcome to the captivating world of Bitcoin, a revolutionary digital currency that has transformed the global financial landscape. At the heart of this extraordinary phenomenon lies a mysterious figure known as Satoshi Nakamoto, the elusive creator of Bitcoin. In this book, we embark on a journey to unravel the enigma of Satoshi Nakamoto, exploring the story behind their creation, the impact of their ideas, and the enduring mystery that continues to captivate the world.

From the origins of Satoshi Nakamoto to the birth of Bitcoin, we delve into the early influences that shaped their thinking and the vision that gradually took shape. Each chapter unveils a different facet of this intriguing tale, examining the genesis block, the mining of the first bitcoins, and the connections to the Cypherpunks movement. We delve into Satoshi's early collaborators, their disappearance from the public eye, and the last known correspondences that left us longing for more.

As we journey through the book, we explore the impact of Bitcoin on various aspects of our lives. We witness the initial reactions to this groundbreaking digital currency, its first transactions, and the creation of Bitcoin Talk, a pivotal platform for the Bitcoin community. Satoshi's growing influence on the crypto space becomes apparent, paving the way for the rise of alternative cryptocurrencies and the emergence of a vibrant and evolving ecosystem.

The book takes us through the controversies surrounding Satoshi's identity, the theories that have emerged, and the potential motivations behind their creation. We delve into the intellectual contributions of Satoshi Nakamoto, their economic philosophy, and the enduring legacy they have left on the world of cryptocurrencies and blockchain technology.

Throughout the chapters, we explore Bitcoin's journey beyond a mere currency. We examine its impact on remittances, its role in financial inclusion, and the challenges it has faced in terms of scalability and regulation. We delve into the dark side of Bitcoin, its connection to the Silk Road, and the responses from governments and regulatory bodies. We witness Satoshi's influence on privacy and security, their impact on global politics, and the rise of decentralized finance.

Also, we explore the enduring mysteries that surround Satoshi Nakamoto. We delve into the hunt for their true identity, the controversies that have arisen, and the potential implications of their unspent bitcoins. We examine Bitcoin's integration with social media, its influence on traditional investments, and its potential in peer-to-peer lending.

Finally, we confront the enduring question: Who is Satoshi Nakamoto? We discuss the cultural impact of this enigmatic figure, their intellectual contributions, and the enduring fascination that surrounds their anonymity. From the enduring mysteries to the potential wealth and the impact on developing economies, we leave no stone unturned in our exploration of Satoshi Nakamoto's legacy.

Join us on this captivating journey through the world of Bitcoin and the enduring mystery of Satoshi Nakamoto. As we delve into the intricate details and untangle the complexities, we aim to shed light on the transformative power of this digital currency and the enigma behind its creation. Brace yourself for an exploration that will challenge your understanding of money, technology, and the very fabric of our financial systems. Welcome to the world of Bitcoin Unveiled.

Chapter 1: Origins of Satoshi Nakamoto

In the vast landscape of technological advancements, there are rare instances when a brilliant mind emerges, shrouded in mystery, and leaves an indelible mark on the world. One such enigma is Satoshi Nakamoto, the pseudonymous creator of Bitcoin, whose identity remains unknown to this day. In this chapter, we delve into the origins of Satoshi Nakamoto and the intriguing journey that led to the birth of the revolutionary digital currency.

Satoshi Nakamoto's story begins with a confluence of factors, including the evolving landscape of cryptography, computer science, and a growing concern over the flaws in traditional financial systems. While the exact details of Nakamoto's early life are largely unknown, it is believed that their deep-rooted passion for privacy, cryptography, and decentralized systems laid the foundation for their groundbreaking work.

The roots of Nakamoto's philosophy can be traced back to the Cypherpunk movement of the 1990s. Cypherpunks were a group of activists, mathematicians, and computer scientists who championed the use of strong cryptography as a means to protect privacy and individual freedoms. Their vision was to create a world where individuals could communicate and transact securely without interference from governments or centralized authorities.

As Nakamoto immersed themselves in the Cypherpunk community, they absorbed its ideals and became acutely aware of the vulnerabilities inherent in traditional financial systems. They witnessed firsthand the economic crises, government interventions, and excessive control over people's wealth. These experiences fueled their desire to find an alternative, a system that would democratize finance and empower individuals.

Nakamoto's journey took a significant turn in 2008, when they published a seminal paper titled "Bitcoin: A Peer-to-Peer Electronic Cash System." This white paper, released under the name Satoshi Nakamoto, outlined a revolutionary concept—a decentralized digital currency that would operate on a peer-to-peer network, eliminating the need for intermediaries and central authorities. It presented a groundbreaking solution to the long-standing problem of double-spending in digital currencies through the ingenious use of a blockchain—a transparent, immutable ledger that would validate and record all transactions.

The release of the white paper marked the birth of Bitcoin, and Nakamoto's creation rapidly garnered attention within the cryptographic and computer science communities. It was clear that Bitcoin had the potential to disrupt traditional financial systems, empower individuals, and usher in a new era of decentralized finance.

In January 2009, Nakamoto launched the first version of the Bitcoin software, along with the genesis block—the very first block of the blockchain. Embedded within the genesis block was a message: "The Times 03/Jan/2009 Chancellor on brink of second bailout for banks." This not only commemorated a significant event in financial history but also symbolized Nakamoto's discontent with the traditional banking system and their vision for a new era of financial sovereignty.

As Nakamoto continued to refine the Bitcoin software and collaborate with early adopters, their influence grew exponentially. They engaged in online forums, notably the Bitcointalk forum, where they shared insights, answered technical questions, and discussed the future of Bitcoin with a growing community of enthusiasts. Their commitment to open dialogue and collaborative development set the stage for the decentralized and inclusive nature of the cryptocurrency community that followed.

However, despite the growing interest in Bitcoin, Nakamoto remained an elusive figure. While many attempted to unveil their true identity, Nakamoto took deliberate steps to protect their privacy. They communicated solely through online channels, never revealing personal information or participating in interviews. Their strong desire for anonymity led to countless speculations and conspiracy theories, further adding to the mystique surrounding their persona.

In April 2011, Nakamoto abruptly disappeared from the Bitcoin scene. Their last known correspondence, a message stating that they had "moved on to other things," left the community in shock and curiosity. The void left by Nakamoto's departure sparked a continuous quest for answers and a search for the person or group behind the pseudonym.

Despite Nakamoto's absence, their creation continued to flourish. Bitcoin gained traction and gradually became a force to be reckoned with in the financial world. Its decentralized nature and limited supply captivated investors, entrepreneurs, and visionaries, inspiring the development of a myriad of cryptocurrencies and blockchain-based applications.

The story of Satoshi Nakamoto and Bitcoin is a testament to the power of an idea and the transformative potential of technology. Nakamoto's vision, rooted in privacy, cryptography, and decentralization, challenged the traditional financial system, and sparked a global movement. Their creation has since reshaped our understanding of money, finance, and the very concept of trust.

As we venture further into the fascinating world of Bitcoin, we will explore the intricacies of its technology, the societal impact of decentralized finance, and the ongoing quest to unravel the mystery of Satoshi Nakamoto. Join us on this captivating journey as we delve into the chapters that lie ahead, uncovering the secrets of Bitcoin and its enigmatic creator.

Chapter 2: The Enigma of Satoshi's Identity

Have you ever encountered a puzzle so perplexing that it consumed your thoughts and imagination? Well, imagine a puzzle that has captured the attention of the entire world—the mystery surrounding the true identity of Satoshi Nakamoto, the brilliant mind behind Bitcoin. In this chapter, we dive deep into the enigma of Satoshi's identity, exploring the theories, the investigations, and the countless attempts to unravel this captivating puzzle.

When Satoshi Nakamoto first introduced Bitcoin to the world, they did so under a pseudonym—a name that has since become legendary in the realm of cryptocurrencies. But who is Satoshi Nakamoto? What is their background, their story? These questions have sparked a global quest for answers, attracting amateur sleuths, professional investigators, and curious individuals alike.

To understand the mystery, we must begin with what we know—or rather, what we think we know—about Nakamoto's identity. The name itself, Satoshi Nakamoto, suggests a Japanese origin. However, it soon became clear that the name was likely a pseudonym, carefully chosen to conceal the creator's true identity. As the world began to dig deeper, many realized that finding Satoshi Nakamoto would be akin to searching for a needle in a haystack.

Numerous theories and claims have emerged over the years, each proposing a different person or group as the true Satoshi Nakamoto. One of the earliest and most prominent theories pointed to a computer scientist named Nick Szabo. Szabo's work on digital currencies and smart contracts, combined with his writings on decentralized systems, made him a compelling candidate. However, Szabo has consistently denied being Nakamoto, leaving the theory inconclusive.

Another individual who found themselves in the spotlight was Dorian Nakamoto, a Japanese-American physicist living in California. In 2014, a Newsweek article claimed that Dorian Nakamoto was the creator of Bitcoin. The revelation caused a media frenzy, but Dorian vehemently denied any involvement in Bitcoin's creation. It soon became apparent that the Newsweek article had made a grave mistake, and Dorian Nakamoto was not the elusive Satoshi.

As the search continued, attention turned towards a cryptographic genius named Hal Finney. Finney was an early Bitcoin adopter and worked closely with Nakamoto during Bitcoin's early days. His technical expertise and proximity to Nakamoto made him a compelling candidate. However, Finney's unfortunate battle with ALS and subsequent passing in 2014 ruled him out as the sole creator of Bitcoin.

Amidst the search for Nakamoto's identity, an Australian entrepreneur named Craig Wright made a bold claim in 2016. He declared himself to be Satoshi Nakamoto, providing cryptographic keys and other pieces of evidence to support his assertion. However, scrutiny from the crypto community and the lack of definitive proof cast doubt on Wright's claim, leading many to dismiss it as an elaborate hoax.

While these are just a few examples, the quest to unmask Satoshi Nakamoto has led to countless other individuals being investigated, analyzed, and debated. Some theories suggest that Nakamoto is not an individual at all but a group of people working collectively. This idea is supported by the fact that Nakamoto's original white paper and subsequent software releases displayed a level of expertise in various domains, from cryptography to economics and computer science.

The more we explore the mystery, the more we realize the complexity of the puzzle. Satoshi Nakamoto, whoever they may be, exhibited an astoundingly deep understanding of various fields, seamlessly blending them to create Bitcoin. Their ability to remain anonymous, coupled with their technical prowess, suggests a deliberate and meticulous effort to protect their identity.

As the years pass, Nakamoto's true identity remains elusive, leaving us with a captivating enigma that continues to fascinate and intrigue. It is a testament to the power of anonymity and the mystery surrounding genius minds. Satoshi Nakamoto's legacy transcends their identity, as their creation, Bitcoin, has evolved into a global phenomenon that has transformed the way we perceive and interact with money.

Ultimately, the quest to discover Satoshi Nakamoto's true identity may continue indefinitely. Perhaps it is the very nature of this mystery that adds to the allure of Bitcoin and the fascination surrounding its enigmatic creator. Regardless of whether Nakamoto's identity is ever revealed, their impact on the world of finance and technology is undeniable, forever altering the course of history.

So, my friend, as we embark on this journey into the world of Satoshi Nakamoto and Bitcoin, let us embrace the mystery and appreciate the wonders that lie within the unknown. The story of Satoshi's identity is one that continues to captivate us, inviting us to explore, speculate, and marvel at the brilliance that birthed a revolution.

Chapter 3: Early Influences on Satoshi's Thinking

Every great mind is shaped by the experiences, knowledge, and influences they encounter throughout their journey. Satoshi Nakamoto, the mysterious creator of Bitcoin, is no exception. In this chapter, we delve into the early influences that played a pivotal role in shaping Satoshi's thinking and laying the foundation for the revolutionary concept of a decentralized digital currency.

Satoshi Nakamoto's intellectual journey began against the backdrop of a rapidly evolving technological landscape. The early days of the internet, the birth of cryptography, and the rise of the Cypherpunk movement all contributed to the formation of Nakamoto's ideas and ideals.

Cryptography, the science of encoding and decoding information, proved to be a fundamental building block for Satoshi Nakamoto. The world of cryptography fascinated Nakamoto, offering a means to secure information and protect individual privacy. The works of prominent cryptographers like Whitfield Diffie, Martin Hellman, and Ralph Merkle influenced Nakamoto's understanding of cryptographic protocols and laid the groundwork for their groundbreaking use of cryptography in Bitcoin.

The Cypherpunk movement of the 1990s, which advocated for the use of strong encryption and privacy-enhancing technologies, played a significant role in shaping Nakamoto's philosophy. The movement attracted a diverse group of individuals, including mathematicians, computer scientists, and activists, who were united in their belief that cryptography could empower individuals and challenge oppressive systems. Nakamoto immersed themselves in the Cypherpunk community, absorbing its ideals of privacy, decentralization, and individual sovereignty.

One of the key principles that Nakamoto embraced from the Cypherpunk movement was the concept of decentralized systems. They recognized that traditional centralized structures, whether in finance or governance, were susceptible to corruption, censorship, and control. Inspired by the ideals of personal freedom and autonomy, Nakamoto sought to create a decentralized digital currency that would enable individuals to transact directly with one another, free from the interference of intermediaries or centralized authorities.

Another significant influence on Nakamoto's thinking was the growing discontent with the flaws of traditional financial systems. Nakamoto witnessed firsthand the economic crises, government interventions, and excessive control over people's wealth. They recognized the need for an alternative, a system that could democratize finance and provide a level playing field for all individuals, regardless of their background or geographic location.

The idea of digital cash was not new, but Nakamoto was driven to overcome the long-standing challenge of double-spending—the ability to spend the same digital currency unit more than once. Previous attempts at digital cash had relied on centralized authorities to prevent double-spending, but Nakamoto saw the potential of utilizing a decentralized network and the power of consensus to address this issue. This vision laid the foundation for Bitcoin's underlying technology, the blockchain—a transparent, immutable ledger that records and verifies all transactions.

It is also worth noting the influence of the Austrian School of Economics on Nakamoto's thinking. The Austrian economists emphasized the importance of sound money and criticized the flaws of fiat currencies controlled by central banks. Nakamoto's decision to introduce a limited supply of bitcoins into the system, coupled with the decentralized nature of Bitcoin, aligned with the Austrian School's principles and their belief in the importance of individual liberty and free markets.

The combination of these early influences—cryptography, the Cypherpunk movement, dissatisfaction with traditional financial systems, and the Austrian School of Economics—converged in Satoshi Nakamoto's mind, giving birth to the revolutionary concept of Bitcoin. Nakamoto's ability to synthesize these ideas into a cohesive vision demonstrated their deep understanding of technology, economics, and the societal implications of their creation.

As we reflect on the early influences that shaped Satoshi Nakamoto's thinking, we gain insight into the factors that led to the development of

Bitcoin. Their fascination with cryptography, immersion in the Cypherpunk movement, disillusionment with traditional finance, and alignment with the principles of the Austrian School of Economics all played a crucial role in shaping Nakamoto's philosophy.

In the subsequent chapters, we will explore the technical intricacies of Bitcoin, its impact on the financial world, and the far-reaching implications of Satoshi Nakamoto's creation. Join us as we unravel the mysteries of blockchain technology, dive into the decentralized revolution, and witness the transformative power of an idea that emerged from the influences that shaped Satoshi's thinking.

Chapter 4: A Vision Takes Shape

In the vast landscape of human ingenuity, there are rare moments when a vision takes shape—a vision that has the potential to reshape industries, challenge the status quo, and empower individuals on a global scale. Such was the case with Satoshi Nakamoto, the mysterious creator of Bitcoin. In this chapter, we delve into the genesis of Nakamoto's vision, tracing the steps that led to the birth of the revolutionary digital currency.

As Satoshi Nakamoto delved deeper into the realms of cryptography, decentralized systems, and the flaws of traditional financial systems, a seed of an idea began to germinate. Nakamoto envisioned a future where financial transactions could be conducted directly between individuals, without the need for intermediaries or centralized authorities. They dreamed of a world where individuals could have full control over their financial destiny, free from the whims of governments and the limitations of traditional banking systems.

The core concept that drove Nakamoto's vision was decentralization—a paradigm shift from the traditional models of power and control. They envisioned a network where every participant had an equal say, where trust was built not on the authority of a central entity, but on the transparency and immutability of a distributed ledger.

The formation of this vision took shape in Nakamoto's seminal white paper, titled "Bitcoin: A Peer-to-Peer Electronic Cash System." Released in 2008, this document outlined the technical framework for a decentralized digital currency that would revolutionize the way we think about money and finance.

At the heart of Nakamoto's vision was the solution to the long-standing problem of double-spending—a vulnerability that had plagued previous attempts at digital currencies. Nakamoto's breakthrough lay in the ingenious use of a blockchain—a public ledger that would record and validate all transactions in a secure and transparent manner.

The blockchain, a concept that Nakamoto synthesized from existing cryptographic research, would serve as the backbone of the Bitcoin network. It would ensure that each unit of the digital currency, called a bitcoin, could only be spent once, preventing fraudulent activity, and ensuring the integrity of the system.

But Nakamoto's vision extended beyond the technical aspects of Bitcoin. They saw the potential for this decentralized digital currency to empower individuals across the globe. They recognized the barriers faced by the unbanked and underbanked populations, who were excluded from the benefits of traditional financial systems. Nakamoto envisioned Bitcoin as a tool for financial inclusion, enabling individuals without access to traditional banking services to participate in the global economy.

Furthermore, Nakamoto's vision encompassed the ideals of privacy and autonomy. They believed that individuals should have control over their own financial information and the ability to transact privately, without fear of surveillance or interference. Bitcoin provided an avenue for individuals to reclaim their financial privacy, offering a level of autonomy that was previously unimaginable in traditional banking systems.

As Nakamoto refined their vision, they recognized the importance of adoption and collaboration. They released the Bitcoin software as open-source, inviting developers and enthusiasts from around the world to contribute to its growth and development. This open and inclusive approach fostered a community of like-minded individuals who shared Nakamoto's vision and worked together to advance the principles of decentralization, transparency, and financial sovereignty.

The release of the Bitcoin software in January 2009 marked a pivotal moment in Nakamoto's journey. The genesis block, the first block of the blockchain, not only served as a technical milestone but also carried a symbolic message: "The Times 03/Jan/2009 Chancellor on brink of second bailout for banks." This message encapsulated Nakamoto's disillusionment with the traditional banking system and their vision for a decentralized alternative.

As Nakamoto's vision began to take shape, it sparked a global movement. Bitcoin gained traction, attracting early adopters, entrepreneurs, and enthusiasts who recognized the transformative potential of this nascent technology. Its decentralized nature and limited supply captivated investors, while its potential to reshape industries and empower individuals ignited the imaginations of visionaries across the globe.

Nakamoto's vision, rooted in the principles of decentralization, transparency, and financial inclusivity, laid the groundwork for a revolution. They challenged the notion that money must be controlled by central authorities and envisioned a future where individuals could transact freely, securely, and without barriers.

In the chapters that follow, we will explore the technical intricacies of Bitcoin, the societal impact of decentralized finance, and the ongoing quest to unravel the mystery of Satoshi Nakamoto. Join us on this exhilarating journey as we witness the realization of a vision—one that emerged from the depths of Nakamoto's mind and has the power to reshape the very foundations of our financial world.

Chapter 5: The Birth of Bitcoin

In the realm of groundbreaking inventions, few have captured the world's attention quite like Bitcoin. The birth of this revolutionary digital currency marked a turning point in the way we perceive money, finance, and the potential for decentralized systems. In this chapter, we delve into the intricate details of how Bitcoin came to be, from its early development to its launch, and the significance of its historic genesis block.

After years of refining their vision, Satoshi Nakamoto, the pseudonymous creator of Bitcoin, embarked on the challenging task of bringing their concept to life. Nakamoto's objective was to create a digital currency that was decentralized, secure, and immune to the flaws of traditional financial systems. With a clear vision in mind, Nakamoto began developing the foundational elements of what would become Bitcoin.

The first step in building Bitcoin was the creation of its underlying technology—the blockchain. Nakamoto recognized the need for a transparent and immutable ledger that could record and validate all transactions in a secure and decentralized manner. This led to the development of a novel consensus mechanism known as proof-of-work. Proof-of-work involved miners using computational power to solve complex mathematical puzzles, thereby validating transactions, and securing the network. Miners would compete to find the solution, and the first miner to solve the puzzle would be rewarded with newly minted bitcoins. This incentivized miners to contribute their computing power to the network, ensuring its security and integrity.

With the foundational elements in place, Nakamoto began working on the Bitcoin software. They programmed the software to implement the rules and protocols that governed the creation, transfer, and verification of bitcoins. This software, released as an open-source project, allowed anyone to participate in the Bitcoin network and interact with the digital currency.

In January 2009, Nakamoto took a historic step—the launch of the first version of the Bitcoin software. This marked the official birth of Bitcoin and the beginning of a journey that would transform the world of finance. With the software released, Nakamoto also introduced the very first block of the blockchain—the genesis block.

The genesis block, or Block 0, holds a special significance in the Bitcoin story. It serves as the foundation upon which the entire blockchain is built. Nakamoto embedded a unique message within the genesis block, adding a touch of symbolism to their creation. The message read, "The Times 03/Jan/2009 Chancellor on brink of second bailout for banks," referencing a headline from The Times newspaper on the day of the block's creation. This message not only commemorated a notable event but also emphasized Nakamoto's motivation—a disillusionment with traditional banking systems and a desire for a decentralized alternative.

With the Bitcoin network live and the genesis block established, Nakamoto began mining and transacting bitcoins alongside a small group of early adopters. The first transactions on the network included Nakamoto sending bitcoins to Hal Finney, a renowned cryptographer and early contributor to Bitcoin's development.

As the network gained traction and more individuals joined the Bitcoin community, Nakamoto's creation began to capture the attention of enthusiasts and technologists around the world. Their innovative solution to the double-spending problem, coupled with the decentralized nature of Bitcoin, resonated deeply with those who saw the potential for a transformative shift in the way we think about money.

In the months following the launch, Nakamoto's involvement in the Bitcoin community continued. They engaged in online forums, particularly the Bitcointalk forum, where they shared insights, answered technical questions, and discussed the future of Bitcoin. Nakamoto's open and collaborative approach set the tone for the inclusive and decentralized nature of the Bitcoin community, fostering an environment where ideas could be exchanged freely.

Despite their involvement in the early stages of Bitcoin's development, Nakamoto gradually began to withdraw from the public eye. By 2010, their presence in the Bitcoin community diminished, and in April 2011, Nakamoto ceased all communication, leaving the community with an enduring mystery—their true identity.

The birth of Bitcoin was not just the creation of a digital currency; it was the manifestation of a visionary's dream. Satoshi Nakamoto's ingenuity, technical expertise, and commitment to decentralization brought forth a paradigm-shifting concept that challenged the traditional financial systems and ignited a global movement.

As we continue our exploration of the Bitcoin journey, we will delve deeper into its technological intricacies, its impact on finance and society, and the ongoing quest to unveil the identity of Satoshi Nakamoto. Join us on this captivating adventure as we uncover the remarkable tale of Bitcoin—the digital currency that emerged from the depths of Nakamoto's imagination and forever changed the way we perceive money.

Type This URL in Your Browser → **https://bit.ly/Guess_What_This**

Chapter 6: The Genesis Block

In the vast realm of blockchain technology and cryptocurrencies, few elements hold as much significance as the genesis block. This inaugural block represents the birth of a blockchain network and sets the stage for all future transactions and developments. In the case of Bitcoin, the genesis block holds a special place in history, carrying a symbolic message that encapsulates the motivations and aspirations of its creator, Satoshi Nakamoto. Join us in this chapter as we explore the intricacies of the Bitcoin genesis block and the profound impact it had on the world of finance and technology.

The genesis block, also known as Block 0, is the very first block in a blockchain. In the case of Bitcoin, it was created on January 3, 2009, when Satoshi Nakamoto launched the network. This inaugural block not only marks the birth of Bitcoin but also lays the foundation for all subsequent transactions and blocks that are added to the blockchain.

Embedded within the Bitcoin genesis block is a symbolic message carefully chosen by Nakamoto. The message, "The Times 03/Jan/2009 Chancellor on brink of second bailout for banks," refers to a headline from The Times newspaper published on the same day. By including this message, Nakamoto paid homage to a significant event in financial history—the potential need for a government bailout of banks during the global financial crisis.

This message serves as a powerful statement, encapsulating Nakamoto's disillusionment with the flaws of traditional banking systems and their desire to create a decentralized alternative. It represents the underlying motivations and vision that drove the development of Bitcoin—a system that would operate outside the control of centralized authorities and provide individuals with financial sovereignty.

The inclusion of the headline from The Times not only adds a historical context but also demonstrates Nakamoto's intention to create a transparent and immutable ledger. By permanently etching this message into the blockchain, Nakamoto ensured that the genesis block and its embedded message would forever be a part of Bitcoin's history, visible to anyone who explores the blockchain.

Beyond its symbolic significance, the Bitcoin genesis block also contains important technical elements. It establishes the initial parameters and characteristics of the blockchain network. For example, the genesis block sets the difficulty level for mining new blocks, the block reward, and other critical protocol parameters.

The genesis block also provides the starting point for the creation and distribution of bitcoins. In the case of Bitcoin, the genesis block rewarded Nakamoto with 50 bitcoins, which were the first coins ever mined. These initial coins would go on to circulate within the Bitcoin network and serve as the foundation for future transactions and economic activity.

As the blockchain grows, each new block added to the chain references the previous block, creating a chain of blocks that forms an unbroken sequence of transactions. The existence of the genesis block ensures that all subsequent blocks can be traced back to the very beginning of the Bitcoin network, establishing a chronological record of transactions and enabling the validation of ownership and the prevention of double-spending.

The creation of the Bitcoin genesis block marked a significant milestone in the development of decentralized digital currencies. Nakamoto's innovative use of the blockchain, coupled with the symbolic message it carried, set the stage for a financial revolution—one that would challenge the existing financial order and redefine our understanding of money.

In the years that followed, the Bitcoin network expanded, attracting a growing community of enthusiasts, miners, developers, and entrepreneurs. As the blockchain grew longer and more secure with each new block, Bitcoin became a global phenomenon, capturing the attention of mainstream media and institutions.

While the identity of Satoshi Nakamoto remains a mystery, their creation—the Bitcoin genesis block—has forever transformed the landscape of finance and technology. It sparked a movement that transcended borders and empowered individuals to take control of their own financial destiny.

The Bitcoin genesis block serves as a reminder of the revolutionary power of decentralized technologies. It represents the triumph of transparency over opacity, empowerment over dependency, and resilience over fragility. It stands as a testament to the vision and ingenuity of Nakamoto, whose creation continues to inspire and shape the ever-evolving world of cryptocurrencies.

As we move forward in our exploration of the Bitcoin journey, we will uncover the technical intricacies of the blockchain, the impact of decentralization on finance and society, and the ongoing quest to unveil the identity of Satoshi Nakamoto. Join us on this captivating adventure as we delve deeper into the mysteries and marvels of the Bitcoin genesis block—a cornerstone of innovation that forever changed the way we perceive and interact with money.

Chapter 7: Mining the First Bitcoins

In the realm of cryptocurrencies, the process of mining holds a vital role in validating transactions, securing the network, and minting new coins. In the case of Bitcoin, the mining of the first bitcoins was an essential step in the early stages of the network's development. In this chapter, we explore the fascinating world of Bitcoin mining, from the initial blocks to the early miners who played a pivotal role in bringing this revolutionary digital currency to life.

When Satoshi Nakamoto launched Bitcoin in 2009, they laid the foundation for a decentralized network that would rely on a unique consensus mechanism known as proof-of-work. This mechanism incentivized miners to contribute their computing power to the network in exchange for the opportunity to earn newly minted bitcoins.

In the early days of Bitcoin, mining was a relatively straightforward process that could be carried out on a regular computer. Nakamoto and a small group of early enthusiasts began mining the first blocks, validating transactions, and securing the network. These early miners played a crucial role in the development of Bitcoin, contributing their computing power to maintain the integrity of the blockchain.

The first block, known as the genesis block, was mined by Nakamoto themselves. This block, which marked the birth of Bitcoin, rewarded Nakamoto with 50 bitcoins. These initial bitcoins, known as the coinbase reward, were the very first coins ever mined and laid the foundation for the Bitcoin economy.

As more miners joined the network, the difficulty of mining increased. Nakamoto had designed the protocol to automatically adjust the difficulty level to ensure that new blocks were added to the blockchain approximately every ten minutes. This adjustment aimed to maintain a stable mining environment, regardless of the total computational power dedicated to the network.

In the early days, mining could be done using a central processing unit (CPU) or a graphics processing unit (GPU). Miners would run the Bitcoin software on their computers and contribute their computational power to solve complex mathematical puzzles known as hashes. The first miner to find a solution to the puzzle would be rewarded with the coinbase reward and the honor of mining the next block.

As Bitcoin gained popularity and more miners joined the network, competition increased, leading to the rise of specialized mining hardware. Miners realized that using more powerful equipment would provide a competitive advantage and increase their chances of mining new blocks.

This realization led to the development of application-specific integrated circuits (ASICs), which are custom-built devices designed solely for the purpose of mining cryptocurrencies. ASICs offered significantly higher hashing power and energy efficiency compared to traditional computer hardware. With the introduction of ASICs, the mining landscape underwent a significant transformation, becoming more specialized and competitive.

While early mining could be carried out by individuals on their personal computers, the rise of ASICs made mining a more industrialized process. Mining farms, consisting of vast arrays of specialized hardware, emerged in regions with access to cheap electricity. These mining farms harnessed enormous computational power, rivaling the collective computing power of entire countries.

Mining became an integral part of the Bitcoin ecosystem, not only validating transactions and securing the network but also serving as a mechanism for the distribution of new bitcoins. The issuance of new coins acted as an incentive for miners to continue dedicating their resources to the network, ensuring its stability and growth.

In addition to the coinbase reward, miners also earned transaction fees for including transactions in the blocks they mined. Transaction fees serve as an additional incentive for miners, encouraging them to prioritize transactions with higher fees attached.

As the Bitcoin network evolved, mining became an increasingly competitive and specialized field. The rise of mining pools—groups of miners who combine their resources to increase their chances of mining new blocks—further intensified the competition. Mining pools allowed individual miners to collectively work towards finding solutions to the mathematical puzzles and share the rewards proportionally based on their contributions.

The mining of the first bitcoins not only established the initial supply of the digital currency but also laid the groundwork for the Bitcoin mining industry as it exists today. Over time, the mining process has become more sophisticated, requiring specialized hardware and significant computational power. However, the underlying principles of validating transactions, securing the network, and earning rewards remain the same.

The early miners who participated in the mining of the first bitcoins played a crucial role in bringing Bitcoin to life. Their dedication and contributions helped establish the foundation of a decentralized network that has transformed the world of finance and technology.

As we continue our exploration of the Bitcoin journey, we will delve deeper into the technical intricacies of mining, the evolving dynamics of the mining industry, and the broader implications of this essential process. Join us on this captivating adventure as we uncover the mysteries and marvels of Bitcoin mining—the backbone of a revolutionary digital currency.

Chapter 8: The Cypherpunk Connection

In the fascinating realm of cryptography and digital privacy, a movement emerged in the 1990s that would have a profound impact on the development of Bitcoin. This movement, known as Cypherpunk, fostered a community of activists, mathematicians, and computer scientists who shared a common goal—to protect individual privacy and promote the use of strong cryptography. In this chapter, we delve into the Cypherpunk connection and its influence on the creation and philosophy of Bitcoin.

The roots of Bitcoin can be traced back to the ideals and principles championed by the Cypherpunk movement. Cypherpunks believed that cryptography could empower individuals, protect privacy, and challenge the oppressive control of governments and centralized authorities. Their vision aligned closely with the motivations of Satoshi Nakamoto, the pseudonymous creator of Bitcoin.

One of the key figures within the Cypherpunk movement was David Chaum, a renowned cryptographer who introduced the concept of digital cash in the 1980s. Chaum's work focused on creating protocols that would enable secure and private electronic transactions. His ideas laid the groundwork for the development of cryptocurrencies and influenced Nakamoto's thinking regarding the need for a digital currency that prioritized privacy.

Timothy C. May, another influential figure within the Cypherpunk community, authored the "Crypto Anarchist Manifesto" in 1992. This manifesto articulated the vision of a future where cryptographic tools would enable individuals to protect their privacy, engage in anonymous transactions, and liberate themselves from the surveillance of governments and corporations. The Crypto Anarchist Manifesto's emphasis on decentralization and individual autonomy resonated with Nakamoto's vision for a peer-to-peer electronic cash system.

The work of Wei Dai, a computer scientist and Cypherpunk enthusiast, also had a significant impact on Nakamoto's thinking. Dai proposed the concept of "b-money" in 1998—a digital currency system that relied on a decentralized network of participants to validate transactions. The ideas presented in Dai's b-money paper, which emphasized the use of cryptographic techniques and decentralized consensus, were foundational to Nakamoto's design of the Bitcoin network.

The Cypherpunk movement provided Nakamoto with a community of like-minded individuals who shared their passion for privacy, cryptography, and decentralized systems. Online forums and mailing lists became spaces for vibrant discussions and the exchange of ideas. The ideas and debates within the Cypherpunk community undoubtedly influenced Nakamoto's thinking as they embarked on the creation of Bitcoin.

Nakamoto's white paper, "Bitcoin: A Peer-to-Peer Electronic Cash System," released in 2008, represented the culmination of their deep understanding of cryptography, decentralized systems, and the flaws of traditional financial systems. This seminal document outlined a vision for a decentralized digital currency that would operate on a peer-to-peer network, free from intermediaries and centralized control.

The core principles of the Cypherpunk movement were intricately woven into the fabric of Bitcoin. Nakamoto sought to enable individuals to transact directly with one another, without the need for trusted third parties. By utilizing cryptographic techniques and the transparent, immutable nature of the blockchain, Nakamoto aimed to create a system that would provide security, privacy, and financial autonomy to its users.

The influence of the Cypherpunk movement on the development of Bitcoin extended beyond the technical aspects. The movement also shaped Nakamoto's philosophical and political beliefs regarding the nature of money, individual sovereignty, and the role of governments in financial systems. Cypherpunks believed that individuals should have control over their own data and be able to engage in private transactions without interference or surveillance.

Nakamoto's creation of Bitcoin represented a powerful fusion of technological innovation and ideological principles. Their vision for a decentralized digital currency aligned with the core tenets of the Cypherpunk movement, challenging the traditional power structures and providing individuals with a means to reclaim their financial freedom.

The Cypherpunk connection continues to resonate within the Bitcoin community today. The emphasis on privacy, decentralization, and individual autonomy remains ingrained in the ethos of the cryptocurrency space. The legacy of the Cypherpunks lives on, inspiring the development of privacy-enhancing technologies, secure digital wallets, and decentralized applications that empower individuals in their control over financial assets and personal data.

As we navigate the fascinating world of Bitcoin, it is crucial to recognize the profound influence of the Cypherpunk movement. The ideals and principles espoused by the Cypherpunks found fertile ground in Nakamoto's creation, shaping the trajectory of Bitcoin and its impact on the world of finance and technology.

In the chapters to come, we will further explore the technical intricacies of Bitcoin, the societal implications of decentralized finance, and the ongoing quest to unveil the identity of Satoshi Nakamoto. Join us on this captivating journey as we uncover the mysteries and marvels of the Bitcoin network—a testament to the power of cryptography, decentralization, and the legacy of the Cypherpunks.

Chapter 9: The Mysterious Forum Posts

In the cryptic world of Bitcoin's origin, a series of forum posts shrouded in mystery and intrigue played a significant role in the early development and dissemination of the revolutionary digital currency. These posts, attributed to the enigmatic figure known as Satoshi Nakamoto, have captivated the imagination of enthusiasts, journalists, and researchers alike. In this chapter, we delve into the mysterious forum posts that shed light on the creation and philosophy of Bitcoin, while leaving the true identity of its creator obscured.

The story of the forum posts begins in November 2008, when an individual using the pseudonym Satoshi Nakamoto registered an account on the P2P Foundation forum. Nakamoto's posts initially discussed the concept and technical details of Bitcoin, sparking the curiosity of those who stumbled upon them. What followed was a series of forum interactions that would shape the understanding and perception of this nascent digital currency.

Nakamoto's forum posts demonstrated a deep understanding of cryptography, decentralized systems, and the flaws of traditional financial systems. They shared insights into the technical aspects of Bitcoin, answering questions and engaging in discussions about the intricacies of its design. The clarity of Nakamoto's explanations and their ability to address complex concepts with precision added to the air of intrigue surrounding their identity.

One of the early forum discussions revolved around the concept of the proof-of-work consensus mechanism—a fundamental component of the Bitcoin network. Nakamoto explained the rationale behind using proof-of-work, emphasizing its role in securing the network and preventing double-spending. These insights provided valuable context for the development and understanding of Bitcoin's underlying technology.

Another notable forum post from Nakamoto shed light on the limited supply of bitcoins. They revealed that the total supply would be capped at 21 million coins, a design choice aimed at ensuring scarcity and preventing inflation. This decision aligned with the principles of the

Austrian School of Economics, a philosophy that emphasizes the importance of sound money and individual liberty.

The forum posts not only covered technical aspects but also addressed broader societal and economic implications. Nakamoto discussed the potential of Bitcoin to revolutionize the financial landscape, enabling individuals to transact directly with one another without the need for intermediaries. They highlighted the ability of Bitcoin to empower the unbanked and underbanked populations, fostering financial inclusion on a global scale.

One of the most intriguing aspects of Nakamoto's forum posts was their commitment to privacy and pseudonymity. Despite being the driving force behind the creation of Bitcoin, Nakamoto remained anonymous and encouraged others to focus on the ideas and technology rather than their personal identity. This emphasis on privacy resonated deeply with the ideals of the Cypherpunk movement, further fueling speculation about Nakamoto's background and motivations.

As the forum discussions gained momentum, Nakamoto's reputation grew within the Bitcoin community. Their technical expertise, unwavering commitment to decentralization, and willingness to engage in open dialogue earned them the respect and admiration of early adopters and enthusiasts.

However, Nakamoto's involvement in the forums gradually diminished. In April 2011, they ceased all communication, leaving the community with an enduring mystery—the true identity of Satoshi Nakamoto. Speculation and attempts to uncover Nakamoto's identity have persisted to this day, with numerous individuals and media outlets claiming to have unraveled the enigma, only to be met with inconclusive evidence.

The enduring anonymity of Nakamoto has added a layer of mystique to the story of Bitcoin. It has allowed the technology to flourish independently of any individual's reputation or authority. Bitcoin's decentralized nature is a testament to the power of collaborative efforts and the shared belief in the potential for a new financial paradigm.

The forum posts attributed to Satoshi Nakamoto remain a crucial piece of Bitcoin's history. They provide a window into the early days of the network's development, offering insights into the motivations, design choices, and philosophy behind this groundbreaking digital currency.

Despite the uncertainty surrounding Nakamoto's true identity, their contributions continue to shape the trajectory of Bitcoin and inspire the ongoing exploration of blockchain technology.

The mysterious forum posts remind us that the power of ideas transcends the individual. Bitcoin's emergence as a global phenomenon is a testament to the transformative potential of decentralized systems and the collective pursuit of innovation.

As we progress further into the Bitcoin journey, we will unravel more of its technical intricacies, the societal impact of decentralized finance, and the quest to uncover the identity of Satoshi Nakamoto. Join us on this captivating adventure as we navigate through the mysteries and marvels of the Bitcoin network—a testament to the power of anonymous ingenuity and the enduring spirit of invention.

Type This URL in Your Browser → *https://bit.ly/Guess_What_This*

Chapter 10: Satoshi's Early Collaborators

In the captivating journey of Bitcoin's creation, Satoshi Nakamoto, the elusive figure behind its inception, did not work alone. While Nakamoto is often credited as the sole creator of Bitcoin, their early collaborators played an essential role in shaping the development and dissemination of this revolutionary digital currency. In this chapter, we explore the key individuals who collaborated with Nakamoto in the early days, their contributions, and the lasting impact they had on the Bitcoin ecosystem.

Hal Finney:

One of the closest collaborators and early adopters of Bitcoin was Hal Finney. Finney, a renowned cryptographer, and a pioneer in the field of public-key cryptography, was one of the first individuals to engage with Nakamoto in the Bitcointalk forum and actively contribute to the development of the Bitcoin software. He played a pivotal role in testing and providing feedback on the initial versions of the software. Finney was also the recipient of the first-ever bitcoin transaction from Nakamoto, demonstrating the practical application and functionality of the digital currency.

Martti Malmi:

Martti Malmi, known by his online handle "Sirius," was an early contributor to the Bitcoin project. Malmi became involved with Bitcoin shortly after its launch, collaborating with Nakamoto on various aspects of the software development and providing valuable insights into its usability and user experience. Malmi's contributions extended to designing and developing the initial version of the Bitcoin client interface. His involvement in the early stages of Bitcoin's development highlights the collaborative nature of the project and the diverse skills required to bring it to fruition.

Gavin Andresen:

Gavin Andresen is perhaps one of the most well-known early collaborators with Nakamoto. Andresen became heavily involved in the Bitcoin project in 2010 when he took over as the lead developer of the Bitcoin client from Nakamoto. Nakamoto trusted Andresen with administrative access to the Bitcoin.org domain and the Bitcoin source code repository on SourceForge. Under Andresen's guidance, the

Bitcoin software continued to evolve, becoming more user-friendly and secure. Andresen also established the Bitcoin Foundation, an organization that supported the growth and adoption of Bitcoin worldwide.

Wei Dai:

Although not a direct collaborator with Nakamoto, Wei Dai's contributions to the field of cryptography and decentralized systems played a significant role in the development of Bitcoin. Dai's concept of "b-money," introduced in 1998, laid the foundation for many of the ideas that Nakamoto incorporated into the design of Bitcoin. The b-money proposal highlighted the need for a decentralized digital currency system and outlined the use of cryptographic techniques and decentralized consensus mechanisms. Nakamoto acknowledged Dai's influence in the Bitcoin white paper, further solidifying the connection between their work.

Nick Szabo:

Nick Szabo, a legal scholar, and computer scientist, is another influential figure whose work intersected with Nakamoto's vision for Bitcoin. Szabo's concept of "bit gold," proposed in 1998, explored the idea of a decentralized digital currency that utilized proof-of-work as a consensus mechanism. The similarities between bit gold and Bitcoin are striking, with both concepts emphasizing the decentralized nature of the currency and the use of cryptographic techniques to secure transactions. While there is no direct evidence of collaboration between Nakamoto and Szabo, their parallel ideas highlight the broader intellectual environment that influenced Bitcoin's development.

These early collaborators, among others, formed a collective brain trust that contributed to the growth and maturation of Bitcoin. Their expertise, technical insights, and dedication helped shape the trajectory of the digital currency, establishing a solid foundation for its widespread adoption and success.

While the exact dynamics and extent of collaboration between Nakamoto and these individuals may vary, their collective contributions highlight the collaborative nature of Bitcoin's evolution. The open-source nature of the Bitcoin software and the inclusive mindset of its early developers fostered an environment of shared knowledge, feedback, and collaboration. This ethos continues to resonate within the Bitcoin community today.

The contributions of Nakamoto's early collaborators extended beyond the technical realm. Their involvement helped build a supportive community around Bitcoin, furthering its adoption and awareness. Their active participation in forums, discussions, and outreach efforts played a crucial role in the dissemination of Bitcoin's ideas and principles.

The legacy of these early collaborators lives on in the ongoing development and evolution of Bitcoin. Their work set the stage for subsequent generations of developers and contributors, ensuring the continued advancement and innovation within the Bitcoin ecosystem.

As we navigate further into the Bitcoin journey, we will uncover more about the technical intricacies of the cryptocurrency, its societal impact, and the ongoing quest to unveil the identity of Satoshi Nakamoto. Join us on this captivating adventure as we explore the remarkable collaborative spirit that propelled Bitcoin from an idea to a global phenomenon—a testament to the power of collective genius and shared vision.

Chapter 11: The White Paper Revealed

In the world of cryptocurrencies, few documents have had as profound an impact as the Bitcoin white paper. Authored by the enigmatic figure known as Satoshi Nakamoto, this concise and visionary document laid out the blueprint for a revolutionary digital currency and blockchain technology. In this chapter, we explore the details and significance of the Bitcoin white paper, revealing the ideas and principles that have reshaped the world of finance and technology.

The Bitcoin white paper, titled "Bitcoin: A Peer-to-Peer Electronic Cash System," was released by Nakamoto in October 2008. This seminal document, spanning just nine pages, presented a groundbreaking solution to the long-standing problem of creating a digital currency that operated on a decentralized network without the need for intermediaries.

The white paper began by identifying the inherent flaws of traditional financial systems—centralization, lack of privacy, and susceptibility to double-spending. Nakamoto proposed Bitcoin as an alternative, envisioning a peer-to-peer electronic cash system that would bypass intermediaries, enable secure transactions, and ensure privacy.

At the core of the white paper was the concept of a blockchain—a transparent and immutable ledger that recorded all Bitcoin transactions. Nakamoto explained how the blockchain would solve the problem of double-spending, a challenge that had plagued previous attempts at creating digital currencies. By utilizing a decentralized network of nodes, the blockchain ensured the validity and integrity of transactions, eliminating the need for trust in a centralized authority.

The white paper also introduced the concept of proof-of-work as the mechanism for achieving consensus within the Bitcoin network. Nakamoto detailed how miners, through their computational efforts, would validate transactions and secure the network. This innovative approach not only provided security but also served as an incentive for miners to contribute their computational power, ensuring the continuous operation and growth of the network.

Nakamoto's vision for Bitcoin extended beyond the technical aspects. They emphasized the importance of privacy, pseudonymity, and individual control over financial transactions. The white paper highlighted how Bitcoin allowed users to transact directly with one another, without the need for trusted intermediaries or the exposure of personal information. This focus on privacy and user empowerment resonated deeply with those who valued financial autonomy and the protection of personal data.

The release of the white paper marked a pivotal moment in the history of cryptocurrencies. Its publication ignited a spark within the cryptography and technology communities, capturing the attention of enthusiasts and experts around the world. The concise yet comprehensive nature of the document made it accessible to a wide audience, allowing the ideas to spread rapidly and generate excitement about the potential of Bitcoin.

As the white paper gained recognition, individuals began to realize the profound implications of Nakamoto's creation. Bitcoin represented more than just a digital currency; it embodied a fundamental shift in the way we perceive and interact with money. The decentralized nature of the system challenged the status quo, questioning the authority of central banks and governments over monetary policy and financial transactions.

The white paper served as a rallying point for early adopters and developers who were captivated by Nakamoto's ideas. It provided a clear roadmap for the development of the Bitcoin software, enabling individuals to collaborate and contribute to the growth of the network. The open-source nature of Bitcoin fostered an environment of innovation and collaboration, amplifying the impact of the white paper and propelling the cryptocurrency forward.

The release of the white paper also signaled the birth of a vibrant community centered around Bitcoin. Enthusiasts, developers, and researchers gathered in online forums and discussion groups to explore the technical intricacies, share ideas, and debate the potential applications and future of the digital currency. The white paper acted as a catalyst, sparking a global movement that continues to thrive to this day.

While the white paper laid the foundation for Bitcoin, its impact extended beyond this singular cryptocurrency. The principles outlined in the document—decentralization, cryptographic security, and the use of blockchain technology—inspired the development of numerous other cryptocurrencies and blockchain-based projects. Nakamoto's ideas spurred a wave of innovation and exploration, reshaping entire industries and paving the way for the decentralized revolution.

The significance of the Bitcoin white paper cannot be overstated. It is a testament to the power of ideas and the impact that a well-articulated vision can have on the world. Nakamoto's concise yet comprehensive document provided a roadmap for a new era of finance and technology—one that transcended borders, challenged the existing financial order, and empowered individuals to take control of their own financial destinies.

As we continue our exploration of the Bitcoin journey, we will delve deeper into the technical intricacies of the cryptocurrency, its societal implications, and the ongoing quest to unveil the true identity of Satoshi Nakamoto. Join us on this captivating adventure as we uncover the mysteries and marvels of the Bitcoin network—a testament to the power of a visionary's ideas and the transformative potential of decentralized technologies.

Type This URL in Your Browser ⟶ ***https://bit.ly/Guess_What_This***

Chapter 12: Initial Reactions to Bitcoin

When Bitcoin emerged onto the scene in 2009, it sparked a wave of curiosity, skepticism, and excitement. The innovative concept of a decentralized digital currency operating outside the control of governments and financial institutions challenged the status quo and captivated the attention of individuals around the world. In this chapter, we delve into the initial reactions to Bitcoin, exploring the range of responses it elicited and the impact it had on various stakeholders.

Technology Enthusiasts and Cypherpunks:

For technology enthusiasts and members of the Cypherpunk movement, Bitcoin was met with intrigue and excitement. Its alignment with the ideals of privacy, decentralization, and cryptographic security resonated deeply with this community. Bitcoin was seen as a revolutionary advancement, providing a potential solution to long-standing challenges in the fields of finance and digital privacy. Many early adopters embraced Bitcoin as an embodiment of their beliefs and actively contributed to its development and dissemination.

Skeptics and Naysayers:

As with any disruptive innovation, Bitcoin faced its fair share of skeptics. Critics questioned its viability as a currency, raising concerns about its volatility, lack of intrinsic value, and potential for use in illicit activities. Some dismissed it as a passing fad, or a speculative bubble destined to burst. Additionally, the anonymous nature of Satoshi Nakamoto, the pseudonymous creator of Bitcoin, added an element of suspicion for those skeptical of the project's legitimacy. These skeptics remained cautious and were often hesitant to embrace or invest in the nascent digital currency.

Financial Institutions and Governments:

Bitcoin's emergence presented a unique challenge for traditional financial institutions and governments. The decentralized nature of the cryptocurrency threatened their control over monetary policy and financial transactions. Initially, many financial institutions and government authorities viewed Bitcoin with skepticism and apprehension. Concerns about its potential for money laundering, tax evasion, and lack of regulation raised eyebrows among regulators. Some even saw Bitcoin as a threat to the stability of the existing financial system. As the technology matured and gained broader recognition, financial institutions and governments began to explore ways to engage with and regulate the cryptocurrency space.

Early Adopters and Entrepreneurs:

A subset of individuals recognized the potential of Bitcoin and seized the opportunity to be early adopters and entrepreneurs in the space. These pioneers saw the potential for financial innovation, technological disruption, and economic empowerment. They embraced Bitcoin as a means of diversifying their portfolios, exploring new business models, and participating in a burgeoning ecosystem. Early adopters and entrepreneurs played a crucial role in building the infrastructure, developing services, and spreading awareness about Bitcoin, contributing to its growth and mainstream adoption.

Media and Public Perception:

The media played a significant role in shaping public perception of Bitcoin. In its early days, Bitcoin was often portrayed in the media as a tool for criminals or associated with illicit activities due to its pseudonymous nature. However, as more individuals and businesses began to recognize the potential benefits of Bitcoin, the media's coverage gradually shifted. News articles and features highlighted the technological innovations, the potential for financial inclusion, and the transformative power of decentralized currencies. Positive media coverage helped to dispel some of the initial skepticism and broaden the understanding of Bitcoin among the general public.

Over time, as Bitcoin's network grew, its value increased, and its use cases expanded, initial reactions began to evolve. Skeptics became more open-minded, financial institutions started exploring blockchain technology, and governments began developing regulatory frameworks to address the challenges and opportunities presented by cryptocurrencies.

Bitcoin's initial reactions and the subsequent evolution of public perception laid the foundation for the broader adoption and recognition of cryptocurrencies. The journey from skepticism to acceptance required education, awareness, and a growing body of evidence demonstrating the practical applications and potential benefits of Bitcoin.

Type This URL In Your Browser → **https://bit.ly/Guess_What_This**

As we continue to explore the Bitcoin journey, we will delve deeper into the evolution of public perception, the ongoing regulatory landscape, and the transformative impact of cryptocurrencies on finance and society. Join us on this captivating adventure as we uncover the mysteries and marvels of the Bitcoin network—an embodiment of the transformative power of decentralized technologies.

Chapter 13: The First Transactions

With the creation of Bitcoin, Satoshi Nakamoto set in motion a new era of decentralized digital currency. As the network gained traction and more individuals became interested in this groundbreaking technology, the first transactions using Bitcoin took place. In this chapter, we delve into the details of these inaugural transactions, exploring their significance and the impact they had on the nascent Bitcoin ecosystem.

The first recorded transaction in Bitcoin's history occurred on January 12, 2009, when Satoshi Nakamoto sent 10 bitcoins to Hal Finney, an early collaborator and notable figure in the cryptography community. This transaction marked the transfer of value on the Bitcoin network, demonstrating the practical application of the digital currency. It showcased the potential for individuals to transact directly, without the need for intermediaries or centralized control.

The transaction between Nakamoto and Finney was not a random event but a deliberate act to test the functionality and viability of Bitcoin. Finney, an active participant in the early development of the cryptocurrency, had contributed valuable insights and feedback to Nakamoto's work. The transaction served as a testament to the collaborative nature of the Bitcoin project, highlighting the trust and camaraderie that existed among its early participants.

The first transaction showcased the transparent and immutable nature of the blockchain, the underlying technology behind Bitcoin. Every transaction on the network is recorded on the blockchain, creating a public ledger that can be viewed by anyone. This transparency ensures accountability and helps prevent fraud or double-spending.

As word of Bitcoin spread and more individuals joined the network, additional transactions took place. One notable transaction occurred on May 22, 2010, when Laszlo Hanyecz, a Bitcoin enthusiast, made history by purchasing two pizzas for 10,000 bitcoins. This transaction, which took place on the Bitcointalk forum, became known as the "Bitcoin Pizza Day", and is celebrated annually by the cryptocurrency community. The transaction exemplified the use of Bitcoin as a medium of exchange, further validating its potential as a currency.

In the early days of Bitcoin, transactions were primarily conducted among the community of enthusiasts and early adopters. Bitcoin was used as a means of exchanging goods and services within this niche community. Online marketplaces, such as the now-defunct Silk Road, also emerged, facilitating transactions involving illegal goods and services. While these activities brought attention to the darker side of Bitcoin's use, they also demonstrated the censorship-resistant nature of the network.

Over time, as Bitcoin gained broader recognition, more businesses and merchants began accepting the digital currency as a form of payment. This marked an important milestone in the adoption of Bitcoin, as it allowed individuals to use the cryptocurrency for everyday purchases. Companies like Overstock.com and Newegg embraced Bitcoin, paving the way for mainstream acceptance.

The first transactions using Bitcoin were not without challenges. The limited infrastructure, scalability concerns, and volatility of the cryptocurrency posed hurdles to widespread adoption. However, the early transactions served as a proof of concept, demonstrating the potential for a decentralized digital currency to disrupt traditional financial systems.

The significance of these initial transactions extends beyond their individual value. They represented the birth of a new financial paradigm—one that challenged the authority of central banks and governments, and empowered individuals with greater control over their finances. The early adopters who engaged in these transactions played a pivotal role in shaping the narrative and spreading awareness about the transformative power of Bitcoin.

The first transactions also fueled speculation and interest in Bitcoin as an investment. As the value of Bitcoin increased over time, early adopters and investors realized significant returns on their initial transactions. The stories of those who became Bitcoin millionaires captured the imagination of the public, further fueling the interest and curiosity surrounding the digital currency.

As we venture further into the Bitcoin journey, we will explore the evolution of transactions, the advancements in payment infrastructure, and the ongoing quest for scalability and usability. Join us on this captivating adventure as we uncover the mysteries and marvels of the Bitcoin network—an embodiment of the transformative power of decentralized technologies.

Type This URL in Your Browser → **https://bit.ly/Guess_What_This**

Chapter 14: The Creation of BitcoinTalk

In the early days of Bitcoin, when the community was still small but growing rapidly, a forum emerged that would become the epicenter of discussions, collaborations, and the exchange of ideas—the BitcoinTalk forum. Created by Satoshi Nakamoto, the mysterious creator of Bitcoin, BitcoinTalk played a vital role in fostering the nascent cryptocurrency community. In this chapter, we explore the creation of BitcoinTalk, its impact on the Bitcoin ecosystem, and the vibrant discussions that unfolded within its virtual halls.

BitcoinTalk was launched on November 22, 2009, as an online forum dedicated to Bitcoin and related topics. It provided a platform for enthusiasts, developers, investors, and curious individuals to come together and engage in discussions surrounding the innovative digital currency. The forum quickly gained popularity, attracting users from around the world who were eager to participate in the burgeoning Bitcoin community.

Satoshi Nakamoto's vision for BitcoinTalk was to create a space where individuals could exchange knowledge, share insights, and collaborate on the development and adoption of Bitcoin. The forum featured various sections covering technical discussions, project development, marketplace activities, and even a section dedicated to off-topic discussions. This structure allowed for a diverse range of topics to be explored, fostering a vibrant and inclusive community.

One of the key features of BitcoinTalk was the introduction of user ranks and a merit system. As users contributed valuable content and engaged in meaningful discussions, they could earn merits from other forum members. This system helped distinguish knowledgeable and respected individuals within the community and encouraged active participation.

BitcoinTalk became the go-to platform for Bitcoin enthusiasts to share their ideas, showcase their projects, and seek feedback from the community. It served as a breeding ground for innovation, with developers showcasing their early implementations of Bitcoin wallets, exchanges, and other tools. These discussions and collaborations within the forum were instrumental in driving the growth and improvement of the Bitcoin ecosystem.

One notable aspect of BitcoinTalk was the "Services" section, where users could offer their goods and services in exchange for bitcoins. This section became a hub for early Bitcoin adoption, as individuals could now use the digital currency to purchase a wide range of products and services. BitcoinTalk acted as a catalyst for the development of a Bitcoin-based economy, demonstrating the practical applications of the digital currency beyond speculative investment.

The forum also played a crucial role in disseminating important updates and announcements related to Bitcoin. Nakamoto used BitcoinTalk to make significant announcements, including software updates and the transfer of administrative control to Gavin Andresen, who became the lead developer of the Bitcoin client. These announcements not only provided important information but also fostered transparency and accountability within the community.

BitcoinTalk was not without its challenges. As the popularity of Bitcoin grew, so did the forum's user base, resulting in a significant increase in spam, scams, and malicious activity. Despite efforts to moderate and regulate the forum, these challenges persisted. However, the community remained resilient, with dedicated users continuing to contribute valuable content and engage in meaningful discussions.

The creation of BitcoinTalk laid the groundwork for the development of a strong and vibrant Bitcoin community. It provided a space for individuals to connect, collaborate, and learn from one another. The forum's inclusive nature welcomed newcomers and seasoned veterans alike, fostering an environment of shared knowledge and camaraderie.

As BitcoinTalk flourished, it became a source of inspiration for other cryptocurrency communities and forums. It set a precedent for open discussions and the exchange of ideas, promoting the decentralized ethos that underpins the world of cryptocurrencies. BitcoinTalk's influence extended far beyond its virtual walls, as individuals who met and collaborated on the forum went on to contribute to various Bitcoin-related projects and initiatives.

While BitcoinTalk has gradually diminished in prominence over the years, its impact on the early Bitcoin ecosystem cannot be overstated. It played a crucial role in shaping the narrative, fostering collaboration, and spreading awareness about the transformative potential of Bitcoin. The forum acted as a catalyst, propelling the cryptocurrency forward and laying the groundwork for the broader adoption and recognition of Bitcoin.

As we journey further into the Bitcoin narrative, we will explore the evolution of communication channels within the cryptocurrency community, the rise of social media platforms, and the ongoing quest for open and inclusive discussions. Join us on this captivating adventure as we uncover the mysteries and marvels of the Bitcoin network—a testament to the power of community, collaboration, and the decentralized revolution.

Chapter 15: Satoshi's Growing Influence

As Bitcoin gained traction and the community around it grew, Satoshi Nakamoto's influence as the creator of Bitcoin began to extend far beyond the initial stages of development. Despite Nakamoto's enigmatic nature and the decision to step away from the project in 2010, their ideas and vision continued to shape the trajectory of Bitcoin and the broader world of cryptocurrencies. In this chapter, we explore the growing influence of Satoshi Nakamoto, the enduring impact of their contributions, and the ongoing quest to unravel the mystery of their true identity.

The Bitcoin White Paper:

Satoshi Nakamoto's most significant contribution was the Bitcoin white paper, which outlined the principles and technical details of the cryptocurrency. The white paper served as a blueprint for the development and implementation of Bitcoin, providing a comprehensive overview of its decentralized nature, the consensus mechanism, and the vision for a peer-to-peer electronic cash system. Nakamoto's clear and concise explanations in the white paper laid the foundation for the subsequent growth and adoption of Bitcoin.

The Bitcoin Software:

Nakamoto's creation of the original Bitcoin software, which served as the backbone of the network, was instrumental in establishing the infrastructure for the digital currency. The open-source nature of the software allowed for collaboration and improvement from developers around the world. While Nakamoto handed over the reins to other developers, their early work and the core principles embedded in the software laid the groundwork for subsequent advancements and iterations.

Early Collaborators:

The relationships and collaborations Nakamoto formed with early Bitcoin enthusiasts and developers further extended their influence. Collaborators such as Hal Finney, Gavin Andresen, and Martti Malmi played crucial roles in the early stages of Bitcoin's development. Their technical expertise, contributions, and ongoing advocacy for Bitcoin helped solidify its legitimacy and foster its growth.

The influence of these early collaborators, combined with Nakamoto's original vision, propelled Bitcoin forward and attracted a broader audience.

Visionary Principles:

Nakamoto's vision for Bitcoin extended beyond the technical aspects of the cryptocurrency. They emphasized the importance of decentralization, individual control over financial transactions, and the potential for a more inclusive and transparent financial system. These principles resonated with individuals seeking alternatives to traditional financial institutions, and they continue to inspire the development of new decentralized technologies and the exploration of blockchain's potential in various industries.

Satoshi's Anonymity:

The enigma surrounding Nakamoto's true identity added a layer of intrigue and mystique to their growing influence. Satoshi Nakamoto's decision to remain anonymous, communicating only through online channels and disappearing from public view, fueled speculation, and heightened interest in Bitcoin. The anonymity of Nakamoto allowed the technology to stand on its own merits, free from associations with any particular individual's reputation or motives.

Unraveling the Mystery:

Despite Nakamoto's withdrawal from the Bitcoin project, the quest to uncover their true identity has persisted. Numerous individuals and organizations have attempted to unveil the person or group behind the pseudonym, with various theories and claims emerging. However, to this day, the true identity of Satoshi Nakamoto remains unknown. The mystery surrounding Nakamoto's identity has become a part of Bitcoin's narrative, capturing the imagination of enthusiasts, and sparking countless debates and investigations.

Satoshi Nakamoto's growing influence transcends the individual and embodies the power of ideas and decentralized innovation. The enduring impact of Nakamoto's contributions is evident in the widespread adoption and recognition of Bitcoin as the pioneer of the cryptocurrency movement. Nakamoto's influence extends beyond Bitcoin itself, inspiring the development of numerous other cryptocurrencies and blockchain-based projects.

As we delve deeper into the Bitcoin journey, we will explore the ongoing developments in the cryptocurrency space, the evolving role of decentralization in finance and technology, and the quest for Satoshi Nakamoto's true identity. Join us on this captivating adventure as we uncover the mysteries and marvels of the Bitcoin network—a testament to the power of innovation, collaboration, and the transformative potential of decentralized technologies.

Type This URL in Your Browser → **https://bit.ly/Guess_What_This**

Chapter 16: The Rise of Alternative Cryptocurrencies

Bitcoin's emergence in 2009 as the world's first decentralized cryptocurrency laid the foundation for a new era of digital currencies. As the Bitcoin community grew, so did the desire for alternative cryptocurrencies that could address different use cases, improve upon Bitcoin's limitations, or experiment with new technologies. In this chapter, we explore the rise of alternative cryptocurrencies, also known as altcoins, their diverse features, and the impact they have had on the cryptocurrency landscape.

The Birth of Altcoins:

The first alternative cryptocurrency to gain significant traction was Namecoin, launched in 2011. Namecoin aimed to create a decentralized domain name system (DNS) that would allow for censorship-resistant and pseudonymous domain name registrations. This marked the beginning of a wave of altcoin creations that sought to explore different applications and improve upon Bitcoin's design.

Litecoin and Scrypt-Based Coins:

Litecoin, created by Charlie Lee in 2011, was one of the earliest altcoins to gain widespread recognition. It introduced several improvements over Bitcoin, including faster block generation times and a different hashing algorithm called Scrypt. The use of Scrypt made Litecoin resistant to the specialized mining hardware used in Bitcoin mining, promoting a more decentralized mining landscape. Litecoin's success paved the way for the development of numerous other Scrypt-based altcoins.

Ethereum and Smart Contract Platforms:

In 2015, Ethereum burst onto the scene, introducing the concept of smart contracts—a revolutionary technology that enables programmable and self-executing contracts on the blockchain. Ethereum's blockchain became a platform for building decentralized applications (DApps) and launching new cryptocurrencies through initial coin offerings (ICOs). The Ethereum platform empowered developers to create complex blockchain-based applications, fueling a surge of innovation and the rise of a vibrant ecosystem of altcoins.

Privacy-Focused Coins:

Privacy has been a recurring theme in the world of cryptocurrencies, and altcoins emerged to address the need for enhanced privacy and anonymity. Monero, launched in 2014, focused on privacy by implementing advanced cryptographic techniques such as ring signatures and stealth addresses. Zcash, introduced in 2016, pioneered the use of zero-knowledge proofs to allow for private transactions while still maintaining a transparent blockchain. These privacy-focused altcoins aimed to provide users with increased confidentiality in their financial transactions.

Stablecoins:

Stablecoins entered the cryptocurrency scene to address the issue of price volatility that often plagues cryptocurrencies like Bitcoin. These altcoins are designed to maintain a stable value by pegging their price to an external asset, such as a fiat currency or a commodity. Tether, launched in 2014, was one of the first stablecoins to gain significant traction. It sought to provide stability by maintaining a 1:1 ratio with the US dollar. Since then, several other stablecoins, such as USDC and DAI, have emerged, offering stability, and acting as a bridge between the traditional financial system and the world of cryptocurrencies.

Niche and Experimental Altcoins:

The altcoin landscape is not limited to specific categories but encompasses a wide range of niche and experimental cryptocurrencies. Some altcoins aim to target specific industries or use cases, such as Ripple for cross-border payments or IOTA for the Internet of Things (IoT). Others explore novel consensus mechanisms, governance models, or scalability solutions. These altcoins offer opportunities for innovation, experimentation, and the exploration of new possibilities beyond the scope of Bitcoin.

The rise of alternative cryptocurrencies has expanded the possibilities and use cases within the broader cryptocurrency ecosystem. Altcoins have provided avenues for technological experimentation, specialization, and innovation, fostering healthy competition, and pushing the boundaries of what is possible with blockchain technology.

However, it is important to note that not all altcoins have gained equal success or stood the test of time. The cryptocurrency market is highly volatile and constantly evolving, with new altcoins entering and exiting the scene regularly. Investors and enthusiasts need to exercise caution and conduct thorough research before engaging with any altcoin.

As we venture further into the cryptocurrency landscape, we will explore the ongoing developments in altcoins, the emergence of new categories, and the evolution of the cryptocurrency market. Join us on this captivating adventure as we uncover the mysteries and marvels of alternative cryptocurrencies—a testament to the ever-evolving nature of decentralized technologies.

Chapter 17: Satoshi's Disappearance

One of the enduring mysteries surrounding Bitcoin is the sudden disappearance of its creator, Satoshi Nakamoto. After introducing the world to Bitcoin and playing an instrumental role in its early development, Nakamoto vanished from the public eye in 2010, leaving behind a legacy and a trail of unanswered questions. In this chapter, we delve into the details surrounding Nakamoto's disappearance, the theories and speculations that emerged, and the ongoing quest to uncover their true identity.

The last known communication from Nakamoto occurred in early 2010 when they handed over control of the Bitcoin project to Gavin Andresen, one of the early collaborators. Nakamoto's final public message was a brief email stating, "I've moved on to other things." Since then, Nakamoto has not made any public appearances or communicated directly with the Bitcoin community.

The sudden disappearance of Nakamoto raised eyebrows and fueled intense speculation about their true identity and motives. Many theories emerged, ranging from Nakamoto being an individual to being a group of individuals working under a pseudonym. Some speculated that Nakamoto might have decided to step away to preserve their privacy or to avoid potential legal implications associated with their creation. Others believed that Nakamoto's disappearance was a deliberate act to empower the decentralized nature of Bitcoin, freeing it from any centralized authority or influence.

Over the years, several individuals have been accused of being Nakamoto, but none of these claims have been definitively proven. Names such as Dorian Nakamoto, Hal Finney, and Nick Szabo have been linked to Nakamoto based on various pieces of evidence and circumstantial connections. However, each of these individuals has either denied being Nakamoto or had their involvement debunked. The true identity of Satoshi Nakamoto remains one of the most captivating mysteries in the cryptocurrency world.

Nakamoto's disappearance did not halt the progress of Bitcoin or dampen the enthusiasm surrounding it. Instead, it further fueled the curiosity and passion of the growing Bitcoin community. Developers, entrepreneurs, and enthusiasts carried the torch forward, continuing to build upon Nakamoto's initial vision and contribute to the growth and development of the cryptocurrency ecosystem.

Nakamoto's absence also highlighted the decentralized nature of Bitcoin. Unlike traditional financial systems, which often rely on central figures, Bitcoin operates on a peer-to-peer network without a single point of control. This absence of a central authority contributes to the censorship resistance and resilience of the network. Nakamoto's disappearance underscored the notion that Bitcoin was designed to exist and thrive independently of any single individual or group.

Despite their withdrawal from the public eye, Nakamoto's influence on the world of cryptocurrencies remains profound. The Bitcoin white paper and the original Bitcoin software continue to serve as the foundation for countless blockchain-based projects and digital currencies. Nakamoto's revolutionary ideas, such as decentralized consensus, transparent ledgers, and the potential for financial empowerment, have inspired a wave of innovation and transformed the financial landscape.

The search for Nakamoto's true identity has become a topic of fascination and intrigue within the cryptocurrency community and beyond. Journalists, researchers, and cryptocurrency enthusiasts have devoted countless hours to unraveling the mystery, exploring connections, analyzing writing styles, and digging into historical records. While there have been promising leads and tantalizing clues, the true identity of Nakamoto remains elusive.

The anonymity of Nakamoto has also become a symbol of the broader ethos of privacy and decentralization within the cryptocurrency movement. Nakamoto's decision to remain anonymous ensures that Bitcoin stands on its own merits, divorced from any particular individual's reputation or motives. It reinforces the notion that cryptocurrencies are not reliant on central figures, but rather on the collective efforts and consensus of the community.

As the years pass, the mystery surrounding Nakamoto's disappearance continues to captivate the imagination of individuals around the world. Speculation and theories persist, with new claims and evidence emerging periodically. The quest for Nakamoto's true identity serves as a reminder of the enigmatic nature of the cryptocurrency world and the transformative power of decentralized technologies.

As we journey deeper into the world of Bitcoin and cryptocurrencies, we will explore the ongoing developments, advancements, and challenges faced by the decentralized revolution. Join us on this captivating adventure as we uncover the mysteries and marvels of the Bitcoin network—an embodiment of the transformative potential of decentralized technologies and the enduring legacy of Satoshi Nakamoto.

Type This URL in Your Browser → ***https://bit.ly/Guess_What_This***

Chapter 18: Satoshi's Last Correspondence

In the early days of Bitcoin, Satoshi Nakamoto was an active and influential figure, guiding the development of the cryptocurrency and engaging in discussions with the growing community. However, as Bitcoin gained traction and the community expanded, Nakamoto gradually withdrew from the public eye. In this chapter, we explore the circumstances surrounding Nakamoto's last known correspondence, the content of their final messages, and the impact they had on the Bitcoin ecosystem.

Nakamoto's last known communication occurred in early 2010. On April 23rd of that year, Nakamoto sent an email to Gavin Andresen, who had become the lead developer of the Bitcoin project. In the email, Nakamoto expressed concerns about the growing visibility of Bitcoin and their intention to step back from the project. They wrote, "I've moved on to other things. It's in good hands with Gavin and everyone." This brief message signaled a turning point in Nakamoto's involvement with Bitcoin and marked the beginning of their withdrawal from public communication.

The content of Nakamoto's final messages reflected a sense of detachment from the project they had birthed. In their correspondence, Nakamoto reiterated the decentralized nature of Bitcoin, emphasizing that they were not the sole authority or decision-maker. They encouraged the Bitcoin community to take ownership of the project and continue its development independently. Nakamoto's departure was a deliberate act to ensure that Bitcoin would thrive as a decentralized network free from any single individual's influence.

The impact of Nakamoto's last known correspondence on the Bitcoin ecosystem was significant. It symbolized a transition from a founder-led project to a community-driven endeavor. Nakamoto's departure challenged the community to embrace their individual roles and responsibilities in the development and adoption of Bitcoin. The community responded by rallying around the principles outlined in the Bitcoin white paper and collaborating to further the growth of the cryptocurrency.

Nakamoto's withdrawal from the public eye left a void in the Bitcoin community, as many had grown accustomed to their insights and guidance. However, the community adapted and continued to build upon Nakamoto's foundational work. Developers, entrepreneurs, and enthusiasts stepped up to contribute their expertise, leading to advancements in various areas such as scalability, privacy, and usability. The absence of Nakamoto also sparked a renewed sense of curiosity and fascination within the cryptocurrency community and beyond. People became intrigued by the mystery surrounding Nakamoto's true identity, and numerous theories and investigations emerged. Journalists, researchers, and enthusiasts dedicated significant time and resources to uncovering the person or group behind the pseudonym. The search for Nakamoto became a topic of ongoing debate and speculation, generating a sense of intrigue and captivation that persists to this day.

Nakamoto's last correspondence also highlighted the broader ethos of privacy and decentralization that underpins the cryptocurrency movement. By choosing to remain anonymous and eventually stepping away from the project, Nakamoto ensured that Bitcoin stood on its own merits, divorced from any centralized authority or individual influence. This decision reinforced the principles of decentralization, transparency, and individual empowerment that remain integral to the cryptocurrency ecosystem.

While Nakamoto's last correspondence signaled their withdrawal from public communication, it did not diminish their impact on the development and trajectory of Bitcoin. The Bitcoin white paper and the original software laid the foundation for subsequent advancements and inspired countless individuals to join the cryptocurrency revolution. Nakamoto's visionary ideas, including decentralized consensus, transparent ledgers, and the potential for financial empowerment, continue to shape the broader landscape of decentralized technologies.

As we continue our exploration of the Bitcoin journey, we will delve deeper into the ongoing developments, challenges, and innovations within the cryptocurrency ecosystem. We will also delve into the enduring quest to uncover the true identity of Satoshi Nakamoto, a mystery that continues to captivate the imagination of individuals around the world. Join us on this captivating adventure as we uncover the mysteries and marvels of the Bitcoin network—an embodiment of the transformative potential of decentralized technologies and the lasting legacy of Satoshi Nakamoto.

Chapter 19: Satoshi's Legacy in the Crypto Community

The legacy of Satoshi Nakamoto, the pseudonymous creator of Bitcoin, extends far beyond the creation of the world's first decentralized cryptocurrency. Nakamoto's ideas, vision, and contributions have had a profound and lasting impact on the broader crypto community. In this chapter, we delve into the legacy of Satoshi Nakamoto, exploring their influence on the development of cryptocurrencies, blockchain technology, and the decentralized revolution.

Pioneering Decentralization:

Satoshi Nakamoto's most significant contribution was the introduction of the concept of decentralization. Bitcoin was designed to operate without a central authority, enabling individuals to transact directly with one another without the need for intermediaries. Nakamoto's vision of a peer-to-peer electronic cash system laid the foundation for the broader decentralization movement, inspiring the development of countless cryptocurrencies and blockchain-based projects.

Transparency and Immutable Ledgers:

The transparent and immutable nature of the blockchain, the underlying technology behind Bitcoin, has become a hallmark of cryptocurrencies. Nakamoto's design ensured that every transaction on the Bitcoin network would be recorded on the blockchain, creating a public ledger that can be viewed by anyone. This transparency promotes trust, accountability, and the prevention of fraud. The concept of a transparent and immutable ledger has been embraced by various industries and has the potential to revolutionize systems beyond finance.

Proof-of-Work Consensus:

Bitcoin introduced the revolutionary consensus mechanism known as proof-of-work (PoW), which ensures the security and integrity of the blockchain. By requiring miners to solve complex mathematical puzzles, PoW prevents malicious actors from gaining control over the network. Nakamoto's innovative use of PoW not only secured the Bitcoin network but also inspired the development of other consensus mechanisms, such as proof-of-stake (PoS) and delegated proof-of-stake (DPoS), which are now used by many other cryptocurrencies.

Cryptographic Innovations:

Nakamoto's understanding of cryptography played a pivotal role in the design of Bitcoin. The use of cryptographic algorithms, such as hash functions and digital signatures, ensures the security and privacy of transactions on the network. Nakamoto's cryptographic innovations have not only facilitated secure and efficient financial transactions but have also influenced the broader field of cryptography and its applications in various domains.

Fostering Innovation and Collaboration:

Nakamoto's creation of Bitcoin inspired a wave of innovation and collaboration within the crypto community. Developers, entrepreneurs, and enthusiasts were motivated by Nakamoto's vision and the potential of decentralized technologies. The open-source nature of Bitcoin's software encouraged collaboration, allowing individuals from around the world to contribute to its development and improvement. Nakamoto's legacy of fostering innovation and collaboration continues to shape the crypto community today.

Financial Empowerment:

Nakamoto's vision of financial empowerment resonated with individuals seeking alternatives to traditional financial systems. By enabling individuals to have direct control over their funds and transact without the need for intermediaries, Nakamoto sought to empower individuals economically. This vision has influenced the rise of decentralized finance (DeFi) and has opened up new possibilities for financial inclusion and economic empowerment, particularly in regions with limited access to traditional banking services.

Philosophical Implications:

Beyond the technological advancements, Nakamoto's work has sparked philosophical discussions and reflections on the nature of money, trust, and governance. Bitcoin challenged the prevailing notions of centralized control, highlighting the potential for decentralized systems to provide alternatives to traditional institutions. Nakamoto's ideas have prompted individuals to question established power structures, explore new economic models, and imagine a future where decentralized technologies play a central role.

Nakamoto's Enigma:

The enigmatic nature of Nakamoto's true identity has added an element of intrigue and fascination to their legacy. The anonymity of Nakamoto has allowed the technology to stand on its own merits, free from associations with any particular individual. Nakamoto's decision to step away from the project and remain anonymous reinforces the decentralized ethos of cryptocurrencies and emphasizes the collective effort and consensus-driven nature of their development.

The legacy of Satoshi Nakamoto is deeply intertwined with the evolution of cryptocurrencies, blockchain technology, and the decentralized revolution. Nakamoto's ideas and contributions continue to shape the crypto community, inspiring further innovation, collaboration, and exploration of the potential of decentralized technologies.

As we journey further into the world of cryptocurrencies, we will continue to uncover the impact of Nakamoto's legacy on the development and adoption of decentralized technologies. Join us on this captivating adventure as we explore the mysteries and marvels of the crypto community—a testament to the transformative power of Satoshi Nakamoto's vision and the ongoing pursuit of a decentralized future.

Chapter 20: The Hunt for Satoshi Nakamoto

The search for the true identity of Satoshi Nakamoto, the enigmatic creator of Bitcoin, has captivated the imagination of countless individuals within and beyond the cryptocurrency community. Since Nakamoto's disappearance from the public eye in 2010, numerous theories, investigations, and claims have emerged, each attempting to unveil the person or group behind the pseudonym. In this chapter, we delve into the fascinating world of the hunt for Satoshi Nakamoto, exploring the key players, intriguing leads, and the ongoing quest to unravel this captivating mystery.

The quest to uncover the true identity of Satoshi Nakamoto began soon after their departure from the Bitcoin project. As Bitcoin gained wider recognition and the community expanded, curiosity grew, and individuals became increasingly intrigued by the persona behind the creation of the world's first decentralized cryptocurrency.

One of the early figures implicated as Nakamoto was Dorian Nakamoto, a Japanese-American physicist living in California. In 2014, a Newsweek article claimed that Dorian Nakamoto was the elusive creator of Bitcoin, leading to a frenzy of media attention. However, Dorian Nakamoto denied any involvement in Bitcoin and emphasized the misunderstanding caused by the misinterpretation of his words.

Another individual who drew attention was Hal Finney, an early cryptographer and one of the first individuals to interact with Nakamoto in the Bitcoin community. Finney's involvement with Bitcoin and his close proximity to the project's early stages fueled speculation about his potential role as Nakamoto. However, Finney vehemently denied being Nakamoto and maintained that he was just an early supporter and contributor to the project.

Nick Szabo, a computer scientist, and cryptographer, has also been linked to Nakamoto. Szabo's work on "bit gold," a precursor to Bitcoin, and his expertise in decentralized technologies made him a subject of speculation. However, Szabo has consistently denied being Nakamoto and maintains that he is an independent researcher and not the creator of Bitcoin.

The search for Nakamoto intensified with the emergence of Craig Wright, an Australian entrepreneur and computer scientist. In 2016, Wright publicly claimed to be Nakamoto, presenting cryptographic evidence to support his assertion. However, his claims were met with skepticism and met with widespread scrutiny within the cryptocurrency community and the broader tech industry. Many experts and community members challenged Wright's evidence, leading to ongoing debates and a lack of consensus regarding his claims.

While these individuals garnered significant attention, the true identity of Satoshi Nakamoto remains unknown. The hunt for Nakamoto has extended beyond investigating potential individuals to exploring linguistic patterns, coding styles, and other forensic analyses in an attempt to unveil the truth. Some researchers have analyzed Nakamoto's writings and compared them to those of suspected candidates to identify linguistic similarities or distinctive patterns that could provide clues.

The pursuit of Nakamoto has not been limited to individuals but has also involved media organizations, independent researchers, and dedicated enthusiasts. The efforts to uncover Nakamoto's identity have taken various forms, including online forums, investigations, and even bounty programs offering rewards for verifiable information leading to the unmasking of Nakamoto.

Despite the numerous theories and claims, no definitive evidence has been produced to confirm the true identity of Satoshi Nakamoto. Nakamoto's decision to remain anonymous, coupled with their deliberate withdrawal from the Bitcoin project, has ensured that the creator's identity remains a captivating mystery—a testament to the power of decentralized technologies and the allure of the unknown.

The ongoing hunt for Nakamoto serves as a reminder of the decentralized nature of cryptocurrencies. Bitcoin operates without reliance on any central figure, making it a truly decentralized network. Nakamoto's anonymity reinforces the idea that cryptocurrencies can thrive independently of any single individual or group, inspiring trust and fostering a sense of community ownership.

While the hunt for Nakamoto continues, it is important to acknowledge the legacy they have left behind. Nakamoto's creation of Bitcoin and their vision of a peer-to-peer electronic cash system have reshaped the

Type This URL in Your Browser → **https://bit.ly/Guess_What_This**

financial landscape, inspiring innovation and sparking a global movement towards decentralized technologies.

As we conclude this chapter, we embrace the mystery surrounding Satoshi Nakamoto's identity and reflect on the enduring legacy they have imparted upon the crypto community. The hunt for Nakamoto serves as a reminder of the power of decentralization, the collaborative nature of cryptocurrencies, and the boundless potential for innovation within the ever-evolving world of blockchain technology.

Chapter 21: The Satoshi Nakamoto Controversies

Satoshi Nakamoto, the pseudonymous creator of Bitcoin, has left an indelible mark on the world of cryptocurrencies. However, the legacy of Nakamoto is not without its fair share of controversies. Over the years, various controversies have arisen surrounding Nakamoto's identity, their motivations, and even the future of Bitcoin itself. In this chapter, we delve into the intriguing controversies that have surrounded Satoshi Nakamoto, shedding light on the debates and challenges that have emerged within the crypto community.

Identity Debates:

One of the primary controversies surrounding Nakamoto revolves around their true identity. Numerous individuals have been accused of being Nakamoto, sparking intense debates and media scrutiny. However, despite the claims and investigations, the true identity of Nakamoto remains unknown. This lack of clarity has fueled skepticism and raised questions about the credibility and legitimacy of Bitcoin. Some critics argue that the anonymity of Nakamoto undermines the transparency and trustworthiness of the cryptocurrency.

Bitcoin's Original Vision:

As Bitcoin grew in popularity, debates arose regarding whether the cryptocurrency had strayed from Nakamoto's original vision. Some members of the community believed that the focus on Bitcoin as a store of value and an investment vehicle had diverged from the initial goal of creating a peer-to-peer electronic cash system. This controversy highlighted the tension between those who sought to preserve the original intent of Bitcoin and those who saw potential in its evolution as a digital asset.

Scaling and Governance:

Bitcoin's scalability challenges and the debate over its governance model have been ongoing points of contention within the community. Disagreements regarding the best approach to scale Bitcoin and handle transaction congestion have led to contentious debates and even the creation of alternative cryptocurrencies. These controversies reflect differing opinions on how to balance decentralization, security, and scalability, and have resulted in the emergence of competing factions within the crypto community.

Forks and Hard Forks:

The introduction of forks, both soft and hard, has stirred controversy in the Bitcoin ecosystem. Forks occur when a cryptocurrency splits into two separate chains with different rule sets. Soft forks are generally less contentious, while hard forks can result in the creation of entirely new cryptocurrencies. Controversial hard forks, such as the Bitcoin Cash and Bitcoin SV forks, have sparked debates around community consensus, market fragmentation, and the overall stability of the Bitcoin ecosystem.

Satoshi's Stash:

The question of what happened to Nakamoto's early Bitcoin holdings, often referred to as "Satoshi's stash," has been a subject of speculation and controversy. It is estimated that Nakamoto mined and held a significant number of early bitcoins. Some argue that if Nakamoto were to sell or utilize these holdings, it could have a significant impact on the Bitcoin market. Others believe that Nakamoto's decision to hold onto their bitcoins demonstrates a long-term commitment to the project and a belief in its potential value.

Patent Controversies:

In 2018, Craig Wright, who claims to be Nakamoto, filed for various Bitcoin-related patents, sparking a new wave of controversies. Many in the crypto community opposed the idea of one individual claiming intellectual property rights over a decentralized technology like Bitcoin. The patent controversies brought to the forefront the tension between open-source collaboration and the desire to protect intellectual property within the crypto space.

Influence on Altcoins:

As alternative cryptocurrencies, or altcoins, gained popularity, controversies arose regarding Nakamoto's influence on these projects. Some argue that Nakamoto's absence and the lack of direct guidance allowed for the development of altcoins that deviated from the original vision of a decentralized, peer-to-peer electronic cash system. The proliferation of altcoins raised questions about the potential dilution of

Nakamoto's influence and the cohesiveness of the broader cryptocurrency movement.

These controversies surrounding Satoshi Nakamoto and Bitcoin serve as reminders of the challenges inherent in navigating a decentralized and rapidly evolving ecosystem. They also reflect the passionate debates and diverse perspectives within the crypto community, highlighting the need for open dialogue, collaboration, and ongoing governance discussions.

While controversies may bring forth differing viewpoints and challenges, they also present opportunities for growth, learning, and the refinement of ideas. The controversies surrounding Nakamoto and Bitcoin have spurred conversations on topics such as identity, governance, scalability, and the future of decentralized technologies.

As we conclude this chapter, it is important to recognize that controversies are an inherent part of any revolutionary technology. The controversies surrounding Nakamoto and Bitcoin have not only shaped the narrative of cryptocurrencies but have also contributed to the resilience and evolution of the broader crypto community. They serve as reminders that the path to innovation is often accompanied by challenges, debates, and controversies—a testament to the transformative potential of Satoshi Nakamoto's vision and the ongoing pursuit of a decentralized future.

Chapter 22: Theories on Satoshi's True Identity

The enigmatic figure of Satoshi Nakamoto, the pseudonymous creator of Bitcoin, has spurred countless theories and speculations regarding their true identity. Over the years, individuals, researchers, and enthusiasts have put forward various theories and potential candidates in an attempt to unravel the mystery behind Nakamoto's persona. In this chapter, we delve into some of the most intriguing theories surrounding the identity of Satoshi Nakamoto, exploring the clues, evidence, and controversies that have emerged in the quest to unmask the creator of Bitcoin.

Single Individual Theory:

One prevailing theory suggests that Satoshi Nakamoto is an individual who developed Bitcoin alone. This theory posits that Nakamoto used a pseudonym to protect their identity and maintain privacy. Supporters of this theory believe that Nakamoto's deep understanding of cryptography, coding expertise, and the coherent narrative presented in the Bitcoin white paper indicate the work of a single, highly skilled individual. However, the true identity of this individual remains unknown, adding to the mystique surrounding Nakamoto.

Group of Collaborators Theory:

Another theory proposes that Satoshi Nakamoto is not an individual but a collective effort by a group of collaborators. Advocates of this theory argue that the complexity and breadth of the Bitcoin project would require the input of multiple experts in cryptography, computer science, economics, and more. They suggest that Nakamoto's use of the singular pronoun "I" in their communications could be a deliberate strategy to create the illusion of an individual creator. However, concrete evidence supporting this theory remains elusive.

Nick Szabo:

Nick Szabo, a renowned computer scientist and cryptographer, has been the subject of speculation regarding his potential connection to Satoshi Nakamoto. Szabo's work on "bit gold," a concept that shares similarities with Bitcoin, has led some to believe that he may be the true identity behind Nakamoto. Additionally, linguistic and writing style analyses have drawn parallels between Szabo's writings and Nakamoto's early communications. However, Szabo has consistently denied being Nakamoto, asserting that he is an independent researcher.

Hal Finney:

Hal Finney, a cryptographic pioneer, and an early contributor to the Bitcoin project, has also been linked to the identity of Satoshi Nakamoto. Some believe that Finney's close association with Nakamoto during Bitcoin's early days, as well as his technical expertise and involvement in the cypherpunk movement, make him a plausible candidate. However, Finney consistently denied being Nakamoto, and his role in the Bitcoin project was that of a dedicated supporter rather than the creator.

Dorian Nakamoto:

Dorian Nakamoto, a Japanese-American physicist, briefly gained attention as a potential candidate for being the creator of Bitcoin. In 2014, a Newsweek article claimed that Dorian Nakamoto was the elusive figure behind the pseudonym. However, Dorian Nakamoto vehemently denied any involvement in Bitcoin and emphasized the misunderstanding caused by the misinterpretation of his words. The controversy surrounding Dorian Nakamoto's brief association with Nakamoto's identity serves as a cautionary tale about the dangers of prematurely assuming someone's involvement.

Craig Wright:

Craig Wright, an Australian entrepreneur, and computer scientist, has made controversial claims of being Satoshi Nakamoto. In 2016, Wright publicly asserted that he was Nakamoto and provided cryptographic evidence to support his claim. However, his claims were met with skepticism and widespread scrutiny within the crypto community and the broader tech industry. Many experts and community members have challenged the validity of Wright's evidence, leading to ongoing debates and a lack of consensus regarding his assertions.

It is important to approach these theories with a critical eye, as concrete evidence linking any individual to the true identity of Nakamoto remains elusive. The search for Nakamoto's identity has been marked by numerous false leads, misinterpretations, and unsubstantiated claims. While it is natural to speculate and explore potential connections, it is crucial to maintain skepticism and rely on substantial evidence before drawing definitive conclusions.

The allure of uncovering Nakamoto's true identity stems from the desire to understand the motivations, experiences, and insights behind the creation of Bitcoin. However, it is worth noting that Nakamoto deliberately chose to remain anonymous, allowing Bitcoin to stand on its own merits without association with any particular individual. Nakamoto's anonymity reinforces the decentralized ethos of cryptocurrencies, emphasizing the collective efforts and collaborative nature of their development.

As we delve further into the world of cryptocurrencies, we will continue to witness the emergence of new theories and potential candidates for the identity of Satoshi Nakamoto. The mystery surrounding Nakamoto's true identity serves as a reminder of the enigmatic nature of the crypto community and the ongoing pursuit of knowledge within this ever-evolving landscape.

Chapter 23: Satoshi's Possible Motivations

The motivations behind Satoshi Nakamoto's creation of Bitcoin have been a subject of much speculation and curiosity within the crypto community. While the true identity of Nakamoto remains unknown, researchers, enthusiasts, and analysts have explored various theories to understand what might have driven the enigmatic figure to develop the world's first decentralized cryptocurrency. In this chapter, we delve into some of the possible motivations that could have inspired Satoshi Nakamoto's creation of Bitcoin.

Desire for Financial Empowerment:

One prevailing theory suggests that Nakamoto's motivation stemmed from a desire to empower individuals financially. Traditional financial systems are often centralized, with intermediaries controlling the flow of funds and limiting access to financial services. Nakamoto may have envisioned a system that would enable individuals to transact directly with one another, bypassing the need for intermediaries and promoting financial inclusion and empowerment on a global scale.

Distrust in Centralized Institutions:

Another possible motivation for Nakamoto could be a lack of trust in centralized financial institutions. The 2008 global financial crisis, which exposed vulnerabilities and corruption within the traditional banking system, occurred around the same time Nakamoto was developing Bitcoin. This event may have fueled Nakamoto's desire to create a decentralized system that operated independently of centralized authorities, providing an alternative to the traditional financial landscape.

Privacy and Anonymity:

The pseudonymous nature of Nakamoto suggests a strong emphasis on privacy and anonymity. Nakamoto's decision to remain anonymous allowed Bitcoin to stand on its own merits, free from association with any particular individual. This focus on privacy aligns with the broader ethos of cryptocurrencies, which aim to provide individuals with greater control over their financial information and transactions.

Technical Curiosity and Cryptographic Expertise:

Nakamoto's deep understanding of cryptography and their technical expertise played a crucial role in the development of Bitcoin. It is possible that Nakamoto's motivation stemmed from a personal interest in exploring the potential of cryptographic technologies and their application to financial systems. By combining their technical prowess with an innovative vision, Nakamoto created a groundbreaking solution to longstanding challenges in the realm of digital currencies.

Ideological Beliefs:

Cryptocurrencies, including Bitcoin, have been associated with various ideological movements and principles. Nakamoto may have been motivated by a belief in concepts such as decentralization, individual sovereignty, and the democratization of financial systems. These principles align with the cypherpunk movement, which sought to use cryptography and other technologies to protect privacy and promote individual freedoms.

Experimentation and Innovation:

Nakamoto's creation of Bitcoin can also be seen as an experiment and a form of innovation. The concept of a decentralized digital currency had been explored by researchers and developers before Nakamoto, but it was their implementation of a decentralized consensus mechanism and the introduction of the blockchain that brought the idea to fruition. Nakamoto's motivation may have been driven by a desire to test and push the boundaries of existing technologies, paving the way for the development of a new paradigm in finance.

Long-Term Vision:

Nakamoto's long-term vision for Bitcoin and the cryptocurrency ecosystem is another possible motivation. By providing a decentralized and transparent financial infrastructure, Nakamoto may have envisioned a future where cryptocurrencies could disrupt traditional financial systems, foster economic inclusivity, and facilitate global financial transactions. The impact of Nakamoto's vision can be seen in the ongoing growth and adoption of cryptocurrencies, as well as the advancements in blockchain technology across various industries.

It is important to note that these possible motivations are speculative, and the true intentions of Satoshi Nakamoto may never be fully known. Nakamoto's anonymity and lack of public communication make it challenging to definitively determine their motivations. Nonetheless, the impact of Nakamoto's creation cannot be understated, as Bitcoin and the subsequent cryptocurrency revolution have transformed the financial landscape and inspired further innovation in decentralized technologies.

As we continue our exploration of the crypto world, we recognize the importance of understanding the motivations behind the creation of Bitcoin. By examining the possible motivations of Satoshi Nakamoto, we gain insight into the transformative power of decentralized technologies, the desire for financial empowerment, and the potential for individuals to shape the future of finance.

Chapter 24: Satoshi's Economic Philosophy

Satoshi Nakamoto's creation of Bitcoin not only revolutionized the world of finance but also introduced a new economic philosophy. Nakamoto's vision of a decentralized, peer-to-peer electronic cash system was underpinned by certain economic principles and ideals. In this chapter, we delve into the economic philosophy that guided Nakamoto's creation of Bitcoin, exploring concepts such as scarcity, sound money, and the potential for financial empowerment.

Scarcity and Limited Supply:

One fundamental aspect of Nakamoto's economic philosophy is the concept of scarcity. Bitcoin was designed to have a limited supply, with a maximum of 21 million coins that can ever be created. This fixed supply is in contrast to traditional fiat currencies, which can be printed or created at the discretion of central banks. By introducing scarcity, Nakamoto sought to create a digital asset that was resistant to inflation and maintained its value over time.

Sound Money and Monetary Policy:

Nakamoto's economic philosophy embraced the idea of sound money. Sound money refers to a form of currency that holds its value over time and is resistant to manipulation. Nakamoto designed Bitcoin to have a decentralized monetary policy, where the issuance of new coins was governed by mathematical algorithms rather than the discretion of a central authority. This approach aimed to create a predictable and transparent monetary system that could not be easily influenced by external factors.

Decentralization and Trustlessness:

Decentralization is a core tenet of Nakamoto's economic philosophy. By removing the need for intermediaries and central authorities, Nakamoto sought to create a trustless system where individuals could transact directly with one another. The decentralized nature of Bitcoin ensures that no single entity or group has control over the network, promoting trust, transparency, and resilience.

Financial Empowerment and Inclusion:

Nakamoto's economic philosophy also emphasized the potential for financial empowerment and inclusion. Traditional financial systems often exclude individuals who lack access to banking services or are subject to strict regulations and limitations. Bitcoin provides an alternative that enables anyone with an internet connection to participate in the global financial system, regardless of their background or location. Nakamoto's vision of financial empowerment aimed to give individuals greater control over their money and financial destinies.

Privacy and Individual Sovereignty:

Privacy and individual sovereignty were important considerations in Nakamoto's economic philosophy. Bitcoin transactions are pseudonymous, with users identified by cryptographic keys rather than personal information. This focus on privacy aligns with the broader ideals of personal freedom and autonomy. Nakamoto's design aimed to provide individuals with the ability to transact privately and securely, without unnecessary intrusions or surveillance.

Economic Incentives and Mining:

Nakamoto's economic philosophy also incorporated the concept of economic incentives through the mining process. Miners, who validate transactions and secure the network, are rewarded with newly minted bitcoins. This incentive structure encourages participation in the network and ensures the security and integrity of the blockchain. Nakamoto's design aligns with the principles of game theory and provides economic incentives for individuals to contribute to the decentralized network.

Long-Term Thinking and Sustainability:

Nakamoto's economic philosophy exhibited a long-term perspective and emphasized the importance of sustainability. The limited supply of bitcoins, coupled with the diminishing block rewards over time, encourages a mindset of long-term investment and value preservation. Nakamoto's design intended to create a system that would be sustainable and incentivize individuals to hold and utilize bitcoins as a form of value exchange.

Openness, Collaboration, and Innovation:

Nakamoto's economic philosophy fostered a spirit of openness, collaboration, and innovation. By releasing the Bitcoin software as open source, Nakamoto invited developers and enthusiasts from around the world to contribute to the project's development and improvement. This open and collaborative approach has fueled innovation and allowed the crypto community to build upon Nakamoto's original vision.

It is important to note that Nakamoto's economic philosophy is not set in stone and can be interpreted and applied in different ways. As the crypto landscape evolves, various perspectives and adaptations of Nakamoto's original ideas emerge. The economic philosophy underlying Bitcoin continues to shape discussions around the future of finance, the role of decentralized technologies, and the potential for economic empowerment on a global scale.

As we explore the world of cryptocurrencies, we continue to witness the impact of Nakamoto's economic philosophy. By embracing concepts such as scarcity, sound money, decentralization, and financial empowerment, Nakamoto's vision has inspired a global movement towards reimagining and reshaping economic systems. Through their innovative approach, Nakamoto has left an enduring legacy that challenges traditional economic paradigms and fosters a greater sense of autonomy and control over personal finances.

Chapter 25: The Evolution of Bitcoin's Technology

Since its inception, Bitcoin has undergone significant technological evolution. From its early days as a concept outlined in a white paper by Satoshi Nakamoto to its current status as the most prominent cryptocurrency, Bitcoin has seen advancements in various aspects of its technology. In this chapter, we explore the key milestones and developments that have shaped the evolution of Bitcoin's technology, from its underlying blockchain to improvements in scalability, privacy, and user experience.

The Blockchain: The foundational technology underlying Bitcoin is the blockchain, a decentralized and immutable ledger that records all Bitcoin transactions. In the early days of Bitcoin, the blockchain served as a ledger for recording transactions, ensuring transparency, and preventing double spending. Over time, the blockchain has evolved to incorporate additional features, such as the ability to embed small pieces of data through mechanisms like OP_RETURN and the integration of smart contracts through second-layer solutions like the Lightning Network.

Scalability Solutions: Scalability has been a persistent challenge for Bitcoin as its popularity and transaction volume increased. To address this issue, several scalability solutions have emerged. The introduction of Segregated Witness (SegWit) in 2017 improved transaction throughput and enabled the development of layer-two protocols like the Lightning Network. Layer-two solutions operate on top of the Bitcoin blockchain and facilitate faster and cheaper transactions by reducing the load on the main chain.

Privacy Enhancements: Privacy has been another area of focus in the evolution of Bitcoin's technology. While Bitcoin transactions are pseudonymous, they are publicly recorded on the blockchain, allowing anyone to view transaction details. To enhance privacy, techniques like CoinJoin, which combines multiple transactions to obfuscate the link between inputs and outputs, have been developed. Additionally, advancements such as Zero-Knowledge Proofs, as implemented in privacy-focused cryptocurrencies like Zcash, are being explored to provide stronger privacy guarantees in Bitcoin transactions.

User Experience Improvements: Bitcoin's early user experience was often challenging, requiring technical expertise to interact with the network. However, efforts have been made to enhance the user experience and make Bitcoin more accessible to a broader audience. User-friendly wallets and intuitive interfaces have been developed to simplify the process of sending and receiving bitcoins. Mobile wallets and hardware wallets have also emerged, providing convenient and secure options for managing Bitcoin holdings.

Cross-Chain Interoperability: Bitcoin's evolution has also seen advancements in cross-chain interoperability, allowing the seamless transfer of assets and data between different blockchain networks. Projects like Atomic Swaps enable users to exchange assets directly between Bitcoin and other compatible cryptocurrencies without the need for intermediaries. These developments have the potential to foster greater liquidity and expand the use cases for Bitcoin.

Smart Contracts and Layer-Two Solutions: While Bitcoin's scripting language is intentionally limited, efforts have been made to enable more complex smart contract functionality. Layer-two solutions like the Lightning Network provide a platform for fast and inexpensive off-chain transactions, fostering microtransactions and enabling the development of decentralized applications on top of the Bitcoin network. These developments open up new possibilities for innovation and expand the utility of Bitcoin beyond simple transactions.

Second-Layer Protocols and Sidechains: Second-layer protocols and sidechains offer additional avenues for innovation within the Bitcoin ecosystem. Sidechains are separate blockchains that are interoperable with the Bitcoin network, allowing for experimentation with different features and functionalities. Projects like RSK and Liquid have implemented sidechains to explore applications such as smart contracts and faster settlement times.

Ongoing Research and Development: Bitcoin's technology continues to evolve through ongoing research and development efforts. Improvements in areas such as privacy, scalability, and user experience remain active areas of exploration. Innovations like Schnorr signatures,

Taproot, and the ongoing work on the Lightning Network continue to push the boundaries of what is possible with Bitcoin.

The evolution of Bitcoin's technology is a testament to the collaborative nature of the crypto community. Developers, researchers, and enthusiasts around the world have contributed to the improvement and refinement of Bitcoin's technology stack. Through open-source collaboration, peer review, and iterative development, the Bitcoin ecosystem continues to adapt and evolve to meet the changing needs and demands of its users.

As we navigate the ever-evolving landscape of cryptocurrencies, we can expect Bitcoin's technology to continue to mature, bringing forth innovations that enhance scalability, privacy, usability, and interoperability. These advancements serve to solidify Bitcoin's position as a leading digital currency and pave the way for a future where decentralized technologies play a central role in our financial and economic systems.

Type This URL in Your Browser ⤳ ***https://bit.ly/Guess_What_This***

Chapter 26: Scaling Challenges and Solutions

As Bitcoin gained popularity and adoption, it faced significant challenges related to scalability—the ability to handle an increasing number of transactions without compromising network performance and transaction speed. Bitcoin's original design was not optimized for handling a large volume of transactions, leading to issues such as high fees and delays. In this chapter, we explore the scaling challenges that Bitcoin has faced and the solutions that have been proposed and implemented to address them.

Increased Transaction Volume:

As Bitcoin gained mainstream attention, the number of transactions being processed on the network grew exponentially. The original Bitcoin blockchain had a limited block size, resulting in a maximum capacity of approximately 7 transactions per second. This limitation led to congestion, delayed confirmations, and rising transaction fees during periods of high demand.

The Block Size Debate:

One of the primary challenges in scaling Bitcoin was the debate surrounding the block size. Increasing the block size would allow more transactions to be included in each block, thus increasing the network's throughput. However, proposals to increase the block size faced opposition, as it could lead to centralization by requiring more storage and processing power, potentially making it more difficult for individual users to participate in the network.

Segregated Witness (SegWit):

Segregated Witness, or SegWit, was a proposed solution to the scaling challenges of Bitcoin. It was implemented in 2017 and aimed to increase the block size limit indirectly by removing signature data from transactions. This change allowed more transactions to fit within a block, effectively increasing the network's capacity. SegWit also introduced other benefits, such as improved transaction malleability and enhanced security.

Layer-Two Solutions: Lightning Network:

The Lightning Network is a second-layer protocol built on top of the Bitcoin blockchain. It addresses scalability by enabling off-chain transactions, which are faster and have lower fees. The Lightning Network leverages payment channels, allowing users to conduct numerous transactions without directly involving the main blockchain. Once the channel is closed, only the final transaction details are recorded on the Bitcoin blockchain, reducing congestion, and increasing transaction throughput.

Sidechains and Drivechains:

Sidechains and drivechains are additional solutions that have been proposed to address scalability. Sidechains are separate blockchains that operate alongside the main Bitcoin blockchain, enabling the development of specific applications or functionalities without congesting the main network. Drivechains, a variation of sidechains, enable assets to be moved between different blockchains in a decentralized manner, expanding the utility of Bitcoin while maintaining the security of the main chain.

Schnorr Signatures:

Schnorr signatures, an upcoming improvement to Bitcoin's cryptographic signatures, offer benefits in terms of scalability and privacy. By aggregating multiple signature data into a single signature, Schnorr signatures reduce the size of transactions, allowing more transactions to be included within a block. This optimization improves the overall efficiency and capacity of the network.

Fee Estimation and Dynamic Pricing:

To address the issue of high transaction fees during peak times, various fee estimation algorithms and dynamic pricing mechanisms have been developed. These tools help users gauge the appropriate fee to include with their transactions, taking into account factors such as network congestion and transaction urgency. This approach allows users to prioritize their transactions based on their desired confirmation times and fee budgets.

Ongoing Research and Innovation:

The scaling challenges faced by Bitcoin are ongoing, and the search for further solutions continues. Researchers and developers are exploring novel ideas and improvements, such as the use of sharding, sidechains with merged mining, and advanced layer-two protocols. These ongoing efforts demonstrate the commitment of the Bitcoin community to addressing scalability challenges and ensuring the long-term viability and growth of the network.

It is worth noting that scalability is a multifaceted issue with no one-size-fits-all solution. Achieving scalability requires balancing factors such as decentralization, security, transaction speed, and network efficiency. The solutions implemented and proposed for Bitcoin aim to strike this delicate balance, allowing the network to handle increased transaction volumes without compromising its core principles.

As Bitcoin evolves and new solutions are implemented, it is crucial to maintain open dialogue and collaboration within the community. The challenges of scaling are not unique to Bitcoin and are shared by many other cryptocurrencies. By sharing knowledge and building upon collective experiences, the crypto community can work together to overcome these challenges and pave the way for a more scalable and inclusive financial future.

So, the scaling challenges faced by Bitcoin prompted the exploration and implementation of various solutions. From SegWit to the Lightning Network, sidechains, and Schnorr signatures, each advancement has contributed to increasing Bitcoin's capacity, enhancing user experience, and mitigating scalability concerns. The ongoing research and innovation within the Bitcoin community highlight the collective commitment to address scalability challenges and ensure the continued growth and success of the world's leading cryptocurrency.

Chapter 27: Bitcoin's Adoption by Merchants

Bitcoin's journey from a niche digital currency to a globally recognized form of payment has been marked by its adoption by merchants around the world. In the early days, Bitcoin was primarily used by tech enthusiasts and early adopters, but as its popularity grew, more businesses began to accept Bitcoin as a legitimate payment option. In this chapter, we delve into the factors that have driven Bitcoin's adoption by merchants, the challenges they faced, and the benefits they have reaped from embracing this digital currency.

Global Reach and Borderless Transactions:

One of the key advantages of accepting Bitcoin for merchants is its ability to facilitate global transactions without the need for intermediaries or traditional banking systems. Bitcoin transcends borders and enables merchants to reach customers in any part of the world, bypassing the challenges associated with cross-border transactions. This global reach has attracted merchants seeking to expand their customer base and tap into new markets.

Lower Transaction Fees:

Traditional payment methods often involve fees imposed by intermediaries, such as credit card companies and banks. Bitcoin, on the other hand, offers the potential for lower transaction fees, particularly for cross-border transactions. By eliminating the need for intermediaries, merchants can avoid hefty fees associated with international payments. This cost-saving aspect has been particularly appealing to businesses operating in industries with tight profit margins.

Chargeback Prevention:

One challenge that merchants face when accepting traditional payment methods is the risk of chargebacks—when customers reverse their payments after receiving goods or services. Chargebacks can result in financial losses and administrative burdens for merchants. Bitcoin transactions, once confirmed on the blockchain, are irreversible, reducing the risk of fraudulent chargebacks. This aspect provides a level of security and peace of mind for merchants, especially for high-value transactions.

Exposure to a New Customer Base:

By accepting Bitcoin, merchants open themselves up to a unique customer base consisting of tech-savvy individuals and early adopters of cryptocurrencies. These customers actively seek out merchants that accept Bitcoin as a form of payment and may prioritize businesses that align with their digital and decentralized values. Accepting Bitcoin can attract a loyal following of cryptocurrency enthusiasts who are eager to support businesses that embrace this emerging technology.

Enhanced Privacy and Security:

Bitcoin transactions offer a certain level of privacy and security that can be appealing to both merchants and customers. While Bitcoin transactions are recorded on the blockchain, the identities of individuals involved are pseudonymous, providing a degree of privacy. Additionally, the decentralized nature of Bitcoin reduces the risk of fraud and hacking, offering merchants a secure payment option in an increasingly digital and interconnected world.

Promotional Opportunities and Media Attention:

For some businesses, accepting Bitcoin has brought them valuable media attention and promotional opportunities. Embracing Bitcoin as a payment method can attract positive media coverage and position a business as innovative and forward-thinking. This exposure can lead to increased brand visibility, attracting both Bitcoin users and mainstream customers interested in supporting businesses at the forefront of technological advancements.

Innovation and Future-Proofing:

By accepting Bitcoin, merchants position themselves at the forefront of technological innovation. Bitcoin represents a fundamental shift in how value is exchanged, and businesses that embrace this change early on demonstrate their willingness to adapt to evolving customer preferences. By adopting Bitcoin as a payment option, merchants future-proof their businesses, ensuring they remain relevant as cryptocurrencies continue to gain acceptance and adoption.

Challenges and Volatility:

While there are benefits to accepting Bitcoin, merchants also face challenges associated with its volatility. Bitcoin's price can fluctuate significantly, which can pose risks for businesses if they do not promptly convert their Bitcoin holdings into fiat currency. Additionally, the technical aspects of accepting Bitcoin, such as setting up wallets and managing transactions, may require initial investment in infrastructure and staff training.

As Bitcoin continues to mature and gain mainstream acceptance, more businesses are likely to consider accepting it as a payment option. The benefits of global reach, lower transaction fees, chargeback prevention, exposure to new customer bases, enhanced privacy and security, promotional opportunities, and future-proofing make Bitcoin an attractive choice for forward-thinking merchants.

It is important to note that Bitcoin's adoption by merchants is not limited to traditional brick-and-mortar establishments. Online retailers, service providers, and even charitable organizations have embraced Bitcoin as a means of payment, expanding the use cases and possibilities for this digital currency.

As we move forward, the adoption of Bitcoin by merchants will play a crucial role in solidifying its position as a legitimate form of payment. By creating a robust ecosystem where individuals can use Bitcoin seamlessly for everyday transactions, merchants contribute to the mainstream acceptance and long-term success of this transformative digital currency.

Chapter 28: The Silk Road and Bitcoin's Dark Side

Bitcoin's association with the Silk Road, an online marketplace known for illicit activities, has become an indelible part of its history. While Bitcoin itself is a decentralized digital currency with legitimate use cases, its pseudonymous nature and global reach have also made it appealing to those engaged in illegal activities. In this chapter, we explore the connection between Bitcoin and the Silk Road, the challenges it posed, and how the broader crypto community has responded to ensure the responsible use of cryptocurrencies.

The Silk Road's Emergence:

The Silk Road was an online marketplace founded by Ross Ulbricht in 2011. Operating on the dark web, it gained notoriety for facilitating the sale of drugs, counterfeit documents, and other illicit goods using Bitcoin as the primary form of payment. The Silk Road's utilization of Bitcoin as a means of exchange was driven by its pseudo-anonymous nature and the perception of increased security and privacy.

Bitcoin's Role as a Currency of Choice:

Bitcoin's decentralized and borderless nature made it an attractive currency for those operating on the Silk Road. It allowed users to make transactions without the involvement of traditional financial intermediaries, making it more challenging for authorities to trace and seize funds. Bitcoin's digital nature also facilitated quick and seamless transactions, further facilitating the Silk Road's illicit activities.

Regulatory and Legal Challenges:

Bitcoin's association with the Silk Road presented regulatory and legal challenges for both the cryptocurrency and law enforcement agencies. The anonymous nature of Bitcoin transactions made it difficult to identify the individuals involved in illegal activities. Additionally, the borderless nature of cryptocurrencies posed jurisdictional challenges, as multiple countries were involved in combating the Silk Road's operations.

Impact on Bitcoin's Reputation:

The association with the Silk Road had a negative impact on Bitcoin's reputation, as it reinforced the perception that cryptocurrencies were primarily used for illicit activities. Mainstream media coverage often focused on the illicit use cases, overshadowing the legitimate and transformative potential of cryptocurrencies. This perception posed a significant hurdle to broader adoption and acceptance of Bitcoin.

Response from the Crypto Community:

The crypto community recognized the importance of addressing the negative associations with Bitcoin and took several steps to promote responsible use and separate the technology from its illicit use cases. Organizations and individuals within the community actively engaged in initiatives to educate the public, advocate for regulatory compliance, and promote transparency in the use of cryptocurrencies.

Enhanced Regulatory Measures:

In response to the challenges posed by illicit activities, governments and regulatory bodies around the world implemented measures to increase oversight and combat money laundering and illicit transactions involving cryptocurrencies. Know Your Customer (KYC) and Anti-Money Laundering (AML) regulations were introduced to exchanges and service providers to ensure greater transparency and accountability in cryptocurrency transactions.

Blockchain Analytics and Forensics:

The development of blockchain analytics and forensic tools has played a crucial role in identifying and tracking illicit activities involving cryptocurrencies. These tools allow law enforcement agencies and blockchain analysts to trace the flow of funds on the blockchain, enabling them to identify patterns and link transactions to individuals. The use of these tools has become an important component in investigating and prosecuting illicit activities involving Bitcoin and other cryptocurrencies.

Focus on Legitimate Use Cases:

Despite the negative association with the Silk Road, the broader crypto community has continued to focus on promoting the legitimate use cases and benefits of cryptocurrencies. From facilitating cross-border remittances to providing financial services to the unbanked, cryptocurrencies have the potential to transform various sectors. By highlighting these positive aspects, the crypto community aims to shift the narrative away from the dark side of Bitcoin.

It is important to note that the association between Bitcoin and the Silk Road does not define the entire cryptocurrency ecosystem. Bitcoin, like any other form of currency, can be used for both legal and illegal purposes. The actions of a few should not overshadow the immense potential for positive change that cryptocurrencies offer.

As the crypto industry continues to evolve, responsible use, compliance with regulations, and collaboration with law enforcement agencies remain critical. By fostering transparency, educating users, and working alongside regulatory bodies, the crypto community can help ensure that cryptocurrencies are used responsibly and for the betterment of society. Bitcoin's association with the Silk Road served as a learning experience for the broader crypto community. It highlighted the need for proactive measures to combat illicit activities and to promote the responsible use of cryptocurrencies. By addressing these challenges head-on, the community aims to build a stronger foundation of trust and foster wider acceptance of cryptocurrencies as a legitimate and transformative force in the global economy.

Chapter 29: Government and Regulatory Responses

The rise of cryptocurrencies, including Bitcoin, has prompted governments and regulatory bodies around the world to develop frameworks and responses to address the unique challenges and opportunities presented by these digital assets. As cryptocurrencies gained popularity, regulators grappled with issues such as consumer protection, financial stability, money laundering, and the prevention of illicit activities. In this chapter, we explore the evolving landscape of government and regulatory responses to cryptocurrencies, highlighting key initiatives and their impact on the broader crypto ecosystem.

Early Recognition and Caution:

In the early days of Bitcoin, many governments took a cautious approach, closely monitoring the development and adoption of cryptocurrencies. Regulators recognized the potential benefits and risks associated with digital assets, acknowledging their disruptive potential while expressing concerns about investor protection, market manipulation, and the use of cryptocurrencies in illicit activities.

Regulatory Frameworks and Licensing:

As cryptocurrencies gained mainstream attention, governments began introducing regulatory frameworks to provide clarity and oversight. Countries such as Japan, Switzerland, and Malta enacted comprehensive regulations, establishing licensing schemes for cryptocurrency exchanges and service providers. These frameworks aimed to promote transparency, consumer protection, and the prevention of financial crimes, while fostering innovation and industry growth.

Know Your Customer (KYC) and Anti-Money Laundering (AML) Requirements:

To combat money laundering and illicit activities, governments introduced KYC and AML requirements for cryptocurrency exchanges and service providers. These measures seek to enhance transparency and traceability by mandating the collection of customer identification information and reporting suspicious transactions. KYC and AML regulations have played a crucial role in addressing concerns surrounding the potential misuse of cryptocurrencies.

Cryptocurrency Taxation:

Governments worldwide have started developing taxation frameworks for cryptocurrencies, aiming to ensure that individuals and businesses comply with existing tax laws. Tax authorities require individuals to report their cryptocurrency holdings, capital gains, and losses for tax purposes. These tax regulations vary across jurisdictions, ranging from treating cryptocurrencies as property to considering them as financial assets subject to capital gains tax.

Central Bank Digital Currencies (CBDCs):

The emergence of cryptocurrencies has also prompted central banks to explore the concept of central bank digital currencies (CBDCs). CBDCs are digital representations of a country's fiat currency issued and controlled by the central bank. Governments and central banks view CBDCs as a way to enhance financial inclusion, reduce costs, and maintain control over the monetary system. Several countries, including China and Sweden, are actively researching and piloting CBDC initiatives.

International Cooperation and Standardization:

Cryptocurrencies operate in a global, decentralized environment, making international cooperation crucial. Regulatory bodies and governments have sought to collaborate on a global scale to address common challenges posed by cryptocurrencies. Organizations such as the Financial Action Task Force (FATF) have issued guidelines to promote consistent AML and counter-terrorism financing standards. The International Organization for Standardization (ISO) has also developed standards related to blockchain and digital currencies.

Investor Protection and Consumer Education:

Regulators have placed a strong emphasis on investor protection and consumer education in the crypto space. Authorities have warned the public about the risks associated with investing in cryptocurrencies, including price volatility, scams, and fraudulent schemes. Educational campaigns and initiatives have been launched to inform the public about the potential risks and benefits of engaging with cryptocurrencies, empowering individuals to make informed decisions.

Evolving and Adapting Regulations:

As the crypto landscape evolves, regulations continue to adapt to emerging challenges and technological advancements. Regulators are constantly reviewing and refining existing frameworks to strike a balance between fostering innovation and safeguarding financial systems. They engage in dialogue with industry participants, researchers, and stakeholders to understand the evolving needs of the crypto ecosystem and adjust regulatory approaches accordingly.

It is important to note that regulatory responses to cryptocurrencies vary significantly across jurisdictions. Some countries have embraced cryptocurrencies, creating favorable environments for innovation and industry growth, while others have taken a more restrictive approach. The diversity in regulatory responses highlights the global nature of cryptocurrencies and the need for ongoing collaboration and harmonization.

The evolving government and regulatory responses to cryptocurrencies reflect the recognition that these digital assets are here to stay. Regulators strive to strike a balance between fostering innovation, protecting investors, and mitigating risks. As the regulatory landscape continues to mature, it is crucial for governments, regulators, and the crypto community to maintain an open and constructive dialogue to ensure responsible growth and widespread adoption of cryptocurrencies.

By implementing robust regulatory frameworks, enhancing consumer protection measures, and fostering international cooperation, governments aim to create an environment that balances innovation and stability, enabling the benefits of cryptocurrencies to be realized while mitigating potential risks.

Chapter 30: Satoshi's Influence on Blockchain Technology

The emergence of Bitcoin and its underlying technology, the blockchain, has revolutionized the way we think about decentralized systems, trust, and value transfer. At the heart of this transformation is the enigmatic figure known as Satoshi Nakamoto, the pseudonymous creator of Bitcoin. In this chapter, we explore Satoshi's profound influence on blockchain technology, examining the key concepts and innovations introduced in the Bitcoin white paper that continue to shape the evolution of blockchain technology.

Decentralization and Trust:

Satoshi Nakamoto's groundbreaking contribution was the creation of a decentralized system that allows individuals to transact directly with one another, eliminating the need for intermediaries such as banks or payment processors. This decentralized approach revolutionized the concept of trust, as it shifted the reliance from centralized authorities to a network of distributed nodes that collectively verify and validate transactions. By removing the need for a central authority, Satoshi introduced a paradigm shift in how we perceive and establish trust in digital systems.

The Blockchain Technology:

Satoshi Nakamoto introduced the concept of the blockchain—a public, append-only ledger that records all transactions in a transparent and immutable manner. The blockchain serves as a foundational technology for Bitcoin, ensuring the integrity of transactions and preventing double spending. By using cryptographic techniques, the blockchain provides a secure and tamper-resistant ledger that can be independently verified by anyone. This innovation laid the groundwork for a wide range of applications beyond digital currency, including supply chain management, identity verification, and decentralized finance.

Proof-of-Work Consensus:

To maintain the security and integrity of the blockchain, Satoshi Nakamoto introduced the concept of proof-of-work (PoW) consensus.

PoW requires network participants, known as miners, to solve complex mathematical puzzles to validate transactions and add blocks to the blockchain. This consensus mechanism ensures that the majority of network participants agree on the order and validity of transactions, making it extremely difficult for malicious actors to manipulate the system. PoW has become the foundation for many blockchain networks, providing a robust and resilient mechanism for achieving consensus.

Cryptographic Signatures:

Satoshi Nakamoto's white paper also introduced the use of cryptographic signatures to verify the authenticity of transactions. Each participant in the network has a unique private key, which they use to sign transactions. The recipient can then verify the transaction's authenticity using the sender's public key. This cryptographic approach ensures the integrity and security of transactions without revealing sensitive information. Cryptographic signatures have become a fundamental component of blockchain technology, enabling secure and verifiable transactions in various applications.

Pseudonymity and Privacy:

Satoshi Nakamoto's decision to remain pseudonymous has had a lasting impact on the blockchain community. By choosing not to reveal their true identity, Satoshi emphasized the importance of privacy and pseudonymity in the decentralized world. This choice resonated with the ethos of decentralization and permissionless innovation, as individuals can participate in the blockchain network without revealing their personal identities. While subsequent advancements have focused on enhancing privacy features, Satoshi's commitment to pseudonymity set the stage for discussions on privacy and self-sovereign identity in the blockchain space.

Open-Source Collaboration:

Satoshi Nakamoto's decision to release the Bitcoin software as open source was a critical factor in the rapid growth and development of blockchain technology. By making the code accessible to anyone, Satoshi invited collaboration and innovation from a global community of developers, researchers, and enthusiasts. This open-source ethos has fostered a culture of transparency, peer review, and continuous improvement in the blockchain space. It has allowed for the creation of numerous blockchain platforms, protocols, and applications that build upon Satoshi's original vision.

The Genesis of Cryptocurrencies:

Bitcoin's creation by Satoshi Nakamoto paved the way for the emergence of a vast ecosystem of cryptocurrencies. Satoshi's innovative design and the decentralized nature of Bitcoin inspired countless developers to create their own cryptocurrencies and blockchain networks. This proliferation of cryptocurrencies has democratized access to financial services, enabled new forms of economic systems, and fueled innovation in areas such as decentralized finance, non-fungible tokens (NFTs), and tokenized assets.

Inspiration for Distributed Ledger Technologies:

Satoshi Nakamoto's revolutionary ideas have not only shaped the development of cryptocurrencies but also inspired the broader concept of distributed ledger technologies (DLTs). Blockchain, as a specific type of DLT, has influenced various sectors beyond finance. Industries such as supply chain management, healthcare, voting systems, and intellectual property have explored the potential of DLTs to enhance transparency, efficiency, and security.

Satoshi Nakamoto's influence on blockchain technology cannot be overstated. By combining cryptographic principles, decentralization, and a visionary approach, Satoshi laid the foundation for a transformative technology that has the potential to reshape industries, empower individuals, and redefine the way we interact with digital systems. Satoshi's legacy continues to inspire innovation, research, and exploration, as the blockchain community strives to unlock the full potential of this revolutionary technology.

Chapter 31: Bitcoin's Price Volatility

Bitcoin's meteoric rise in popularity and adoption has been accompanied by significant price volatility, making it one of the most volatile assets in the financial markets. The price of Bitcoin can experience rapid and substantial fluctuations within short periods, capturing the attention of investors, traders, and the general public. In this chapter, we delve into the factors that contribute to Bitcoin's price volatility, the impact it has on the crypto ecosystem, and how investors navigate this volatile landscape.

Market Supply and Demand:

Bitcoin's price is primarily driven by the dynamics of market supply and demand. As with any asset, when demand for Bitcoin exceeds its available supply, the price tends to rise. Conversely, when supply surpasses demand, the price may decline. The relative imbalance between buyers and sellers in the market can contribute to sudden price movements, especially when combined with factors such as investor sentiment and market speculation.

Market Perception and Sentiment:

Bitcoin's price is heavily influenced by market perception and sentiment. Positive news, such as regulatory developments or institutional adoption, can lead to increased demand and a surge in prices. Conversely, negative news, such as regulatory crackdowns or security breaches, can trigger selling pressure and cause prices to plummet. The market's reaction to these events, fueled by emotions and sentiment, can amplify price volatility in both directions.

Speculation and Trading Activity:

The speculative nature of Bitcoin attracts traders who seek to profit from short-term price movements. The presence of traders engaging in speculative trading strategies, such as day trading or margin trading, can contribute to increased volatility. These traders often rely on technical analysis, market trends, and short-term price patterns to make trading decisions, which can result in rapid price swings as they execute their strategies.

Market Liquidity and Trading Volumes:

Bitcoin's price volatility is closely tied to its liquidity and trading volumes. Higher liquidity and trading volumes generally lead to greater price stability, as there is a larger pool of buyers and sellers to absorb market orders. However, during periods of low liquidity, such as in the early days of Bitcoin or during specific timeframes with limited trading activity, even a relatively small buy or sell order can cause significant price fluctuations.

Regulatory and Legal Developments:

Bitcoin's price can be affected by regulatory and legal developments. Regulatory actions, such as bans or restrictions on cryptocurrency exchanges, can create uncertainty and dampen market sentiment, leading to increased volatility. Conversely, regulatory clarity and supportive measures can boost investor confidence and stabilize prices. As the regulatory landscape continues to evolve, market participants closely monitor developments that may impact Bitcoin's price dynamics.

Technological Advancements and Innovation:

Technological advancements and innovations within the crypto ecosystem can also contribute to Bitcoin's price volatility. New developments, such as upgrades to the Bitcoin protocol, the introduction of new consensus mechanisms, or the launch of novel applications and platforms, can generate excitement and speculation in the market. The anticipation of these advancements can cause price movements as investors try to position themselves ahead of potential market shifts.

Market Maturity and Institutional Involvement:

Bitcoin's price volatility has historically been exacerbated by its relatively nascent and less mature market compared to traditional asset classes. However, as the market matures and institutional involvement increases, there is a growing expectation that Bitcoin's price volatility may gradually decrease. The entry of institutional investors, with their longer-term investment horizons and risk management strategies, can help stabilize prices and mitigate short-term volatility.

Investor Risk Appetite and Market Psychology:

Bitcoin's price volatility is also influenced by the risk appetite and psychological factors of investors. The fear of missing out (FOMO) can drive buying frenzies and rapid price increases, while fear, uncertainty, and doubt (FUD) can trigger panic selling and price declines. Investor psychology plays a significant role in shaping market trends and can contribute to exaggerated price movements in either direction.

Navigating Bitcoin's price volatility requires a nuanced approach from investors and traders. Strategies such as diversification, risk management, and a long-term perspective can help mitigate the impact of short-term price fluctuations. Additionally, conducting thorough research, staying informed about market developments, and understanding the fundamentals of Bitcoin and the broader crypto market can provide a more informed perspective for making investment decisions.

It is essential to note that while Bitcoin's price volatility can present challenges, it also offers opportunities for profit and growth. Traders who are adept at analyzing market trends and employing appropriate risk management strategies can take advantage of price swings to generate returns. Additionally, for long-term investors, Bitcoin's volatility can be seen as a characteristic of an emerging asset class with high growth potential.

Bitcoin's price volatility reflects its unique position as a digital asset at the intersection of technology, finance, and global adoption. As the market matures, regulatory frameworks evolve, and institutional involvement deepens, the expectation is that Bitcoin's price volatility may gradually stabilize. However, it is important to recognize that price volatility is an inherent aspect of Bitcoin and cryptocurrencies, and market participants should be prepared for potential fluctuations as they engage with this dynamic and evolving ecosystem.

Chapter 32: The Mt. Gox Scandal

The Mt. Gox scandal stands as one of the most significant and notorious events in the history of Bitcoin. Mt. Gox, once the largest Bitcoin exchange in the world, collapsed in 2014, resulting in the loss of hundreds of millions of dollars' worth of customers' funds. In this chapter, we delve into the details of the Mt. Gox scandal, examining its causes, the aftermath, and the lessons learned from this devastating event.

The Rise of Mt. Gox:

Mt. Gox, originally established in 2009 as a platform for trading Magic: The Gathering cards, transitioned into a Bitcoin exchange in 2010. Under the leadership of Mark Karpeles, Mt. Gox quickly rose to prominence, dominating the Bitcoin exchange market and handling a significant portion of Bitcoin trading volume worldwide. Its success was largely attributed to its early entry into the market and the lack of competing exchanges at the time.

Security Breaches and Operational Challenges:

As Mt. Gox grew in popularity, it faced mounting security and operational challenges. The exchange experienced several security breaches, including a significant hacking incident in 2011 that resulted in the theft of thousands of Bitcoins. These security breaches raised concerns about the exchange's ability to protect customer funds and highlighted vulnerabilities in its infrastructure and security practices.

Insolvency and Missing Bitcoins:

In February 2014, Mt. Gox abruptly suspended all trading and filed for bankruptcy protection, citing the loss of approximately 850,000 Bitcoins, both belonging to customers and the exchange itself. The exact circumstances surrounding the disappearance of these funds remain a topic of debate, with investigations pointing to a combination of hacking, internal theft, and operational mismanagement.

Legal Proceedings and Recovery Efforts:

The collapse of Mt. Gox triggered a lengthy legal process and efforts to recover the lost funds. The bankruptcy proceedings involved investigations, lawsuits, and the appointment of a trustee to oversee the distribution of remaining assets to affected customers. Over the years, a portion of the lost Bitcoins has been recovered and returned to users, but the majority of the funds remain unrecovered.

Impact on Bitcoin's Reputation:

The Mt. Gox scandal had a significant impact on Bitcoin's reputation and the public's perception of cryptocurrencies. The collapse of such a prominent exchange shook investor confidence and raised questions about the security, reliability, and regulatory oversight of the nascent cryptocurrency industry. Media coverage of the event largely focused on the negative aspects, leading to increased skepticism and caution surrounding Bitcoin and other digital assets.

Lessons Learned and Industry Improvements:

The Mt. Gox scandal served as a catalyst for improvements within the cryptocurrency industry. It highlighted the need for robust security measures, transparent financial audits, and regulatory oversight to protect users and prevent similar incidents from occurring in the future. The event spurred the development of best practices for exchanges, including cold storage solutions, multi-signature wallets, and enhanced security protocols.

Emergence of Regulated Exchanges:

Following the Mt. Gox scandal, regulators around the world intensified their focus on cryptocurrency exchanges. Governments introduced stricter regulations and licensing requirements to enhance investor protection and promote transparency in the industry. Regulated exchanges with robust security measures and compliance frameworks have emerged, providing users with greater confidence and trust in the cryptocurrency ecosystem.

Importance of Individual Security Measures:

The Mt. Gox scandal highlighted the importance of individual security measures for cryptocurrency users. It underscored the need for individuals to exercise caution and take responsibility for securing their own funds. Best practices, such as using hardware wallets, enabling two-factor authentication, and practicing good password hygiene, have become essential for safeguarding cryptocurrency holdings.

The Mt. Gox scandal remains a cautionary tale within the cryptocurrency industry. It serves as a reminder of the risks associated with centralized exchanges and the importance of adopting security measures and regulatory frameworks that prioritize user protection. While the event had a profound impact on Bitcoin's reputation, the crypto community has learned valuable lessons and taken steps to strengthen the ecosystem, placing a greater emphasis on security, transparency, and regulatory compliance.

As the cryptocurrency industry continues to evolve, the legacy of the Mt. Gox scandal serves as a constant reminder of the need for vigilance, responsible practices, and ongoing improvements in the space. By learning from past mistakes and embracing best practices, the industry aims to build a more resilient and trustworthy environment for users and investors.

Chapter 33: Satoshi's Reemergence?

The mysterious creator of Bitcoin, Satoshi Nakamoto, vanished from the public eye in 2010, leaving behind a revolutionary technology and a community of dedicated supporters. For years, speculation and curiosity surrounded Satoshi's identity and whereabouts. However, every once in a while, rumors and claims of Satoshi's reemergence resurface, sparking excitement and intrigue within the crypto community. In this chapter, we explore the instances where Satoshi's reemergence has been suggested and examine the impact and implications of these events.

The Occasional Satoshi Sightings:

Over the years, there have been sporadic instances where individuals have claimed to be Satoshi Nakamoto or have been identified as such by others. These claims range from anonymous forum posts to public statements and media interviews. However, none of these claims have been definitively proven, leaving the true identity of Satoshi Nakamoto still shrouded in mystery.

The Dorian Nakamoto Misidentification:

In 2014, a Newsweek article named a California resident named Dorian Nakamoto as the creator of Bitcoin, sparking widespread media attention. However, it soon became evident that Dorian Nakamoto was not the true Satoshi Nakamoto. The incident demonstrated the risks of misidentification and the impact it can have on individuals mistakenly associated with Satoshi's identity.

The Craig Wright Controversy:

One of the most prominent claims to Satoshi's identity came in 2016 when Australian computer scientist Craig Wright publicly declared himself as Satoshi Nakamoto. Wright provided cryptographic evidence to support his claim, but many within the crypto community remained skeptical. The ensuing controversy and debate cast doubt on Wright's assertions, with critics citing inconsistencies in his technical knowledge and the lack of conclusive evidence.

The GQ Interview:

In 2021, a British magazine, GQ, published an interview with an anonymous individual claiming to be Satoshi Nakamoto. The interview provided insights into Satoshi's thought process, motivations, and personal experiences, reigniting speculation, and fascination within the crypto community. However, skepticism remained due to the lack of verifiable proof, leaving the authenticity of the interviewee's claim unconfirmed.

Implications and Community Reactions:

The possibility of Satoshi Nakamoto's reemergence carries significant implications for the cryptocurrency industry. Satoshi's return could bring renewed attention, legitimacy, and potential influence to Bitcoin and the broader crypto ecosystem. The involvement of the creator in the development and governance of the technology could shape the future direction of cryptocurrencies, protocols, and blockchain innovation.

However, the potential reemergence of Satoshi also raises questions and concerns. Satoshi's continued anonymity has allowed the crypto community to grow organically and independently, free from centralized influence. The revelation of Satoshi's identity could disrupt the decentralized nature of the community and potentially undermine the principle of distributed decision-making that forms the foundation of cryptocurrencies.

Furthermore, the concept of Satoshi Nakamoto has taken on a mythical status, transcending the individual behind it. Satoshi's anonymity has allowed Bitcoin to be embraced and championed by a diverse community of developers, entrepreneurs, and enthusiasts. Satoshi's reemergence could overshadow this collective effort and shift the focus back to a single individual, potentially altering the dynamics and culture of the crypto community.

As the crypto industry continues to evolve, the question of Satoshi's reemergence remains an intriguing and unresolved mystery. Whether Satoshi will ever choose to reveal their true identity or actively participate in the crypto ecosystem is uncertain. Nonetheless, Satoshi Nakamoto's legacy as the creator of Bitcoin and the underlying blockchain technology remains profound, driving innovation and shaping the future of finance and decentralized systems.

Chapter 34: The Bitcoin Halving Events

Bitcoin's monetary policy is unique among traditional fiat currencies. One crucial aspect of this policy is the occurrence of Bitcoin halving events, which happen approximately every four years. These events have a significant impact on the supply of new Bitcoins entering the market and, consequently, on the dynamics of Bitcoin's value. In this chapter, we will delve into the details of Bitcoin halving events, their purpose, historical occurrences, and their effects on the crypto ecosystem.

Understanding Bitcoin Halving:

Bitcoin halving is a pre-programmed event written into the Bitcoin protocol that reduces the rate at which new Bitcoins are issued. It occurs approximately every 210,000 blocks, which translates to roughly four years. During a halving event, the block reward given to Bitcoin miners is cut in half. This reduction in block reward serves as a mechanism to control the supply of new Bitcoins and has important implications for the overall scarcity and value of Bitcoin.

Scarcity and Inflation Control:

The primary purpose of Bitcoin halving events is to control the inflation rate of the cryptocurrency. By reducing the rate of new Bitcoin issuance, the protocol ensures that the total supply of Bitcoins gradually approaches its ultimate cap of 21 million coins. This deliberate scarcity stands in contrast to traditional fiat currencies, which can be printed and inflated by central banks. The controlled supply of Bitcoin is one of its key attributes and contributes to its store of value characteristics.

Historical Halving Events:

Bitcoin has experienced three halving events since its inception in 2009. The first halving occurred in November 2012, when the block reward was reduced from 50 Bitcoins to 25. The second halving took place in July 2016, further reducing the block reward to 12.5 Bitcoins. The most recent halving occurred in May 2020, cutting the block reward in half once again to 6.25 Bitcoins. Each halving event has had a profound impact on the Bitcoin ecosystem and market dynamics.

Supply and Demand Economics:

Bitcoin halving events create an imbalance between supply and demand dynamics. With the reduction in the block reward, the rate at which new Bitcoins enter circulation decreases. If demand remains constant or increases, this reduction in supply can lead to upward pressure on Bitcoin's price. The expectation of reduced supply often generates anticipation and speculation within the market, as investors and traders adjust their strategies in response to the halving event.

Mining Economics and Network Security:

Bitcoin mining plays a crucial role in the functioning and security of the network. Miners validate transactions, secure the network, and are rewarded with newly minted Bitcoins. Halving events have a direct impact on mining economics, as miners receive fewer Bitcoins for their efforts. This reduction in block rewards can affect the profitability of mining operations, prompting some miners to adjust their strategies, upgrade equipment, or exit the mining industry altogether.

Market Impact and Price Volatility:

Bitcoin halving events have historically been associated with increased price volatility. The anticipation leading up to the event, combined with the reduced supply of newly minted Bitcoins, can create a heightened sense of market speculation and trading activity. This heightened activity can result in significant price movements, both before and after the halving event. However, it is important to note that price volatility is influenced by various factors and cannot be solely attributed to halving events.

Long-Term Effects and Price Appreciation:

While the immediate impact of halving events can lead to short-term price volatility, the long-term effects are more nuanced. Historically, Bitcoin's price has experienced significant appreciation following each halving event. This price appreciation is often attributed to the combination of reduced supply, growing demand, and increasing recognition of Bitcoin as a legitimate asset class. However, it is important to note that past performance is not indicative of future results, and Bitcoin's price is influenced by a multitude of factors.

Halving Events and Market Maturity:

As the number of Bitcoin halving events increases, the market's understanding and anticipation of these events are likely to evolve. Market participants, including investors, traders, and miners, may become more adept at pricing in the impact of halving events, leading to potentially smoother market reactions. Additionally, the increasing maturity of the market, regulatory developments, and institutional involvement can contribute to a more stable and less volatile environment surrounding halving events.

Bitcoin halving events are unique phenomena that shape the supply dynamics, mining economics, and market sentiment within the crypto ecosystem. These events are not only significant milestones in Bitcoin's history but also serve as a reminder of the protocol's robust and deflationary nature. As Bitcoin continues to mature and evolve, halving events will remain an essential aspect of its monetary policy, affecting its value proposition and the dynamics of the broader cryptocurrency market.

Chapter 35: Bitcoin's Impact on Remittances

Remittances, or the transfer of money by individuals working abroad to their home countries, play a crucial role in global economies. Traditional remittance methods often involve high fees, lengthy processing times, and limited accessibility. However, the advent of Bitcoin and other cryptocurrencies has the potential to revolutionize the remittance industry. In this chapter, we explore how Bitcoin is transforming the landscape of remittances, offering faster, cheaper, and more inclusive options for individuals seeking to send money across borders.

The Challenges of Traditional Remittances:

Traditional remittance methods, such as wire transfers or money transfer operators, come with various challenges. These include high fees, particularly for smaller transactions, long processing times, cumbersome paperwork, and limited access for unbanked or underbanked individuals. These barriers often disproportionately affect lower-income workers who rely on remittances as a lifeline for their families back home.

Bitcoin as a Digital Currency:

Bitcoin, as a decentralized digital currency, offers a potential solution to the challenges of traditional remittances. Built on blockchain technology, Bitcoin enables secure, peer-to-peer transactions without the need for intermediaries. The inherent features of Bitcoin, including its speed, low transaction fees, and borderless nature, make it an attractive alternative for cross-border money transfers.

Faster and More Efficient Transactions:

Bitcoin facilitates near-instantaneous transactions compared to traditional remittance methods, which can take several days or even weeks to complete. The decentralized nature of the Bitcoin network allows for direct transfers between individuals, eliminating the need for intermediaries and reducing the time required for processing and verification.

Lower Transaction Costs:

One of the significant advantages of using Bitcoin for remittances is the potential for lower transaction costs. Traditional remittance services often impose high fees, particularly for smaller transfers. In contrast, Bitcoin transactions typically involve lower fees, which can result in more significant savings for both the sender and the recipient. These reduced costs make remittances more accessible and affordable for individuals with limited financial resources.

Financial Inclusion for the Unbanked:

Bitcoin's borderless nature has the potential to bridge the gap for unbanked or underbanked individuals who lack access to traditional financial services. With a Bitcoin wallet and an internet connection, individuals can participate in the global economy and receive remittances directly, without relying on traditional banking infrastructure. This increased financial inclusion has the potential to empower individuals and families, stimulating economic growth and reducing poverty in underserved communities.

Potential Challenges and Volatility:

While Bitcoin offers numerous advantages for remittances, it is important to acknowledge the potential challenges and risks associated with its volatility. Bitcoin's value can fluctuate significantly, which means that the amount received by the recipient in their local currency may vary. This volatility introduces an element of uncertainty, particularly for individuals who rely on stable and predictable income streams.

Regulatory Considerations:

The regulatory landscape surrounding Bitcoin and cryptocurrencies varies across different jurisdictions. Governments are increasingly recognizing the importance of regulating the crypto industry to protect consumers and combat illicit activities. Regulatory frameworks aim to strike a balance between facilitating innovation and safeguarding against potential risks such as money laundering and fraud. The evolving regulatory environment will shape the future of Bitcoin-based remittances and determine the level of adoption and acceptance by financial institutions.

The Role of Bitcoin Exchanges and Wallets:

Bitcoin exchanges and wallets play a crucial role in facilitating Bitcoin-based remittances. These platforms provide users with the necessary infrastructure to convert fiat currency into Bitcoin and vice versa. They also offer services such as secure storage, transaction tracking, and compliance with regulatory requirements. The emergence of user-friendly mobile wallets and the integration of Bitcoin into existing remittance platforms are further driving the adoption of Bitcoin as a remittance tool.

Bitcoin's impact on remittances has the potential to transform the lives of individuals and families around the world. By providing faster, cheaper, and more inclusive options for cross-border money transfers, Bitcoin can empower individuals with greater control over their finances and reduce their reliance on traditional remittance methods. However, it is crucial to consider the potential risks, including volatility and regulatory challenges, as the remittance industry continues to embrace this disruptive technology.

As the global remittance market evolves and the crypto industry matures, the integration of Bitcoin into remittance services is likely to increase. The transformative power of Bitcoin has the potential to reshape the remittance landscape, fostering financial inclusion and driving economic empowerment for individuals and communities worldwide.

Chapter 36: Satoshi's Vision for a Decentralized Future

Satoshi Nakamoto, the enigmatic creator of Bitcoin, not only introduced the world to a revolutionary digital currency but also laid the groundwork for a decentralized future. Satoshi's vision was deeply rooted in the belief that individuals should have control over their own financial transactions and be free from the influence of centralized authorities. In this chapter, we explore Satoshi's vision for a decentralized future, the principles underlying Bitcoin's design, and the potential implications for society.

Empowering Individuals:

At the core of Satoshi's vision was the empowerment of individuals. Traditional financial systems are built on trust in central authorities, such as banks and governments, to facilitate transactions and ensure security. However, Satoshi saw the potential for abuse of power and sought to create a system that removed the need for intermediaries and put individuals in control of their own funds. Bitcoin, with its decentralized nature, allows users to transact directly with one another, fostering financial sovereignty and self-reliance.

Eliminating Third-Party Trust:

Satoshi recognized the inherent risks associated with trusting third parties with our financial transactions. Whether it is banks, payment processors, or other intermediaries, relying on them introduces vulnerabilities such as censorship, hacking, and data breaches. By leveraging blockchain technology, Bitcoin eliminates the need for such trust. Transactions are verified and recorded on a distributed ledger, visible to all network participants, ensuring transparency, accountability, and immutability.

Distributed Consensus and Security:

Bitcoin's consensus mechanism, known as proof-of-work, ensures the security and integrity of the network. By distributing the verification of transactions across a decentralized network of miners, Bitcoin achieves consensus without the need for a central authority. This decentralized consensus mechanism prevents fraud, double-spending, and tampering with transaction history. Satoshi's vision was to create a system that could resist attacks and censorship, ensuring the long-term stability and reliability of the network.

Financial Inclusion:

Another important aspect of Satoshi's vision was to foster financial inclusion for the unbanked and underbanked populations. Around the world, billions of people lack access to traditional banking services, limiting their economic opportunities and financial independence. Bitcoin's decentralized nature and its accessibility through internet-connected devices provide individuals with a means to participate in the global economy, send and receive funds, and store value without the need for a traditional bank account.

Resisting Censorship and Control:

Satoshi was keenly aware of the potential for censorship and control in centralized systems. Governments and authorities can impose restrictions, freeze assets, or monitor transactions in traditional financial systems. By designing Bitcoin as a decentralized and censorship-resistant network, Satoshi aimed to create a system that could not be easily controlled or manipulated. This principle aligns with the ideals of individual freedom, privacy, and the right to control one's financial resources.

Open-Source Collaboration:

Satoshi's vision embraced the power of open-source collaboration and the collective intelligence of a global community. Bitcoin's codebase is open source, meaning that anyone can view, review, and contribute to its development. This transparency fosters innovation, peer review, and the ability to address vulnerabilities or shortcomings in the system. Satoshi believed in the power of decentralized decision-making and the collective effort to shape the future of Bitcoin and its underlying technology.

A Catalyst for Decentralization:

Bitcoin's emergence as the first successful decentralized cryptocurrency has inspired a broader movement toward decentralization across various industries. The principles and technologies introduced by Satoshi have paved the way for the development of decentralized applications (DApps), decentralized finance (DeFi), decentralized governance models, and more. Satoshi's vision has ignited a paradigm shift in how we think about trust, authority, and power, challenging centralized systems in favor of more democratic and inclusive alternatives.

Potential Societal Implications:

Satoshi's vision for a decentralized future extends beyond financial systems. The principles underlying Bitcoin can have far-reaching implications for various sectors, including governance, supply chains, intellectual property, and data privacy. By embracing decentralized technologies, societies have the potential to shift power dynamics, increase transparency, foster innovation, and enable individuals to have greater control over their digital lives.

Satoshi Nakamoto's vision for a decentralized future was a response to the inherent flaws and risks in centralized systems. Through the introduction of Bitcoin and its underlying technology, Satoshi aimed to empower individuals, promote financial inclusion, resist censorship, and foster a more equitable and transparent society. While Satoshi's identity remains a mystery, the impact of their vision has reverberated across the globe, inspiring a movement toward decentralized systems that challenge the status quo and redefine the balance of power.

As the world continues to embrace decentralized technologies, the realization of Satoshi's vision is an ongoing process. It requires the collective efforts of developers, entrepreneurs, policymakers, and individuals to shape the future of decentralization and build systems that empower, protect, and enhance the lives of people worldwide.

Chapter 37: Forks and the Creation of Bitcoin Cash

Bitcoin, as the first decentralized cryptocurrency, has witnessed several forks throughout its history. A fork occurs when a blockchain's underlying protocol is modified, resulting in two separate chains with distinct characteristics and features. One notable fork in the Bitcoin ecosystem led to the creation of Bitcoin Cash (BCH), a digital currency that aimed to address perceived limitations of Bitcoin. In this chapter, we delve into the concept of forks, explore the reasons behind the creation of Bitcoin Cash, and examine the impact of this fork on the crypto ecosystem.

Understanding Forks in Cryptocurrencies:

In the context of cryptocurrencies, a fork is a significant event where a blockchain diverges into two separate chains with different rules and features. This divergence occurs when developers or a community propose changes to the underlying protocol, which may result in conflicting opinions and visions for the cryptocurrency's future. Forks can be categorized into two types: hard forks and soft forks.

Hard Forks and Chain Splits:

A hard fork occurs when the changes proposed to a cryptocurrency's protocol are not backward compatible. This means that nodes that do not upgrade to the new rules will no longer be able to validate transactions on the new chain. As a result, a hard fork can lead to a chain split, where the original chain and the newly created chain coexist as separate entities.

Bitcoin Cash: The Fork from Bitcoin:

In August 2017, the Bitcoin network experienced a significant hard fork, resulting in the creation of Bitcoin Cash. The fork was driven by a group of developers and community members who believed that Bitcoin's block size should be increased to accommodate more transactions and improve scalability. Bitcoin Cash aimed to address perceived limitations of Bitcoin, such as high transaction fees and slow confirmation times.

Differences Between Bitcoin and Bitcoin Cash:

The key difference between Bitcoin and Bitcoin Cash lies in their approach to scaling. Bitcoin Cash increased the block size limit from 1 MB to 8 MB, allowing for more transactions to be processed in each block. This change aimed to enhance transaction capacity and reduce congestion on the network. Bitcoin Cash also implemented some technical changes, such as the removal of the Replace-by-Fee (RBF) feature and the addition of a new difficulty adjustment algorithm.

Market Reaction and Community Response:

The creation of Bitcoin Cash sparked a significant debate within the crypto community. Some saw it as a necessary evolution of Bitcoin, offering improved scalability and lower fees. Others viewed it as a contentious fork that threatened the unity and integrity of the Bitcoin ecosystem. The market reacted with mixed sentiment, and both Bitcoin and Bitcoin Cash garnered their respective communities of supporters, miners, and investors.

Impact on the Crypto Ecosystem:

The creation of Bitcoin Cash had several notable impacts on the wider cryptocurrency ecosystem. It demonstrated the potential for forks to address scalability concerns and offer alternative solutions to the design choices of the original cryptocurrency. It also highlighted the importance of consensus and community support in determining the success and adoption of a forked digital asset.

Forks as a Catalyst for Innovation:

The fork of Bitcoin into Bitcoin Cash showcased the dynamic and innovative nature of the cryptocurrency space. Forks enable developers and communities to experiment with different approaches, address perceived limitations, and iterate on the technology. While not all forks achieve widespread adoption or lasting impact, they serve as catalysts for innovation and drive the evolution of the cryptocurrency ecosystem as a whole.

Coexistence and Future Perspectives:

Bitcoin and Bitcoin Cash have coexisted since the fork, with each maintaining its separate community, development teams, and market presence. Bitcoin Cash has undergone its own updates, including subsequent hard forks that introduced further changes and features. The coexistence of these two cryptocurrencies provides users with choice and allows for continued exploration and development of different scaling solutions.

The creation of Bitcoin Cash through a hard fork of Bitcoin illustrates the dynamic and evolving nature of the cryptocurrency ecosystem. Forks like these serve as a testament to the decentralized and open-source nature of cryptocurrencies, enabling communities to experiment, innovate, and address perceived limitations. While the fork resulted in separate paths for Bitcoin and Bitcoin Cash, both cryptocurrencies continue to shape the broader landscape of digital currencies, each with its own unique characteristics and visions.

As the crypto industry continues to evolve, the occurrence of forks and the subsequent creation of new cryptocurrencies are likely to persist. These forks represent opportunities for further exploration, experimentation, and the pursuit of alternative visions for decentralized systems. Ultimately, forks contribute to the ongoing development and diversification of the cryptocurrency ecosystem, fostering innovation and providing users with a wide range of options and possibilities.

Chapter 38: The Lightning Network and Scalability

Bitcoin, as the first decentralized cryptocurrency, has faced challenges related to scalability, particularly in terms of transaction throughput and confirmation times. These limitations have spurred the development of various solutions, one of the most notable being the Lightning Network. In this chapter, we explore the Lightning Network, its potential to address Bitcoin's scalability issues, and its impact on the broader crypto ecosystem.

Scalability Challenges in Bitcoin:

Bitcoin's underlying blockchain technology has a limited capacity to process transactions. With a block size limit of 1 MB, Bitcoin can handle only a certain number of transactions per block. As adoption and usage of Bitcoin increased, congestion on the network became evident, resulting in slower confirmation times and higher transaction fees during periods of high demand.

Introducing the Lightning Network:

The Lightning Network is a second-layer protocol designed to address Bitcoin's scalability challenges. It operates as an off-chain solution, enabling faster and cheaper transactions by conducting most transactions off the main Bitcoin blockchain. By leveraging payment channels and smart contracts, the Lightning Network aims to enable instant, low-cost transactions with enhanced scalability.

How the Lightning Network Works:

The Lightning Network operates by establishing payment channels between participants. These channels are created by locking a certain amount of Bitcoin in a multi-signature address, which is then used to facilitate off-chain transactions. Participants can transact with each other through these payment channels, and the final settlement is recorded on the Bitcoin blockchain when the channel is closed.

Benefits of the Lightning Network:

The Lightning Network offers several advantages that contribute to Bitcoin's scalability:

- Increased Transaction Throughput: By conducting transactions off-chain, the Lightning Network significantly increases the transaction throughput capacity of the Bitcoin network. It enables a high volume of transactions to be processed quickly and efficiently.
- Reduced Transaction Fees: With the Lightning Network, transaction fees can be significantly lower compared to on-chain transactions. Since most transactions occur off-chain, participants only incur minimal fees when opening or closing payment channels.
- Instant Transactions: The Lightning Network allows for near-instantaneous transactions. Participants can send and receive funds within the Lightning Network without having to wait for block confirmations on the main blockchain.
- Enhanced Privacy: The Lightning Network adds an additional layer of privacy to transactions. Since most transactions occur off-chain and are not recorded on the main blockchain, they offer a higher level of privacy compared to traditional on-chain transactions.

Network Growth and Adoption:

Since its inception, the Lightning Network has seen steady growth in terms of network capacity and adoption. The number of active nodes and payment channels has increased, facilitating a growing number of transactions. Wallet providers, exchanges, and merchants have also begun integrating Lightning Network support, enabling users to leverage its benefits for everyday transactions.

Potential Use Cases:

The Lightning Network has the potential to enable various use cases beyond simple peer-to-peer transactions. Some potential applications include microtransactions, streaming services, content monetization, and machine-to-machine payments. The network's scalability and low transaction costs make it suitable for these types of high-frequency, low-value transactions.

Challenges and Considerations:

While the Lightning Network offers promising solutions to Bitcoin's scalability challenges, it is not without its own considerations:

- Network Liquidity: To transact on the Lightning Network, participants need to have payment channels with sufficient liquidity. As

the network grows, liquidity management and routing become crucial factors in ensuring the smooth operation of the Lightning Network.
- User Experience: The Lightning Network's current user experience is still evolving. Setting up and managing payment channels require technical expertise, which can be a barrier to widespread adoption. However, efforts are underway to improve user-friendly interfaces and simplify the process.
- Centralization Concerns: The Lightning Network's routing mechanism relies on well-connected nodes. Critics argue that this could lead to a centralization of the network, potentially compromising its decentralized nature. Ongoing research and development aim to address these concerns and promote a more decentralized routing ecosystem.

Impact on the Crypto Ecosystem:

The Lightning Network's development has had a positive impact on the broader crypto ecosystem. It has sparked innovation and experimentation with layer-two scaling solutions for other blockchain platforms. Additionally, the Lightning Network has paved the way for the development of decentralized finance (DeFi) applications and services that leverage its scalability and instant settlement features.

The Lightning Network represents a significant step toward addressing Bitcoin's scalability challenges. Its ability to facilitate faster, cheaper, and more scalable transactions offers a promising solution for the broader adoption and use of Bitcoin as a medium of exchange. As the Lightning Network continues to evolve and gain traction, it has the potential to transform the Bitcoin ecosystem and contribute to the development of a more efficient and scalable decentralized financial infrastructure.

Chapter 39: Institutional Adoption of Bitcoin

Bitcoin, once considered a fringe asset, has gained significant attention and adoption from institutional players in recent years. Traditional financial institutions, corporations, and investment firms have recognized the potential of Bitcoin as a store of value and a hedge against inflation. In this chapter, we explore the reasons behind the institutional adoption of Bitcoin, the impact it has had on the cryptocurrency market, and the potential implications for the future.

Recognition of Bitcoin's Value Proposition:

Institutions have started to view Bitcoin as a legitimate asset class due to its unique characteristics. Bitcoin's decentralized nature, limited supply, and censorship-resistant properties make it an appealing hedge against traditional financial systems and inflationary pressures. Institutions recognize the potential of Bitcoin to preserve wealth, diversify portfolios, and provide long-term investment opportunities.

Hedge Against Inflation and Economic Uncertainty:

In times of economic uncertainty, institutions seek assets that can retain value and act as a hedge against inflation. Bitcoin's scarcity, with a limited supply of 21 million coins, provides an alternative to traditional fiat currencies that can be inflated by central banks. As governments around the world implement expansive monetary policies, institutions increasingly turn to Bitcoin as a potential store of value and a means to protect against the erosion of purchasing power.

Growing Market Infrastructure:

The development of robust market infrastructure has played a crucial role in facilitating institutional adoption of Bitcoin. Established financial institutions, including banks, custodians, and exchanges, have entered the crypto space, offering regulated and secure platforms for institutions to buy, sell, and hold Bitcoin. This infrastructure development has provided institutions with the necessary confidence and support to enter the market.

Regulatory Clarity and Compliance:

As regulatory frameworks around cryptocurrencies have become more defined, institutions have gained clarity on how to navigate the legal and compliance aspects of investing in Bitcoin.

Regulatory agencies in various jurisdictions have taken steps to provide guidelines and frameworks for digital assets, reducing uncertainty and providing a more transparent environment for institutional investors. This regulatory clarity has encouraged institutions to consider allocating funds to Bitcoin.

Mainstream Endorsements and Acceptance:

Bitcoin has received endorsements and recognition from influential figures and mainstream institutions. Prominent investors, such as Paul Tudor Jones and Stanley Druckenmiller, have publicly expressed their support for Bitcoin as a hedge against inflation. Additionally, major companies like Tesla and Square have invested significant amounts of capital in Bitcoin, signaling institutional acceptance and adoption.

Diversification of Investment Portfolios:

Institutions recognize the importance of diversifying their investment portfolios to manage risk and capture potential returns. Bitcoin's low correlation to traditional asset classes, such as stocks and bonds, makes it an attractive addition to institutional portfolios. By including Bitcoin, institutions can enhance portfolio diversification and potentially improve risk-adjusted returns.

Enhanced Market Liquidity:

As institutional investors enter the Bitcoin market, liquidity has significantly increased. The presence of large institutional players brings deeper liquidity pools and tighter bid-ask spreads, which improves price stability and reduces execution risks. This increased liquidity provides institutions with greater flexibility in terms of trade execution and portfolio management.

Impact on the Crypto Ecosystem:

The institutional adoption of Bitcoin has had a profound impact on the broader crypto ecosystem. It has brought increased liquidity, improved market efficiency, and heightened credibility to the crypto market. Furthermore, institutional involvement has driven the development of new financial products, such as Bitcoin futures, options, and exchange-traded funds (ETFs), which further enhance market access for institutional investors.

Potential Risks and Challenges:

While institutional adoption brings numerous benefits, there are also risks and challenges to consider. Bitcoin's price volatility remains a concern for institutions that are more accustomed to traditional asset classes. Additionally, cybersecurity and custody solutions need to be robust to protect institutional holdings. Regulatory developments and geopolitical factors can also influence institutional sentiment and investment decisions.

Future Outlook:

The institutional adoption of Bitcoin is likely to continue in the coming years. As more traditional financial institutions enter the market and regulatory frameworks mature, barriers to entry for institutions are expected to decrease. Additionally, the integration of Bitcoin into existing financial infrastructure, such as payment networks and investment platforms, could further drive institutional participation.

The institutional adoption of Bitcoin represents a significant milestone in the evolution of cryptocurrencies. It underscores the growing recognition of Bitcoin as a legitimate asset class with unique value propositions. As institutions continue to allocate funds to Bitcoin and explore its potential, the impact on the crypto market and the broader financial landscape is likely to be transformative, paving the way for a more inclusive and diversified global financial system.

Chapter 40: Satoshi's Intellectual Contributions

Satoshi Nakamoto's intellectual contributions extend far beyond the creation of Bitcoin itself. Satoshi's innovative ideas and groundbreaking concepts have had a profound impact on various fields, including computer science, cryptography, economics, and governance. In this chapter, we delve into Satoshi's intellectual contributions, exploring the principles and ideas that have shaped the trajectory of technology and society.

Decentralization and Distributed Systems:

Satoshi's most significant intellectual contribution lies in the concept of decentralization. By introducing a decentralized peer-to-peer network through Bitcoin, Satoshi challenged the traditional paradigm of centralized systems. Decentralization removes the need for a single point of control, enabling individuals to transact directly with one another without intermediaries. This concept has since influenced the development of blockchain technology, decentralized applications, and distributed computing systems.

Blockchain Technology and Consensus Mechanisms:

Satoshi's introduction of the blockchain as a distributed ledger system has revolutionized the way we record and verify transactions. The blockchain serves as a transparent and immutable record of all Bitcoin transactions, providing security and trust in a decentralized manner. Satoshi's consensus mechanism, proof-of-work, enables agreement among network participants without the need for a central authority. This consensus model has been widely adopted in subsequent blockchain implementations.

Cryptography and Privacy:

Satoshi's expertise in cryptography is evident in the design of Bitcoin. He integrated cryptographic techniques to ensure the security and privacy of transactions. Public-key cryptography, digital signatures, and cryptographic hash functions play vital roles in securing Bitcoin transactions and verifying the integrity of the blockchain. Satoshi's emphasis on privacy and pseudonymity within the Bitcoin network has sparked discussions on the balance between transparency and individual privacy in the digital age.

Economic Incentives and Game Theory:

Bitcoin's economic model, driven by incentives and game theory, is another intellectual contribution of Satoshi. Through Bitcoin's design, Satoshi created a system where participants are incentivized to act in the best interest of the network. Miners are rewarded with newly minted Bitcoin and transaction fees for securing the network, while users benefit from a decentralized and censorship-resistant currency. This economic model has inspired further research and exploration of incentive mechanisms in blockchain systems.

Open-Source Collaboration and Community Development:

Satoshi's decision to release the Bitcoin codebase as open source was instrumental in fostering collaboration and community development. The open-source nature of Bitcoin enabled a global community of developers to review and contribute to its improvement. This model of decentralized collaboration has since become a cornerstone of the broader open-source movement, stimulating innovation, peer review, and the democratization of technology development.

Libertarian Ideals and Individual Empowerment:

Satoshi's writings and the genesis of Bitcoin reflect a strong influence of libertarian ideals. Bitcoin's design, with its emphasis on decentralization, financial sovereignty, and resistance to censorship, aligns with principles of individual empowerment and freedom. Satoshi's vision was to create a system where individuals can transact and store value without reliance on centralized authorities. This emphasis on individual control and autonomy has sparked discussions about the future of money, governance, and personal liberty.

Inspiration for Further Research and Development:

Satoshi's intellectual contributions have inspired further research and development in various fields. Scholars and technologists have delved into topics such as consensus algorithms, scalability solutions, smart contract platforms, and privacy-enhancing technologies. Satoshi's ideas continue to influence the design and evolution of blockchain systems, driving innovation and shaping the future of technology.

Cultural and Societal Implications:

Satoshi Nakamoto's intellectual contributions extend beyond technical and academic realms. Bitcoin and the underlying concepts have sparked conversations about trust, transparency, financial inclusivity, and the role of technology in shaping society. The rise of cryptocurrencies and decentralized systems has prompted discussions on economic systems, governance models, and individual freedoms. Satoshi's intellectual legacy lies in the transformative potential of these ideas to reshape our world.

While Satoshi Nakamoto's true identity remains unknown, the intellectual contributions embedded within Bitcoin's design and philosophy have left an indelible mark on the world. Satoshi's visionary ideas have stimulated interdisciplinary discussions and paved the way for the exploration and development of decentralized technologies. As we continue to unravel the implications of Satoshi's contributions, we enter a new era of innovation, collaboration, and reimagining the possibilities of a decentralized future.

Chapter 41: Bitcoin's Role in Financial Inclusion

Bitcoin, with its decentralized and borderless nature, has the potential to play a significant role in promoting financial inclusion. Around the world, billions of people lack access to traditional banking services, limiting their ability to participate in the global economy and improve their financial well-being. In this chapter, we explore how Bitcoin can address barriers to financial inclusion, empower individuals, and provide opportunities for economic advancement.

Accessibility and Global Reach:

One of Bitcoin's key advantages is its accessibility. All that is needed to participate in the Bitcoin network is an internet connection and a digital wallet. This low barrier to entry makes Bitcoin available to anyone with internet access, regardless of their geographic location. Unlike traditional banking systems that require physical infrastructure and centralized intermediaries, Bitcoin can reach underserved populations in remote areas, enabling them to engage in financial transactions and store value securely.

Empowering the Unbanked and Underbanked:

A significant portion of the global population remains unbanked or underbanked, lacking access to basic financial services such as bank accounts, loans, and payment systems. Bitcoin offers an alternative to traditional banking by providing individuals with a means to store value, send and receive funds, and engage in economic activities without relying on a bank account. This financial empowerment can unlock opportunities for entrepreneurship, savings, and economic stability.

Remittances and Cross-Border Transactions:

Bitcoin has the potential to revolutionize the remittance industry, which often imposes high fees and lengthy processing times. For individuals working abroad and sending money back to their families, Bitcoin offers a more efficient and cost-effective solution. By leveraging Bitcoin's borderless and near-instantaneous transaction capabilities, individuals can bypass traditional remittance channels and transfer funds directly to recipients, reducing costs and improving financial outcomes for families in developing countries.

Protection Against Inflation and Currency Volatility:

In regions with unstable economies and high inflation rates, traditional currencies can rapidly lose value, eroding people's purchasing power and savings. Bitcoin's decentralized nature and limited supply provide a hedge against inflation and currency volatility. Individuals can store their wealth in Bitcoin, mitigating the risk of losing value due to economic fluctuations and political instability. This stability can foster long-term financial security and protect individuals from the negative impacts of hyperinflation.

Financial Services for the "Unscorable":

In many parts of the world, individuals lack access to credit due to a lack of credit history or the absence of formal identification documents. This "unscorable" population is often excluded from traditional financial systems. Bitcoin's decentralized nature allows individuals to establish a financial identity and build a reputation within the network based on their transaction history. This, in turn, can enable them to access alternative lending platforms and financial services that leverage Bitcoin's blockchain technology.

Empowering Entrepreneurs and Startups:

Entrepreneurs and small businesses in underserved regions often face significant challenges in accessing capital and financial services. Bitcoin offers a decentralized fundraising mechanism through Initial Coin Offerings (ICOs) and tokenization, enabling entrepreneurs to raise funds from a global pool of investors. Additionally, Bitcoin can serve as a secure and efficient payment system for startups, enabling them to transact with customers globally without the need for traditional banking intermediaries.

Privacy and Financial Freedom:

Bitcoin's emphasis on privacy and pseudonymity provides individuals with a level of financial freedom and autonomy that is often restricted in traditional financial systems. Individuals can maintain control over their financial transactions and personal information, reducing the risk of identity theft and unauthorized access to their funds. This privacy aspect is particularly relevant in regions where governments impose strict financial controls or where individuals face persecution based on their financial activities.

Education and Financial Literacy:

Bitcoin's rise has sparked interest in digital currencies and blockchain technology, leading to increased awareness and education about financial concepts and technology. Educational initiatives focused on Bitcoin and cryptocurrencies can empower individuals with the knowledge and skills needed to navigate the digital economy. Improved financial literacy can help individuals make informed decisions, manage their finances effectively, and protect themselves against fraudulent schemes.

Challenges and Considerations:

While Bitcoin holds promise for financial inclusion, it is not without challenges. Technical barriers, such as the need for internet access and reliable electricity, can limit adoption in certain regions. The volatility of Bitcoin's price poses risks for individuals who rely on it for day-to-day transactions. Additionally, regulatory frameworks and compliance requirements can vary across jurisdictions, affecting the ability of individuals and businesses to fully utilize Bitcoin's potential.

Collaborative Solutions:

Addressing the challenges of financial inclusion requires collaboration among various stakeholders, including governments, non-profit organizations, and technology providers. Partnerships can facilitate the development of infrastructure, education programs, and policy frameworks that support the responsible use of Bitcoin and promote financial inclusion. Initiatives like Bitcoin wallets designed for low-bandwidth environments and community-led educational programs can bridge the digital divide and empower underserved populations.

Bitcoin's potential for financial inclusion lies in its ability to provide access to financial services, foster economic empowerment, and enable cross-border transactions for individuals who are underserved by traditional banking systems. By leveraging Bitcoin's decentralized and inclusive nature, we can work toward a future where individuals worldwide have equal opportunities to participate in the global economy, improve their financial well-being, and achieve greater economic stability.

Chapter 42: Bitcoin and Energy Consumption Concerns

As Bitcoin has gained popularity and its network has grown, concerns regarding its energy consumption have emerged. Critics argue that the mining process, which secures the Bitcoin network and verifies transactions, requires a significant amount of electricity, and has a negative impact on the environment. In this chapter, we delve into the topic of Bitcoin's energy consumption, examine the factors involved, and explore potential solutions and perspectives.

Understanding Bitcoin Mining:

Bitcoin mining is the process by which new bitcoins are created and transactions are validated on the blockchain. Miners compete to solve complex mathematical problems, and the first miner to find a valid solution is rewarded with newly minted bitcoins. This process requires substantial computational power, which consumes energy.

Energy Consumption and Proof-of-Work:

Bitcoin's consensus mechanism, known as proof-of-work, is designed to secure the network and prevent fraudulent transactions. However, it requires miners to perform numerous calculations, which in turn requires significant computational power and energy consumption. As the Bitcoin network has grown, so has the energy required to mine new blocks and sustain the network's security.

Factors Affecting Bitcoin's Energy Consumption:

Several factors contribute to Bitcoin's energy consumption:

- Hash Rate and Difficulty: As more miners join the network and competition increases, the difficulty of mining new blocks adjusts to maintain a consistent block time. Higher hash rates, which represent the total computational power of the network, require more energy to maintain the required level of security.
- Energy Sources: The energy sources used for Bitcoin mining vary, ranging from fossil fuels to renewable energy. The energy mix can have a significant impact on the environmental footprint of Bitcoin mining. Some miners have started exploring renewable energy options to mitigate their carbon footprint.

- Hardware Efficiency: The efficiency of mining hardware plays a role in energy consumption. More energy-efficient mining equipment can perform computations at a lower energy cost, reducing the overall energy consumption of the network.

Comparing Bitcoin's Energy Consumption to Traditional Systems:

Critics often compare Bitcoin's energy consumption to that of traditional financial systems or other industries. While Bitcoin's energy consumption is substantial, it is worth considering the broader context. Traditional banking systems, for example, consume energy through physical infrastructure, paper-based processes, and data centers. The energy consumption of these systems is difficult to quantify and compare directly to Bitcoin.

Environmental Impact and Sustainability Concerns:

Bitcoin's energy consumption has raised concerns about its environmental impact, particularly in regions where fossil fuels are the predominant energy source. Critics argue that the carbon footprint of Bitcoin mining contributes to climate change and contradicts efforts to reduce greenhouse gas emissions. However, it is important to note that Bitcoin mining is not the sole contributor to global energy consumption, and efforts are being made to increase the use of renewable energy in mining operations.

Technological Innovations and Energy Efficiency:

Bitcoin's energy consumption concerns have driven technological innovations aimed at improving energy efficiency. Some mining companies are developing more energy-efficient mining hardware, while others are exploring alternative consensus mechanisms that consume less energy, such as proof-of-stake. Additionally, advancements in renewable energy technologies and the adoption of greener energy sources by miners can help mitigate Bitcoin's environmental impact.

The Value of Bitcoin's Security and Utility:

Bitcoin's energy consumption must also be evaluated in the context of its value and utility. Bitcoin provides a secure, decentralized, and censorship-resistant store of value and medium of exchange. Supporters argue that the energy consumption is a necessary trade-off for the benefits it offers. They believe that Bitcoin's potential to disrupt traditional financial systems and empower individuals outweighs the energy expended in the mining process.

Potential Solutions and Future Outlook:

Efforts are underway to address Bitcoin's energy consumption concerns. These include:

- Transition to Renewable Energy: Encouraging miners to shift to renewable energy sources can significantly reduce the carbon footprint of Bitcoin mining. Some mining operations are already being powered entirely by renewable energy.
- Energy Recycling and Efficiency: Innovative solutions, such as using excess heat generated by mining equipment for other purposes, can maximize energy efficiency and reduce waste.
- Research and Development: Ongoing research focuses on alternative consensus mechanisms that consume less energy, as well as scaling solutions that increase transaction throughput while maintaining or reducing energy consumption.

The future of Bitcoin's energy consumption depends on a combination of technological advancements, adoption of greener energy sources, and the industry's commitment to sustainability. As the Bitcoin ecosystem evolves, it is crucial to balance the need for security and decentralization with environmental considerations.

It is worth noting that the energy consumption of Bitcoin is not solely a negative aspect. Bitcoin's presence has driven investment in renewable energy projects and incentivized the development of more energy-efficient mining technologies. Additionally, the potential societal and economic benefits of Bitcoin, such as financial inclusion and decentralized finance, must be weighed against the energy consumed.

So, Bitcoin's energy consumption is a complex and multifaceted issue. While concerns exist regarding its environmental impact, ongoing innovations and the adoption of renewable energy sources offer potential solutions. As the cryptocurrency industry continues to evolve, stakeholders must collaborate to ensure that Bitcoin and other blockchain technologies align with sustainable practices, allowing for the realization of their transformative potential.

Type This URL in Your Browser → *https://bit.ly/Guess_What_This*

Chapter 43: The Rise of Bitcoin Exchanges

Bitcoin exchanges play a crucial role in the cryptocurrency ecosystem, serving as platforms where individuals can buy, sell, and trade Bitcoin and other digital assets. Over the years, these exchanges have experienced significant growth, with increased user adoption and the emergence of numerous trading platforms. In this chapter, we explore the rise of Bitcoin exchanges, their evolution, and their impact on the accessibility and liquidity of cryptocurrencies.

Early Days of Bitcoin Exchanges:

In the early days of Bitcoin, exchanges were few and far between. The first Bitcoin exchange, BitcoinMarket.com, was established in 2010, providing a platform for users to trade Bitcoin for fiat currencies. However, these early exchanges faced numerous challenges, including security vulnerabilities, regulatory uncertainties, and limited liquidity.

Mt. Gox and its Impact:

Mt. Gox, launched in 2010, quickly became the dominant Bitcoin exchange, handling the majority of Bitcoin trading volume at its peak. However, it faced severe security breaches and operational issues, culminating in its collapse in 2014. The Mt. Gox incident highlighted the need for robust security measures and regulatory oversight within the cryptocurrency exchange industry.

Evolution of Exchanges:

Following the Mt. Gox incident, the landscape of Bitcoin exchanges began to change. Exchanges started implementing stringent security measures, including cold storage of user funds and two-factor authentication. Additionally, regulatory frameworks for cryptocurrency exchanges began to emerge in various jurisdictions, bringing a level of legitimacy and consumer protection to the industry.

Expansion of Services:

As the cryptocurrency market grew, exchanges expanded their services beyond simple buying and selling. Many exchanges introduced advanced trading features, such as margin trading and futures contracts, catering to the needs of more sophisticated traders. Additionally, exchanges began listing a wide range of altcoins, providing users with opportunities to trade various cryptocurrencies.

Liquidity and Market Depth:

The rise of Bitcoin exchanges significantly improved liquidity and market depth in the cryptocurrency market. With the growing number of exchanges and the increased participation of traders, the availability of buyers and sellers improved, resulting in tighter bid-ask spreads and increased price stability. This enhanced liquidity has attracted institutional investors and facilitated the growth of derivative markets, such as Bitcoin futures and options.

User Experience and Accessibility:

Bitcoin exchanges have made significant strides in improving user experience and accessibility. User-friendly interfaces, mobile applications, and intuitive trading platforms have made it easier for individuals, regardless of their technical expertise, to participate in cryptocurrency trading. Additionally, the integration of payment gateways and fiat-to-crypto onramps has simplified the process of buying Bitcoin, attracting a broader user base.

Regulatory Compliance:

Regulatory compliance has become a critical aspect of operating a cryptocurrency exchange. Exchanges are now subject to Know Your Customer (KYC) and Anti-Money Laundering (AML) requirements, ensuring that users' identities are verified, and transactions are monitored. Compliance with these regulations has instilled confidence in users and facilitated the integration of cryptocurrencies into the traditional financial system.

Security and Trust:

The security of user funds has been a significant concern for cryptocurrency exchanges. High-profile hacking incidents, such as the Mt. Gox and Coincheck breaches, have highlighted the importance of robust security measures. As a result, exchanges have implemented measures like cold storage of funds, multi-signature wallets, and regular security audits to enhance the protection of user assets. The industry has also witnessed the emergence of insurance products specifically designed to cover digital asset losses.

Global Market Expansion:

Bitcoin exchanges have expanded their operations to cater to a global user base. They have established presence in multiple jurisdictions, complying with local regulations and tailoring their services to specific markets. This global expansion has facilitated greater accessibility to cryptocurrencies, allowing individuals from around the world to participate in the digital asset economy.

Decentralized Exchanges:

In recent years, decentralized exchanges (DEXs) have emerged as an alternative to traditional centralized exchanges. DEXs operate on blockchain networks and allow users to trade cryptocurrencies directly from their wallets without relying on a centralized intermediary. These platforms offer increased privacy, control over funds, and resistance to censorship. While DEXs are still in their early stages of development, they represent a potential paradigm shift in the exchange landscape.

Challenges and the Road Ahead:

Despite their growth and progress, Bitcoin exchanges still face challenges. Scalability remains an ongoing concern as exchanges need to handle increasing trading volumes and user demand. Regulatory uncertainty in some jurisdictions creates compliance challenges and restricts market access. Furthermore, maintaining a balance between security and user convenience is an ongoing endeavor for exchanges.

So, the rise of Bitcoin exchanges has played a pivotal role in the growth and maturation of the cryptocurrency ecosystem. These platforms have improved accessibility, liquidity, and security, making it easier for individuals to engage in cryptocurrency trading. As the industry continues to evolve, exchanges will play a vital role in driving adoption, fostering innovation, and bridging the gap between the traditional financial system and the emerging world of digital assets.

Chapter 44: Satoshi's Unspent Bitcoin

The story of Satoshi Nakamoto, the mysterious creator of Bitcoin, is filled with intrigue and speculation. One aspect that adds to the mystique is the fact that Satoshi possesses a significant amount of Bitcoin that remains unspent. In this chapter, we delve into the topic of Satoshi's unspent Bitcoin, examine its potential implications, and explore the various theories surrounding its fate.

The Genesis of Satoshi's Bitcoin:

Satoshi Nakamoto, believed to be an individual or a group, mined the first Bitcoins in the early days of the cryptocurrency. As the sole miner during Bitcoin's inception, Satoshi accumulated a substantial number of coins. These initial coins, known as the "genesis block," serve as a testament to Satoshi's pioneering efforts and hold symbolic value within the Bitcoin community.

The Mystery of Satoshi's Identity:

Satoshi Nakamoto's true identity remains unknown, adding to the allure and speculation surrounding the unspent Bitcoin. Many theories and individuals have been proposed as the possible identity of Satoshi, ranging from renowned cryptographers to technology enthusiasts. However, no conclusive evidence has surfaced to confirm any of these claims.

Satoshi's Bitcoin Holdings:

Estimates suggest that Satoshi's Bitcoin holdings amount to around one million coins, which at the time of writing, would be worth a significant sum. These coins are tied to specific public addresses known to belong to Satoshi. However, Satoshi has not accessed or spent any of these coins, leading to various theories about the reasons behind this decision.

Preservation of Satoshi's Anonymity:

One widely speculated reason for Satoshi's decision to leave the Bitcoin untouched is the desire to preserve their anonymity. Accessing or spending the coins could potentially reveal information that could lead to their identification. By leaving the Bitcoin unspent, Satoshi maintains a level of privacy and protection, allowing them to remain hidden from the public eye.

The Significance of Satoshi's Bitcoin:

Satoshi's unspent Bitcoin holds symbolic value within the Bitcoin community. It serves as a testament to the integrity and selflessness of the creator. Satoshi's decision not to cash out or spend the coins despite their substantial value demonstrates a commitment to the principles of decentralization and the vision of Bitcoin as a global currency free from centralized control.

Potential Impact on the Bitcoin Market:

The existence of a large amount of unspent Bitcoin held by an anonymous figure like Satoshi has the potential to impact the Bitcoin market. If Satoshi were to sell or transfer a significant portion of the coins, it could create substantial price volatility and market uncertainty. However, the mere fact that the coins remain untouched can also contribute to market stability, as they are effectively removed from circulation.

Theories and Speculation:

Numerous theories and speculations surround the fate of Satoshi's unspent Bitcoin. Some believe that Satoshi has lost access to the coins due to technical reasons or the loss of private keys. Others speculate that Satoshi may choose to spend the coins at some point in the future, potentially to support a cause or project aligned with their vision for Bitcoin. However, until concrete evidence emerges, these theories remain speculative.

Satoshi's Intentions and Legacy:

The intentions behind Satoshi's decision to leave the Bitcoin unspent can only be speculated upon. It is possible that Satoshi considers the Bitcoin holdings as a testament to the success and resilience of the network. By not accessing the coins, Satoshi may wish to emphasize the decentralized and self-sustaining nature of Bitcoin, where no single individual holds control over the currency's fate.

Contributions Beyond Bitcoin Holdings:

While Satoshi's unspent Bitcoin has captured attention and intrigue, it is essential to recognize that Satoshi's greatest contributions lie in the creation of Bitcoin and the underlying technology. The ideas, concepts, and principles introduced by Satoshi have sparked a revolution in finance, technology, and governance. The unspent Bitcoin serves as a reminder of the genius behind the creation but pales in comparison to the transformative impact of the technology itself.

The Legacy Continues:

As Bitcoin and the broader cryptocurrency ecosystem continue to evolve, Satoshi Nakamoto's legacy remains influential. Satoshi's vision of a decentralized, peer-to-peer electronic cash system has inspired countless innovators, entrepreneurs, and developers. While Satoshi's unspent Bitcoin may capture the imagination, it is the ongoing development, adoption, and exploration of the technology that truly advances the principles and ideals laid out in the Bitcoin white paper.

So, Satoshi Nakamoto's unspent Bitcoin represents an enigmatic aspect of the Bitcoin story. The unspent coins, held by the anonymous creator, symbolize the integrity and commitment to decentralization that underpins the Bitcoin network. While speculation and theories surround the fate of these coins, the true significance lies in the transformative impact of Bitcoin as a global currency and the ongoing legacy of Satoshi's ideas.

Chapter 45: Government Seizures of Bitcoin

Bitcoin's decentralized and pseudonymous nature has made it an attractive option for individuals seeking financial privacy and autonomy. However, governments around the world have also recognized the potential risks associated with cryptocurrencies, leading to various instances of government seizures of Bitcoin. In this chapter, we explore the topic of government seizures of Bitcoin, examine the reasons behind these actions, and discuss the implications for both individuals and the cryptocurrency ecosystem as a whole.

Legal Basis for Government Seizures:

Government seizures of Bitcoin typically occur within the framework of existing laws and regulations related to asset forfeiture, money laundering, and illicit activities. Governments assert their authority to seize Bitcoin and other cryptocurrencies when they suspect that the funds are involved in criminal activities, such as drug trafficking, money laundering, or terrorist financing. These seizures are conducted by law enforcement agencies with the aim of disrupting illicit activities and recovering illicitly obtained funds.

Publicized Seizures and High-Profile Cases:

Several high-profile cases of government seizures of Bitcoin have garnered significant attention. One notable example is the Silk Road case in 2013, where the United States government seized a substantial amount of Bitcoin from the notorious dark web marketplace. Another prominent case involved the seizure of Bitcoin from the ransomware group, Dark Side, following the Colonial Pipeline attack in 2021. These publicized cases serve as a deterrent and send a message that illegal activities involving cryptocurrencies will not go unpunished.

Methods of Seizure:

Government seizures of Bitcoin can occur through different methods. In some cases, law enforcement agencies may gain access to private keys or wallets associated with illicit activities, allowing them to confiscate the funds. In other instances, exchanges or custodial services holding the funds may be compelled to freeze or hand over the assets following a court order. Additionally, governments may auction seized Bitcoin to convert it into fiat currency.

Impact on Individuals:

Government seizures of Bitcoin can have significant consequences for individuals involved in illicit activities or inadvertently caught up in investigations. Seized funds may be used as evidence in criminal proceedings, and individuals may face legal consequences, including fines and imprisonment. Even innocent users who have their assets seized as part of an investigation may experience difficulties in recovering their funds and proving their innocence.

Legal and Regulatory Challenges:

Government seizures of Bitcoin raise legal and regulatory challenges, as the nature of cryptocurrencies poses unique complexities in asset recovery and forfeiture. The decentralized and pseudonymous nature of Bitcoin makes it challenging for governments to identify and trace funds. Additionally, cross-border transactions and jurisdictional issues further complicate the process. As a result, governments and regulatory bodies are working to establish clear frameworks and guidelines for the handling of seized cryptocurrencies.

Impact on Cryptocurrency Market Sentiment:

Government seizures of Bitcoin can impact market sentiment and investor confidence in cryptocurrencies. The association of Bitcoin with illicit activities may create a perception of increased risk and regulatory scrutiny, leading to short-term market volatility. However, it is worth noting that as the cryptocurrency ecosystem matures, efforts to enhance transparency, compliance, and anti-money laundering measures are being implemented, which can contribute to long-term market stability.

The Dual Nature of Bitcoin:

Government seizures of Bitcoin highlight the dual nature of the cryptocurrency. While Bitcoin is often associated with illicit activities due to its pseudonymous nature, it also offers significant benefits such as financial inclusivity, security, and privacy. Governments and regulatory bodies face the challenge of striking a balance between combating illegal activities and fostering innovation and financial freedom.

International Cooperation:

Given the global nature of cryptocurrencies, international cooperation is crucial in addressing the challenges associated with government seizures. Governments and law enforcement agencies around the world are working together to share information, develop effective investigative techniques, and establish legal frameworks for the seizure and recovery of cryptocurrencies. This collaboration is essential for combating cross-border criminal activities involving Bitcoin.

Asset Management and Auctions:

Following seizures, governments are faced with the task of managing and disposing of the seized Bitcoin. Some governments have held auctions, where the confiscated cryptocurrency is sold to the highest bidder, usually converting it into fiat currency. These auctions provide an opportunity for legitimate buyers to acquire Bitcoin at potentially favorable prices and generate revenue for the government.

Potential Implications for Privacy:

While government seizures of Bitcoin primarily target illicit activities, there is a concern that these actions may encroach upon individuals' financial privacy. As governments develop more sophisticated tools and techniques for tracing transactions on the blockchain, there is a risk of overreach and the potential for unwarranted surveillance. Striking a balance between law enforcement efforts and preserving individual privacy rights is a crucial aspect of navigating the evolving landscape of government seizures.

So, government seizures of Bitcoin are a reflection of the efforts to combat illicit activities and enforce existing laws and regulations. While these seizures can impact individuals involved in illegal activities, they also serve as a deterrent and contribute to the overall integrity and legitimacy of the cryptocurrency ecosystem. Striking a balance between regulatory oversight and individual privacy rights is a complex challenge that requires ongoing collaboration between governments, regulatory bodies, and industry participants.

Chapter 46: Satoshi's Influence on Privacy and Security

Satoshi Nakamoto's creation of Bitcoin not only revolutionized the financial world but also had a profound impact on the concepts of privacy and security. In this chapter, we explore Satoshi's influence on privacy and security within the context of Bitcoin and its underlying technology, the blockchain. We delve into the principles embedded in Bitcoin's design, the implications for individuals and society, and the ongoing developments in the realm of privacy and security.

Pseudonymity and Financial Privacy:

One of the key aspects of Bitcoin is its pseudonymous nature, allowing users to transact without revealing their true identities. Satoshi recognized the importance of financial privacy and designed Bitcoin to provide individuals with greater control over their personal information. By removing the need for intermediaries like banks, Bitcoin enables users to maintain a level of privacy and control over their financial transactions.

Decentralization and Security:

Satoshi's vision of a decentralized network, maintained by a distributed network of miners, contributes to the security of Bitcoin. Traditional financial systems rely on centralized authorities to validate and record transactions, making them vulnerable to single points of failure and potential security breaches. Bitcoin's decentralized nature reduces the risk of hacking and censorship, enhancing the security and integrity of transactions.

Trustless Transactions:

Bitcoin's underlying technology, the blockchain, enables trustless transactions. Transactions are recorded on a public ledger that is transparent and immutable, reducing the need for trust in centralized institutions. By relying on cryptographic protocols and consensus mechanisms, Bitcoin ensures that transactions are verified and recorded accurately without the need for a trusted third party.

Potential for Financial Inclusion:

Satoshi's vision of Bitcoin encompassed financial inclusion for individuals who are unbanked or underbanked. Bitcoin provides an alternative financial system that allows individuals to access financial services and participate in the global economy without the need for traditional banking infrastructure. This has the potential to empower individuals in underserved regions and increase financial autonomy.

Challenges to Privacy:

While Bitcoin offers pseudonymity, it is not inherently anonymous. The public nature of the blockchain means that transactions are visible to anyone. Over time, advancements in blockchain analysis techniques have made it possible to trace and link transactions to specific addresses and individuals. As a result, maintaining privacy on the Bitcoin network requires additional measures, such as using mixing services or privacy-enhancing technologies like CoinJoin.

Advances in Privacy-Enhancing Technologies:

The Bitcoin ecosystem has seen the development of various privacy-enhancing technologies and protocols. For example, advancements such as Confidential Transactions and Schnorr signatures aim to improve privacy by obfuscating transaction amounts and reducing the information exposed on the blockchain. Additionally, second-layer solutions like the Lightning Network enable off-chain transactions, enhancing privacy and scalability.

Regulatory Considerations:

While privacy is an essential aspect of Bitcoin, it has also raised concerns among regulators and law enforcement agencies. The pseudonymous nature of transactions has led to debates about the potential misuse of cryptocurrencies for illicit activities. Striking a balance between privacy and regulatory compliance has become a critical challenge for policymakers, as they seek to prevent illegal activities while not compromising the fundamental principles of privacy and individual autonomy.

Privacy-First Cryptocurrencies:

Satoshi's influence extends beyond Bitcoin itself, inspiring the development of privacy-focused cryptocurrencies. Projects like Monero, Zcash, and Grin implement advanced cryptographic techniques to provide strong privacy guarantees, including obfuscating transaction details and hiding user identities. These privacy-first cryptocurrencies aim to address some of the limitations of Bitcoin's pseudonymity and offer enhanced privacy for users.

User Responsibility and Education:

Privacy and security in the cryptocurrency space require active user participation and education. Individuals must take responsibility for securing their Bitcoin holdings, employing best practices such as using hardware wallets, practicing good password hygiene, and being cautious of phishing attempts. Understanding the potential risks and implementing appropriate security measures are essential for protecting one's privacy and funds.

Evolving Landscape:

The landscape of privacy and security within the cryptocurrency ecosystem is continually evolving. Developers, researchers, and industry participants are actively working on improving privacy features, enhancing security protocols, and exploring innovative solutions to address emerging challenges. Ongoing collaborations and advancements in technology will contribute to the continued evolution of privacy and security in the world of cryptocurrencies.

So, Satoshi Nakamoto's creation of Bitcoin brought forth a paradigm shift in the realm of privacy and security. Bitcoin's pseudonymous nature, decentralization, and trustless transactions have empowered individuals, offering financial privacy, security, and the potential for financial inclusion. While challenges remain and privacy-enhancing technologies continue to evolve, Satoshi's influence has set the stage for ongoing developments that prioritize individual autonomy and secure transactions.

Chapter 47: Bitcoin's Impact on Global Politics

Bitcoin, the decentralized digital currency created by Satoshi Nakamoto, has not only disrupted the financial landscape but also had a significant impact on global politics. In this chapter, we explore the ways in which Bitcoin has influenced global politics, from its potential as a tool for economic empowerment and financial sovereignty to its role in geopolitical dynamics and the challenges it poses for governments and regulatory bodies.

Economic Empowerment and Financial Sovereignty:

Bitcoin has the potential to empower individuals and communities by providing them with an alternative financial system that operates independently of traditional banking institutions. In regions with unstable economies or limited access to financial services, Bitcoin offers a means of conducting peer-to-peer transactions, storing value, and accessing global markets. This economic empowerment can lead to increased financial sovereignty and reduced dependence on centralized financial systems.

Cross-Border Transactions and Remittances:

Bitcoin's borderless nature enables seamless cross-border transactions, making it a viable alternative for remittances. Traditional remittance methods are often costly and time-consuming, requiring intermediaries and incurring high fees. Bitcoin allows individuals to transfer funds directly, quickly, and at a fraction of the cost, potentially reducing the reliance on traditional remittance services and empowering individuals to take control of their own financial transactions.

Geopolitical Implications:

Bitcoin's emergence has geopolitical implications, challenging the status quo of global financial systems. The decentralized nature of Bitcoin bypasses traditional intermediaries and, in turn, reduces the influence of central banks and governments over monetary policy. This can potentially disrupt established power dynamics, especially in regions where governments exert control over their citizens' financial transactions.

Financial Inclusion and Human Rights:

Bitcoin has the potential to promote financial inclusion and protect human rights in areas where citizens face economic instability or political repression. In countries with high inflation rates or authoritarian regimes, Bitcoin can serve as a means of preserving wealth, facilitating transactions, and protecting individuals from arbitrary restrictions on their financial freedom. This can empower individuals and communities to exercise their basic rights, such as freedom of expression and assembly, without fear of financial reprisal.

Regulatory Challenges:

The decentralized nature of Bitcoin poses challenges for governments and regulatory bodies seeking to oversee and control financial transactions. Bitcoin's pseudonymous nature makes it difficult to trace and regulate, raising concerns about its potential misuse for illegal activities, money laundering, and tax evasion. Governments around the world are grappling with the task of striking a balance between preserving the benefits of financial innovation and protecting against potential risks.

Government Adoption and Central Bank Digital Currencies (CBDCs):

As governments recognize the potential of blockchain technology, some are exploring the adoption of digital currencies, including central bank digital currencies (CBDCs). CBDCs are government-backed digital currencies that aim to combine the benefits of cryptocurrencies, such as efficiency and transparency, with the control and regulation of traditional fiat currencies. The emergence of CBDCs can be seen as a response to the growing popularity of cryptocurrencies like Bitcoin.

Economic Sanctions and Bitcoin:

Bitcoin has also gained attention in the context of economic sanctions imposed by countries. In regions where traditional banking systems are limited or where governments impose strict financial controls, Bitcoin can provide an avenue for individuals and businesses to circumvent economic sanctions and access global markets. This presents challenges for governments seeking to enforce sanctions and control the flow of funds.

Political Activism and Fundraising:

Bitcoin has been utilized as a tool for political activism and fundraising. The decentralized and censorship-resistant nature of Bitcoin allows individuals and organizations to receive donations and support political causes without the need for traditional financial intermediaries. This has enabled dissidents and activists to fund their campaigns, raise awareness, and mobilize support on a global scale, bypassing potential restrictions imposed by governments or financial institutions.

Cybersecurity and National Security Considerations:

Bitcoin's rise has also drawn attention to cybersecurity and national security considerations. The secure storage and transfer of Bitcoin require robust cybersecurity measures, as the loss or theft of digital assets can have significant implications for individuals and nations alike. Governments are increasingly recognizing the need to develop strategies to protect their citizens' digital assets and safeguard national interests in the face of potential cyber threats.

Evolving Landscape:

As Bitcoin and the cryptocurrency ecosystem continue to evolve, so will their impact on global politics. Ongoing technological advancements, regulatory developments, and geopolitical shifts will shape the future trajectory of Bitcoin's role in global politics. It is crucial for governments, policymakers, and stakeholders to engage in dialogue and develop frameworks that balance innovation, security, and the protection of individual rights.

So, Bitcoin's impact on global politics is multi-faceted, ranging from economic empowerment and financial sovereignty to geopolitical dynamics and regulatory challenges. Bitcoin has the potential to promote financial inclusion, protect human rights, and disrupt traditional financial systems. While governments navigate the complexities of regulating cryptocurrencies, the ongoing evolution of Bitcoin and its underlying technology will continue to shape the global political landscape.

Chapter 48: The Evolution of Bitcoin Wallets

Bitcoin wallets play a crucial role in facilitating the storage and management of Bitcoin. Over the years, Bitcoin wallets have evolved significantly, offering users more convenience, security, and flexibility. In this chapter, we explore the evolution of Bitcoin wallets, from the early days of software wallets to the emergence of hardware wallets and mobile wallets. We delve into the different types of wallets, their features, and the advancements that have made managing Bitcoin more accessible for users around the world.

The Early Days: Software Wallets

In the early days of Bitcoin, software wallets were the primary means of storing and managing Bitcoin. These wallets were desktop applications that users installed on their computers. The software wallets generated and stored the user's private keys, allowing them to access their Bitcoin. While software wallets provided users with control over their funds, they also introduced security risks, as computers could be vulnerable to malware or hacking attempts.

Web-Based Wallets: Accessibility and Convenience

As Bitcoin gained popularity, web-based wallets emerged, offering users the convenience of accessing their Bitcoin from any device with an internet connection. Web wallets, also known as online wallets, stored the user's private keys on remote servers. While web wallets offered greater accessibility, they also introduced an element of trust, as users had to rely on the security measures implemented by the wallet service provider.

Mobile Wallets: Bitcoin on the Go

The rise of smartphones led to the emergence of mobile wallets, allowing users to manage their Bitcoin on their mobile devices. Mobile wallets offered the convenience of on-the-go access, making it easier for users to send and receive Bitcoin using QR codes or near-field communication (NFC) technology. Mobile wallets typically stored the private keys on the user's device, enhancing security compared to web-based wallets.

Hardware Wallets: Enhanced Security

Hardware wallets revolutionized the security of Bitcoin storage. These devices are specifically designed to securely generate and store private keys offline. Hardware wallets provide an extra layer of protection by keeping the private keys isolated from potentially vulnerable devices like computers or smartphones. Transactions are signed within the hardware wallet itself, ensuring that the private keys never leave the device. This significantly reduces the risk of private key theft and malware attacks.

Paper Wallets: Cold Storage Option

Paper wallets offer an offline storage solution for Bitcoin. They involve generating a Bitcoin address and its corresponding private key, which are then printed on paper. Paper wallets are considered a form of cold storage, as they are not connected to the internet and are, therefore, less susceptible to hacking attempts. However, users must exercise caution when generating and handling paper wallets to ensure the private keys are not compromised.

Multisignature Wallets: Enhanced Security and Control

Multisignature wallets, also known as multisig wallets, add an additional layer of security by requiring multiple signatures to authorize a transaction. This involves setting up a wallet that requires the approval of multiple private keys held by different parties. Multisignature wallets provide enhanced protection against theft or unauthorized transactions, as an attacker would need access to multiple private keys to move the funds.

Custodial Wallets: Convenience with Trade-Offs

Custodial wallets are provided by third-party services that handle the storage and security of the user's Bitcoin. Users trust the service provider to manage their funds securely. While custodial wallets offer convenience, they also introduce counterparty risk, as users are reliant on the security measures and integrity of the service provider. Custodial wallets are often used by novice users or those who prefer convenience over complete control of their funds.

Advances in User Experience and Interface Design

Over time, wallet developers have focused on improving the user experience and interface design of Bitcoin wallets. Wallets now feature intuitive interfaces, simplified setup processes, and user-friendly functionalities. This has made it easier for individuals, regardless of their technical expertise, to manage their Bitcoin holdings effectively.

Privacy-Focused Wallets: Protecting User Identities

Privacy-focused wallets aim to enhance the anonymity and confidentiality of Bitcoin transactions. These wallets prioritize privacy by implementing features such as coin mixing, which obfuscates transaction trails, and the integration of privacy-enhancing technologies. Privacy-focused wallets cater to users who prioritize their anonymity and wish to mitigate the traceability of their transactions.

Ongoing Development and Innovation

The evolution of Bitcoin wallets is an ongoing process. Developers are continually exploring new features, security enhancements, and integration with emerging technologies. Concepts such as decentralized wallets, which allow users to retain complete control over their private keys without relying on third parties, are gaining traction. Innovations in user authentication, integration with hardware security modules, and biometric authentication are further improving the security and usability of Bitcoin wallets.

So, Bitcoin wallets have evolved significantly, offering users a range of options to store, manage, and transact with Bitcoin. From software wallets to hardware wallets, each type of wallet caters to different user preferences and requirements, balancing convenience, security, and control. The ongoing development and innovation in the field of Bitcoin wallets continue to provide users with improved user experiences and enhanced security measures.

Chapter 49: Satoshi's Absence and the Bitcoin Community

The mysterious disappearance of Satoshi Nakamoto, the enigmatic creator of Bitcoin, continues to captivate the imagination of the Bitcoin community and the wider cryptocurrency ecosystem. In this chapter, we delve into the details surrounding Satoshi's absence, explore the impact it has had on the Bitcoin community, and discuss the ongoing efforts to unravel the identity of Satoshi.

Satoshi's Departure:

After launching Bitcoin and leading its development in the early years, Satoshi Nakamoto gradually faded from the public eye. In December 2010, Satoshi made his final public communication and handed over the reins of Bitcoin's development to the community. Since then, Satoshi has remained silent and has not been involved in the project.

Speculations on Satoshi's Identity:

The question of Satoshi's true identity has sparked countless speculations and investigations. Numerous theories and claims have emerged, with individuals and groups purporting to be Satoshi Nakamoto. However, none of these claims have been definitively proven, leaving the true identity of Satoshi shrouded in mystery.

Satoshi's Reasons for Disappearing:

The reasons behind Satoshi's departure remain speculative. Some suggest that Satoshi withdrew from the public eye to protect their privacy, as the increasing attention on Bitcoin and its creator could have exposed them to legal, financial, or personal risks. Others believe that Satoshi's exit was a deliberate act to ensure that Bitcoin remains a decentralized and community-driven project without a central figurehead.

Impact on the Bitcoin Community:

Satoshi's absence has had a profound impact on the Bitcoin community. While Bitcoin has thrived and grown since Satoshi's departure, the absence of a clear leader has allowed the community to shape the direction of the project collectively. This decentralized governance has fostered a sense of ownership and responsibility among Bitcoin enthusiasts, as they work together to build and improve upon Satoshi's vision.

Satoshi's Influence on Bitcoin's Core Principles:

Despite Satoshi's absence, their influence on Bitcoin's core principles remains strong. Satoshi's original white paper, which outlined the concept and technical specifications of Bitcoin, continues to serve as the foundation of the cryptocurrency. The Bitcoin community, guided by these principles, has sought to maintain the integrity of the original vision while adapting and innovating to meet the evolving needs of the ecosystem.

Satoshi's Philosophy of Decentralization:

Satoshi's departure has reinforced the philosophy of decentralization within the Bitcoin community. By stepping away, Satoshi emphasized that Bitcoin should not be reliant on a single individual or central authority. Instead, Bitcoin's success and resilience depend on the collective efforts of its community members who continue to contribute to its development, security, and adoption.

The Search for Satoshi:

The quest to unveil the true identity of Satoshi Nakamoto continues to intrigue and fascinate the cryptocurrency community. Various individuals, journalists, and researchers have dedicated substantial time and resources to unmasking Satoshi's identity, scrutinizing everything from early Bitcoin transactions to linguistic analysis of Satoshi's writings. However, conclusive evidence has yet to surface, leaving the mystery unsolved.

Satoshi's Relevance Today:

While Satoshi's identity remains unknown, their impact on the world of cryptocurrencies and blockchain technology cannot be understated. Satoshi's creation of Bitcoin paved the way for a decentralized digital currency revolution, inspiring a multitude of projects and developments within the broader cryptocurrency ecosystem. Satoshi's vision of a peer-to-peer electronic cash system continues to shape the way we think about money, finance, and trust in the digital age.

Focus on the Technology, Not the Individual:

In the absence of Satoshi, the Bitcoin community has shifted its focus to the technology itself rather than fixating on the identity of its creator. The ongoing development, research, and innovation within the Bitcoin ecosystem are driven by the desire to enhance scalability, privacy, security, and usability. The community's resilience and dedication to the project demonstrate that Bitcoin is more than just the creation of a single individual—it is a collective endeavor.

Embracing the Mystery:

As time passes, the mystery surrounding Satoshi's identity has become an intrinsic part of Bitcoin's story and allure. Satoshi's absence has allowed the community to flourish independently, free from the constraints of a central authority. Rather than dwelling on the unknown, the Bitcoin community has embraced the mystery and focused on the mission of advancing the principles and possibilities that Bitcoin represents.

So, Satoshi Nakamoto's disappearance has had a profound impact on the Bitcoin community and the wider cryptocurrency ecosystem. While the quest to uncover Satoshi's true identity continues, the Bitcoin community has thrived, driven by the core principles and vision laid out in Satoshi's original white paper. Satoshi's absence has empowered the community to take ownership and work collectively towards the decentralized future that Bitcoin envisions.

Chapter 50: The Emergence of Bitcoin ATMs

Bitcoin ATMs have emerged as a convenient and accessible way for individuals to buy and sell Bitcoin using traditional fiat currencies. In this chapter, we explore the evolution of Bitcoin ATMs, their impact on the adoption of cryptocurrencies, and the benefits they offer to both new and seasoned Bitcoin users.

Introduction to Bitcoin ATMs:

Bitcoin ATMs, also known as BTMs or Bitcoin vending machines, are self-service kiosks that allow users to buy or sell Bitcoin using cash or other forms of payment. These machines provide a bridge between the digital world of cryptocurrencies and the physical world of traditional financial systems, making it easier for individuals to interact with Bitcoin.

Early Bitcoin Vending Machines:

The first Bitcoin ATMs appeared in 2013, marking a milestone in the development of cryptocurrency infrastructure. These early machines were primarily one-way ATMs, allowing users to purchase Bitcoin using cash. The user would input the recipient's Bitcoin address, insert cash, and receive a paper receipt containing the transaction details and a redeemable code.

Two-Way Bitcoin ATMs:

As the demand for Bitcoin increased, so did the functionality of Bitcoin ATMs. Two-way ATMs were introduced, allowing users to both buy and sell Bitcoin. Users could deposit Bitcoin into the machine and receive cash in exchange, providing an additional avenue for liquidity and enabling individuals to convert their Bitcoin holdings into fiat currencies when needed.

User Experience and Interface:

Bitcoin ATMs have evolved to offer user-friendly interfaces and streamlined processes. The user experience has improved significantly, with clear instructions and prompts guiding users through the transaction process. Many Bitcoin ATMs now offer multilingual support, ensuring accessibility for users from diverse backgrounds.

Compliance and Regulatory Measures:

Bitcoin ATMs operate within regulatory frameworks, complying with anti-money laundering (AML) and know-your-customer (KYC) regulations. This includes verifying the user's identity and adhering to transaction limits. Compliance measures have been put in place to prevent illicit activities, enhance security, and promote transparency within the cryptocurrency ecosystem.

Increased Accessibility:

Bitcoin ATMs have played a crucial role in increasing the accessibility of Bitcoin and other cryptocurrencies. These machines can be found in various locations, including shopping malls, convenience stores, and airports. By providing physical access points to buy and sell Bitcoin, Bitcoin ATMs have made it easier for individuals to participate in the cryptocurrency economy.

Onboarding New Users:

Bitcoin ATMs have become an important gateway for newcomers to enter the world of cryptocurrencies. For individuals without access to traditional banking services or those who prefer to transact with cash, Bitcoin ATMs offer a straightforward way to acquire Bitcoin. This accessibility helps to lower barriers to entry and foster wider adoption of cryptocurrencies.

Privacy Considerations:

Bitcoin ATMs provide users with varying levels of privacy. Some ATMs require extensive identity verification, while others may only ask for a phone number or email address. This range of privacy options allows users to choose an ATM that aligns with their preferences for privacy or regulatory compliance.

Global Adoption and Market Growth:

Bitcoin ATMs have seen significant global adoption, with machines now available in many countries around the world. The market for Bitcoin ATMs continues to grow, driven by increasing demand for cryptocurrencies and the desire for accessible and convenient on-ramps to the digital asset ecosystem.

Advancements and Innovation:

Bitcoin ATMs are not limited to cash transactions. Some machines offer additional features, such as the ability to purchase other cryptocurrencies or provide services beyond buying and selling, such as sending Bitcoin to external wallets or integrating with mobile apps. Innovations in the field are constantly emerging as the technology evolves.

Limitations and Challenges:

While Bitcoin ATMs have brought increased accessibility and convenience, they also face certain limitations and challenges. These include transaction fees that can be higher than traditional exchanges, limited availability in some regions, and occasional technical issues. However, as the industry continues to mature, these challenges are being addressed and overcome.

Future Outlook:

The future of Bitcoin ATMs looks promising, with continued growth expected in terms of both the number of machines and their capabilities. As the cryptocurrency ecosystem evolves, Bitcoin ATMs will likely incorporate new features, such as enhanced security measures, support for a broader range of cryptocurrencies, and integration with digital wallets and payment systems.

So, Bitcoin ATMs have emerged as an essential part of the cryptocurrency infrastructure, providing individuals with convenient and accessible options for buying and selling Bitcoin. These machines have increased the accessibility of cryptocurrencies, onboarded new users, and contributed to the wider adoption of digital assets. As the technology continues to advance and regulatory frameworks evolve, Bitcoin ATMs will play an important role in shaping the future of the cryptocurrency ecosystem.

Chapter 51: Bitcoin and the Gig Economy

Bitcoin, the decentralized digital currency, has made significant inroads into various sectors, including the gig economy. In this chapter, we explore the intersection of Bitcoin and the gig economy, examining the ways in which Bitcoin is transforming the way freelancers and gig workers send and receive payments, access financial services, and navigate the globalized marketplace.

The Rise of the Gig Economy:

The gig economy refers to a labor market characterized by short-term contracts and freelance work. This sector has witnessed tremendous growth in recent years, driven by technological advancements, changing work preferences, and the desire for flexible employment opportunities. Bitcoin has emerged as a transformative force within this landscape, offering unique advantages for gig workers.

Seamless Cross-Border Transactions:

One of the significant advantages of Bitcoin for gig workers is its ability to facilitate seamless cross-border transactions. Traditional payment methods often involve high fees and lengthy processing times, especially for international transfers. Bitcoin enables gig workers to send and receive payments directly, without the need for intermediaries or the limitations imposed by traditional banking systems.

Lower Transaction Fees:

Bitcoin transactions typically involve lower fees compared to traditional payment methods. For gig workers who rely on regular payments for their services, reduced transaction fees translate to higher earnings and improved financial stability. This is especially beneficial for those working in the gig economy, where small transactions and frequent payments are common.

Financial Inclusion for the Unbanked:

In many parts of the world, access to traditional banking services is limited, leaving a significant portion of the population unbanked or underbanked. Bitcoin provides an alternative financial system that is accessible to anyone with an internet connection and a digital wallet. This inclusivity empowers gig workers who may not have access to traditional financial services to participate in the global gig economy.

Decentralized and Censorship-Resistant Payments:

Bitcoin's decentralized nature ensures that gig workers have full control over their funds. With traditional payment methods, gig workers often face the risk of account freezes, payment reversals, or censorship imposed by centralized authorities. Bitcoin eliminates these risks, allowing gig workers to receive payments directly and without the fear of interference or censorship.

Micropayments and Instant Settlements:

Bitcoin's divisibility allows for micropayments, making it suitable for gig workers who receive small payments for their services. Additionally, Bitcoin transactions settle quickly, enabling gig workers to access their earnings immediately, without having to wait for payment processing or clearing periods.

International Gig Work and Remittances:

Bitcoin also offers advantages for gig workers engaged in international work and remittances. Many gig workers provide services to clients in different countries, which often involves navigating complex payment systems and incurring high fees. Bitcoin simplifies cross-border transactions, enabling gig workers to receive payments from clients worldwide and send remittances to their home countries more efficiently.

Access to Financial Services:

For gig workers in regions with limited access to financial services, Bitcoin provides a pathway to accessing a range of financial products. Through Bitcoin wallets and platforms, gig workers can access services such as lending, savings, and insurance, empowering them to manage and grow their financial resources.

Freelancing Platforms and Bitcoin Integration:

Some freelancing platforms and gig economy marketplaces have recognized the benefits of Bitcoin and integrated it into their payment systems. This integration allows gig workers to receive payments in Bitcoin directly on the platform, providing them with additional flexibility and choice in managing their earnings.

Volatility and Risk Considerations:

While Bitcoin offers unique advantages to gig workers, it is important to consider the inherent volatility and risk associated with the cryptocurrency. Bitcoin's price can fluctuate significantly, impacting the value of earnings held in Bitcoin. Gig workers may choose to convert their Bitcoin earnings to fiat currencies periodically to mitigate this risk or leverage services that offer instant conversion.

Regulatory Considerations:

The gig economy operates within various regulatory frameworks, and gig workers must consider the regulatory implications of using Bitcoin for their payments. Tax obligations, reporting requirements, and compliance with local laws may vary depending on the jurisdiction. Gig workers should consult with legal and tax professionals to ensure compliance with relevant regulations.

Continued Innovation and Adoption:

As the gig economy continues to evolve, so does the integration of Bitcoin and other cryptocurrencies. Innovations in payment systems, digital wallets, and decentralized platforms are reshaping the way gig workers access financial services, manage payments, and engage with clients. The ongoing development and adoption of Bitcoin within the gig economy hold the potential for further transformative changes.

So, Bitcoin has emerged as a powerful tool within the gig economy, empowering freelancers and gig workers with seamless cross-border transactions, lower fees, and financial inclusion. Bitcoin's decentralized and censorship-resistant nature aligns with the ethos of the gig economy, providing gig workers with greater control over their earnings and expanding access to financial services. As the gig economy continues to thrive and Bitcoin adoption grows, the intersection of these two forces will shape the future of work and financial empowerment for gig workers.

Chapter 52: Satoshi's Potential Wealth

The question of Satoshi Nakamoto's wealth is one that has intrigued the cryptocurrency community and beyond. As the creator of Bitcoin, Satoshi is believed to hold a substantial amount of the cryptocurrency. In this chapter, we explore the potential wealth of Satoshi Nakamoto, the factors influencing it, and the implications of such wealth within the broader context of the cryptocurrency ecosystem.

Satoshi's Bitcoin Holdings:

Satoshi Nakamoto is estimated to have mined a significant number of Bitcoins during the early days of the cryptocurrency. The exact number of Bitcoins held by Satoshi remains unknown, as the creator's identity and associated wallet addresses have not been definitively revealed. Some estimates suggest that Satoshi's Bitcoin holdings could be in the range of hundreds of thousands or even millions of Bitcoins.

Unspent Bitcoin and Dormant Wallets:

Satoshi's Bitcoin holdings are often referred to as "unspent" or "dormant" because they have not been moved or spent since the early days of Bitcoin. These untouched Bitcoins add to the intrigue surrounding Satoshi's potential wealth, as they represent a significant portion of the total supply of Bitcoins in circulation.

Market Value and Volatility:

The value of Satoshi's potential Bitcoin holdings is subject to the volatile nature of the cryptocurrency market. Bitcoin has experienced significant price fluctuations over the years, with periods of dramatic growth and periods of price decline. The market value of Satoshi's potential wealth would be heavily influenced by the prevailing Bitcoin price at any given time.

Implications for the Cryptocurrency Ecosystem:

Satoshi's potential wealth carries implications for the broader cryptocurrency ecosystem. The large holdings, if ever moved or liquidated, could impact the market, potentially causing significant price movements. This potential influence on the market has led to speculation and analysis of Satoshi's behavior and the potential impact on Bitcoin's stability and adoption.

Decentralization and Distribution:

Bitcoin's decentralization is a key principle and one of its defining characteristics. Satoshi's large potential wealth, if ever realized, raises questions about the distribution of wealth within the cryptocurrency ecosystem. The concentration of wealth in the hands of a single individual could be seen as contradictory to the decentralized ethos of Bitcoin. However, it is worth noting that Bitcoin's decentralized nature is not contingent upon the actions or holdings of any single individual, including Satoshi.

Satoshi's Possible Motivations:

The reasons behind Satoshi's decision to hold onto their Bitcoin holdings are a subject of speculation. Some believe that Satoshi's intention was to create a decentralized digital currency system that operates independently of any central authority or individual control. By refraining from spending or moving their Bitcoins, Satoshi may have sought to avoid exerting undue influence or disrupting the stability of the ecosystem.

Privacy and Anonymity:

Another factor that may have influenced Satoshi's decision to hold onto their Bitcoin holdings is the desire for privacy and anonymity. Satoshi's anonymity has been a subject of much discussion and speculation. By maintaining their anonymity and not accessing their Bitcoin holdings, Satoshi may have aimed to protect their privacy and avoid potential legal, financial, or personal risks associated with revealing their identity.

Speculation and Investigations:

The potential wealth of Satoshi Nakamoto has sparked intense speculation and investigative efforts to uncover the true identity of the Bitcoin creator. Researchers, journalists, and cryptocurrency enthusiasts have analyzed early Bitcoin transactions and conducted linguistic and technical analyses in an attempt to trace the origins and movements of Satoshi's Bitcoins. However, thus far, conclusive evidence regarding the true identity of Satoshi remains elusive.

The Enigma of Satoshi's Wealth:

The enigma surrounding Satoshi's potential wealth contributes to the mystique of Bitcoin and the ongoing fascination with its creator.

The unknown nature of Satoshi's intentions, actions, and possible access to significant wealth adds to the allure and curiosity surrounding Bitcoin and its origin story.

Focus on Bitcoin's Promise and Technology:

While the question of Satoshi's potential wealth piques interest, it is essential to remember that Bitcoin's significance goes beyond the actions or holdings of any single individual, including its creator. Bitcoin's promise lies in its underlying technology, its decentralized nature, and its potential to transform the way we think about money, finance, and trust in the digital age. Satoshi's potential wealth should be viewed in the context of the broader impact of Bitcoin on the world.

So, the potential wealth of Satoshi Nakamoto remains a captivating aspect of the Bitcoin narrative. Satoshi's Bitcoin holdings, if realized, could have a substantial impact on the cryptocurrency market. However, Bitcoin's value extends beyond the actions or holdings of its creator. The true significance of Bitcoin lies in its decentralized nature, its transformative technology, and the possibilities it offers for a more inclusive and equitable financial system.

Type This URL in Your Browser ⟶ *https://bit.ly/Guess_What_This*

Chapter 53: Bitcoin's Role in Humanitarian Aid

Bitcoin, the decentralized digital currency, has demonstrated its potential to make a positive impact in various sectors, including humanitarian aid. In this chapter, we explore the growing role of Bitcoin in humanitarian efforts, examining how it facilitates financial inclusion, enhances transparency, and empowers individuals and organizations to provide assistance in times of crisis.

Financial Inclusion and Accessibility:

Bitcoin has the potential to improve financial inclusion in areas where traditional banking infrastructure is limited or nonexistent. In humanitarian contexts, where access to financial services can be crucial, Bitcoin offers an alternative means of transacting and receiving funds. It enables individuals in underserved regions to access financial resources, regardless of their geographic location or socioeconomic status.

Rapid and Transparent Aid Distribution:

One of the key benefits of Bitcoin in humanitarian aid is its ability to facilitate rapid and transparent distribution of funds. Traditional aid systems often involve multiple intermediaries, bureaucratic processes, and lengthy delays, which can hinder the timely delivery of assistance. Bitcoin's decentralized nature and fast transaction confirmations allow aid organizations to disburse funds quickly and efficiently, ensuring that help reaches those in need more effectively.

Donor Accountability and Traceability:

Bitcoin's transparency and immutability make it easier to track and verify the flow of funds within the humanitarian aid sector. By utilizing Bitcoin, donors can have greater confidence that their contributions are reaching the intended recipients. The public nature of Bitcoin's blockchain allows for increased accountability and reduces the risk of funds being misused or diverted.

Lower Transaction Costs:

Bitcoin transactions typically involve lower fees compared to traditional banking systems, particularly for cross-border transfers. In humanitarian aid efforts, where every dollar counts, the reduced transaction costs associated with Bitcoin can significantly maximize the impact of donated funds. This cost efficiency allows more resources to be directed towards direct assistance rather than being absorbed by intermediaries.

Disaster Relief and Crisis Response:

Bitcoin has proven to be a valuable tool in disaster relief and crisis response efforts. In emergency situations, such as natural disasters or conflicts, traditional financial infrastructure can be disrupted or inaccessible. Bitcoin offers a decentralized and resilient means of transferring value, allowing aid organizations to quickly mobilize resources and provide immediate support to affected communities.

Empowering Individuals and Communities:

Bitcoin empowers individuals and communities by providing them with greater control over their financial resources. In humanitarian contexts, this empowerment can be particularly impactful, as it enables recipients to make decisions about how to allocate the aid they receive. Bitcoin's peer-to-peer nature allows for direct transactions, bypassing intermediaries and fostering self-reliance.

Remittances and Economic Stability:

Bitcoin can facilitate more efficient and cost-effective remittance transfers, benefiting individuals and families relying on financial support from abroad. In regions with high remittance dependency, such as developing countries, Bitcoin's lower transaction fees and faster settlement times can contribute to economic stability and poverty reduction.

Blockchain-based Aid Tracking:

Blockchain technology, which underlies Bitcoin, can be utilized to enhance aid tracking, and ensure transparency in the distribution process. By recording transactions and information on a public ledger, aid organizations can create a tamper-proof audit trail, providing stakeholders with visibility into the allocation and impact of funds. This transparency can help build trust and accountability in the humanitarian sector.

Overcoming Banking Restrictions and Sanctions:

Bitcoin offers a potential solution for individuals and communities in regions facing banking restrictions or economic sanctions. In such circumstances, traditional financial channels may be limited or entirely cut off, hindering the flow of humanitarian aid.

Bitcoin's decentralized nature allows individuals to bypass these restrictions and access funds, enabling aid to reach those who need it most.

Collaboration and Global Reach:

Bitcoin's global reach and ease of use facilitate collaboration and coordination among individuals, organizations, and donors from around the world. It transcends geographical and political boundaries, enabling humanitarian efforts to leverage a global network of support. This interconnectedness enhances the potential for scalable and sustainable humanitarian aid initiatives.

Challenges and Considerations:

While Bitcoin holds great potential in humanitarian aid, there are challenges and considerations to be addressed. Volatility in the cryptocurrency market can pose risks for both donors and recipients. Additionally, ensuring adequate digital literacy and accessibility to Bitcoin technology among aid beneficiaries is crucial. Collaboration between cryptocurrency experts, aid organizations, and local communities can help address these challenges effectively.

Ethical and Environmental Considerations:

Bitcoin mining and transaction processing consume significant amounts of energy, leading to concerns about the environmental impact. It is essential for the cryptocurrency community and humanitarian organizations to explore and adopt sustainable mining practices and energy-efficient solutions to mitigate any negative ecological consequences.

So, Bitcoin's unique attributes have the potential to revolutionize the way humanitarian aid is provided and received. Its ability to foster financial inclusion, enhance transparency, and facilitate rapid fund distribution empowers both aid organizations and individuals to make a tangible difference in times of crisis. By leveraging Bitcoin's capabilities and collaborating across sectors, we can create a more efficient, accountable, and impactful humanitarian aid ecosystem.

Chapter 54: The Bitcoin Mining Industry

The Bitcoin mining industry plays a crucial role in the functioning of the Bitcoin network. In this chapter, we delve into the world of Bitcoin mining, exploring its purpose, the process involved, the economic incentives for miners, and the challenges and environmental considerations associated with this industry.

The Purpose of Bitcoin Mining:

Bitcoin mining serves two primary purposes: validating and securing transactions and issuing new Bitcoins into circulation. Miners verify the legitimacy of transactions and add them to the blockchain, a decentralized public ledger that records all Bitcoin transactions. Through a process known as proof-of-work, miners compete to solve complex mathematical puzzles, ensuring the integrity of the network.

Mining Hardware and Software:

Bitcoin mining requires specialized hardware and software. Miners use powerful computer systems equipped with specialized mining hardware, such as application-specific integrated circuits (ASICs), to perform the computational tasks necessary for mining. Mining software interfaces with the hardware, coordinating the mining process and communicating with the Bitcoin network.

Mining Pools and Solo Mining:

Mining can be performed individually or in mining pools. In mining pools, multiple miners combine their computational power, increasing the chances of successfully mining a block and receiving the associated rewards. Pool members share the rewards proportionally to their contributed computational power. Solo mining involves an individual miner competing on their own, which can be more challenging but offers the potential for higher rewards.

Block Rewards and Transaction Fees:

Miners are rewarded for their efforts through block rewards and transaction fees. When a miner successfully mines a new block, they are awarded a certain number of Bitcoins. Initially, this reward was 50 Bitcoins per block, but it is halved approximately every four years through a process known as the "Bitcoin halving." In addition to block rewards, miners can also earn transaction fees paid by users for including their transactions in mined blocks.

Mining Difficulty and Network Security:

Bitcoin mining difficulty adjusts approximately every two weeks to maintain a consistent block creation rate. The difficulty level is based on the total computational power in the network, ensuring that blocks are mined at a relatively constant rate. This difficulty adjustment mechanism enhances the security of the Bitcoin network by making it computationally expensive to manipulate or compromise the blockchain.

Economic Incentives for Miners:

The economic incentives in Bitcoin mining provide a key motivation for miners to participate in the network. Block rewards and transaction fees serve as financial rewards for miners' computational work. As the value of Bitcoin increases, so does the potential profitability of mining. However, miners also face operational costs, such as electricity and cooling, which impact their profitability.

Energy Consumption and Environmental Impact:

Bitcoin mining is energy-intensive, and the energy consumption associated with the industry has raised concerns about its environmental impact. Mining operations require significant computational power, which translates into a high electricity demand. Miners are exploring various strategies, such as utilizing renewable energy sources and adopting energy-efficient technologies, to mitigate the environmental footprint of mining.

Geographic Distribution of Mining:

Bitcoin mining is a global industry, with miners distributed across various regions. Factors such as electricity costs, regulatory environments, and access to suitable infrastructure influence the geographic distribution of mining operations. Some regions, such as China, have historically been prominent in Bitcoin mining due to favorable conditions, but the landscape is continually evolving as mining operations emerge in other countries.

Mining Centralization and Decentralization:

Over time, concerns about mining centralization have emerged, as large mining operations with significant computational power can potentially dominate the network. However, Bitcoin's design promotes decentralization by allowing any individual or entity to participate in mining. The entrance of new miners, advancements in mining hardware accessibility, and the ongoing decentralization of mining pools contribute to a more distributed network.

Technological Advancements:

The Bitcoin mining industry is characterized by constant technological advancements. Miners continuously seek more efficient mining hardware, improved cooling solutions, and innovative mining techniques to enhance their competitiveness. Advancements in mining technology, such as the development of more energy-efficient ASICs, contribute to the sustainability and evolution of the industry.

Regulatory Considerations:

Regulatory frameworks for Bitcoin mining vary across jurisdictions. Some countries embrace and support the industry, recognizing its potential economic benefits, while others have imposed restrictions or implemented licensing requirements. Regulatory considerations include issues such as energy consumption, environmental impact, taxation, and financial regulations governing the exchange of mined Bitcoins for fiat currencies.

The Future of Bitcoin Mining:

The future of Bitcoin mining lies in finding a balance between profitability, energy efficiency, and environmental sustainability. Innovations in mining hardware, renewable energy adoption, and the exploration of alternative consensus mechanisms, such as proof-of-stake, could shape the future of mining. Additionally, the ongoing development and adoption of Bitcoin's Lightning Network may impact transaction fees and the economic incentives for miners.

So, the Bitcoin mining industry plays a vital role in maintaining the security and integrity of the Bitcoin network. Miners validate transactions, issue new Bitcoins, and contribute to the decentralization of the network. While mining has faced challenges related to energy consumption and environmental impact, ongoing technological advancements and a growing emphasis on sustainability are shaping the industry's future. As the Bitcoin ecosystem evolves, mining will continue to be a critical component, ensuring the resilience and security of the world's first decentralized digital currency.

Chapter 55: Satoshi's Technical Prowess

Satoshi Nakamoto, the enigmatic creator of Bitcoin, possessed remarkable technical prowess, which was essential in the development of the world's first decentralized digital currency. In this chapter, we delve into Satoshi's technical abilities, exploring their contributions to Bitcoin's design, their understanding of cryptography and computer science, and the lasting impact of their technical innovations.

An Innovative Visionary:

Satoshi Nakamoto's technical prowess was evident in their ability to envision a decentralized digital currency system that operates independently of central authorities. Satoshi's white paper, "Bitcoin: A Peer-to-Peer Electronic Cash System," presented a groundbreaking solution to the double-spending problem, laying the foundation for the development of Bitcoin.

Cryptographic Expertise:

Satoshi's technical knowledge extended to the field of cryptography, a fundamental component of Bitcoin's security. Satoshi's understanding of cryptographic principles, such as asymmetric encryption, hashing algorithms, and digital signatures, allowed them to design a secure and robust system for verifying transactions and protecting the integrity of the blockchain.

Peer-to-Peer Networking:

Satoshi's technical acumen encompassed the design and implementation of peer-to-peer networking protocols, a crucial aspect of Bitcoin's decentralized architecture. Satoshi's ability to leverage existing technologies, such as the BitTorrent protocol, and adapt them to suit Bitcoin's specific requirements showcases their ability to navigate complex technical challenges.

Data Structures and Blockchain Design:

Bitcoin's blockchain, a distributed ledger that records all transactions, is a testament to Satoshi's technical prowess in data structures and database design. Satoshi's innovative use of a linked list, known as the blockchain, to store and organize transactions, allowed for efficient and secure data management within the decentralized framework of Bitcoin.

Consensus Mechanisms:
Satoshi's technical expertise was instrumental in the development of Bitcoin's consensus mechanism, known as proof-of-work. This mechanism ensured agreement and prevented malicious actors from manipulating the blockchain. Satoshi's understanding of game theory and distributed systems was crucial in designing a consensus mechanism that incentivized miners to participate honestly and secure the network.

Practical Implementations:
Satoshi's technical prowess extended beyond theoretical concepts. The release of the Bitcoin software in 2009 demonstrated their ability to implement complex cryptographic and networking principles into a functional software application. Satoshi's programming skills and attention to detail allowed for the successful execution of their vision.

Continuous Improvement:
Satoshi's technical contributions to Bitcoin were not limited to its initial release. Their engagement with the Bitcoin community and subsequent updates to the software showcased their commitment to continuous improvement. Satoshi's technical guidance and involvement fostered the growth and maturation of the Bitcoin ecosystem.

Open-Source Development:
Satoshi's decision to release Bitcoin as open-source software exemplified their technical mindset and collaborative approach. By sharing the codebase with the world, Satoshi encouraged transparency, peer review, and community contributions, which ultimately led to the evolution of Bitcoin as a global, decentralized project.

Legacy in Cryptocurrency Development:
Satoshi's technical prowess has had a lasting impact on the field of cryptocurrency development. Bitcoin's innovative design and underlying technologies, which Satoshi pioneered, have influenced subsequent cryptocurrency projects and blockchain-based applications. The principles and technical foundations laid by Satoshi continue to shape the trajectory of the entire industry.

Inspiration for Future Innovators:
Satoshi's technical achievements continue to inspire individuals to explore and contribute to the field of decentralized technologies.

Satoshi's ability to combine various technical disciplines, such as cryptography, networking, and database management, in the creation of Bitcoin serves as a reminder of the transformative power of interdisciplinary thinking and innovative problem-solving.

Humility and Selflessness:

Beyond their technical prowess, Satoshi's humility and selflessness are qualities that have resonated with the Bitcoin community. Satoshi's decision to remain anonymous and their focus on the collaborative development of Bitcoin highlight their commitment to the greater good rather than personal recognition.

A Catalyst for Innovation:

Satoshi Nakamoto's technical brilliance ignited a global movement towards decentralized technologies. Their contributions set in motion a wave of innovation, sparking the development of numerous cryptocurrencies, blockchain applications, and advancements in computer science. Satoshi's technical prowess continues to inspire and drive progress in the pursuit of decentralized and trustless systems.

So, Satoshi Nakamoto's technical prowess played a pivotal role in the development and success of Bitcoin. Their deep understanding of cryptography, computer science, networking, and database management allowed them to envision and create a decentralized digital currency system that revolutionized the world of finance. Satoshi's technical legacy extends beyond Bitcoin, serving as an inspiration for future innovators and contributing to the ongoing evolution of decentralized technologies.

Chapter 56: Bitcoin's Impact on Financial Institutions

Bitcoin, as a decentralized digital currency, has disrupted traditional financial systems and institutions. In this chapter, we explore the profound impact that Bitcoin has had on financial institutions, including banks, payment processors, and regulatory bodies. We examine how Bitcoin challenges traditional models, fosters innovation, and transforms the relationship between individuals and financial intermediaries.

Disintermediation and Peer-to-Peer Transactions:

One of the key impacts of Bitcoin on financial institutions is the potential for disintermediation. Bitcoin enables direct peer-to-peer transactions without the need for intermediaries such as banks or payment processors. This decentralized nature of Bitcoin has the potential to reduce transaction costs, increase efficiency, and enhance financial inclusivity.

Competition and Innovation:

Bitcoin's emergence has compelled traditional financial institutions to adapt and innovate. The competition posed by cryptocurrencies has prompted banks and other financial intermediaries to explore blockchain technology and develop their own digital payment solutions. This drive for innovation benefits consumers by offering more choices and pushing the boundaries of traditional financial services.

Enhanced Financial Inclusion:

Bitcoin has the potential to address the issue of financial exclusion by providing financial services to individuals who are underserved or unbanked. Through the use of Bitcoin wallets, individuals can access basic financial services, such as sending and receiving money, without relying on traditional banking infrastructure. This empowers individuals with greater control over their finances and fosters financial inclusion on a global scale.

Cross-Border Payments and Remittances:

Bitcoin's borderless nature and lower transaction fees make it an attractive option for cross-border payments and remittances.

Traditional remittance services often impose high fees and lengthy processing times. Bitcoin offers a faster and more cost-effective alternative, allowing individuals to send and receive money across borders with greater ease and affordability.

Challenges and Adaptation:

Financial institutions have faced challenges in adapting to the rise of Bitcoin. The decentralized and pseudonymous nature of Bitcoin transactions poses regulatory and compliance concerns, as it can be used for illicit activities. However, financial institutions are gradually adapting by implementing robust know-your-customer (KYC) and anti-money laundering (AML) measures to ensure compliance with regulations while embracing the transformative potential of cryptocurrencies.

Digital Asset Custody and Security:

As cryptocurrencies gain mainstream acceptance, financial institutions are increasingly providing custody services for digital assets, including Bitcoin. These services offer secure storage and management solutions for individuals and institutional investors, bridging the gap between traditional finance and the digital asset ecosystem. The emergence of regulated custodial services contributes to increased trust and legitimacy within the Bitcoin space.

Central Bank Digital Currencies (CBDCs):

Bitcoin's impact on financial institutions has also prompted central banks to explore the concept of central bank digital currencies (CBDCs). CBDCs are digital representations of national currencies issued and regulated by central banks. The development of CBDCs is driven, in part, by the potential for increased efficiency, enhanced monetary policy, and improved financial inclusion in a rapidly digitizing world.

Regulatory Response:

Bitcoin's disruptive potential has prompted regulatory bodies around the world to grapple with the challenge of balancing innovation and consumer protection. Governments and regulatory agencies have implemented various approaches, ranging from embracing cryptocurrencies to implementing strict regulations. The regulatory landscape continues to evolve as regulators seek to strike a balance between fostering innovation and mitigating potential risks associated with cryptocurrencies.

Collaboration and Partnerships:

Financial institutions are increasingly recognizing the value of collaboration and partnerships with cryptocurrency-related entities. Banks, for instance, have formed alliances with cryptocurrency exchanges or invested in blockchain technology to leverage the benefits of digital currencies while maintaining compliance and regulatory standards. Such collaborations enable financial institutions to explore new business models and stay relevant in a rapidly changing landscape.

Digital Transformation:

Bitcoin's impact on financial institutions extends beyond specific use cases. It has spurred a broader digital transformation within the industry. Financial institutions are adopting digital technologies, including blockchain and distributed ledger technology, to streamline processes, enhance security, and improve customer experience. This digital transformation is driven, in part, by the realization that embracing technological innovation is essential for remaining competitive in the evolving financial landscape.

Trust and Transparency:

Bitcoin's decentralized nature challenges traditional notions of trust in financial transactions. The transparency of the blockchain allows for greater visibility and traceability of transactions, reducing the need for trust in intermediaries. Financial institutions are increasingly exploring ways to leverage blockchain technology to enhance transparency and build trust among their customers.

The Future of Financial Institutions:

The impact of Bitcoin on financial institutions is an ongoing and evolving phenomenon. As cryptocurrencies continue to gain mainstream adoption, financial institutions will need to adapt and innovate further. The integration of blockchain technology, the exploration of digital asset custody solutions, and the development of regulatory frameworks for cryptocurrencies will shape the future relationship between Bitcoin and financial institutions.

So, Bitcoin has disrupted traditional financial institutions by offering an alternative, decentralized, and inclusive financial system. Financial institutions have responded by embracing innovation, exploring blockchain technology, and reevaluating their role as intermediaries. The continued evolution of Bitcoin and the broader cryptocurrency ecosystem will shape the future of financial institutions, paving the way for a more accessible, efficient, and inclusive financial landscape.

Chapter 57: The Cryptocurrency Market Volatility

The cryptocurrency market, including Bitcoin, is known for its inherent volatility. In this chapter, we explore the factors contributing to cryptocurrency market volatility, its impact on investors and the broader financial landscape, and strategies to navigate this dynamic market environment.

Understanding Volatility:

Volatility refers to the degree of price fluctuation in a financial market. Cryptocurrency markets, including Bitcoin, exhibit higher levels of volatility compared to traditional asset classes. The decentralized and speculative nature of cryptocurrencies, combined with factors such as market sentiment, regulatory developments, and technological advancements, contribute to their price volatility.

Market Sentiment and Speculation:

Cryptocurrency markets are heavily influenced by market sentiment and speculative activity. Positive news, such as regulatory endorsements or institutional adoption, can drive prices upward, while negative news or market uncertainty can lead to price corrections. Speculative trading, fueled by the potential for significant returns, can amplify market volatility as investors react to short-term price movements.

Regulatory Developments:

Regulatory announcements and actions play a significant role in cryptocurrency market volatility. News of regulatory scrutiny or potential bans can trigger price declines, as it creates uncertainty and raises concerns about the future of cryptocurrencies. Conversely, regulatory clarity and favorable regulations can boost market confidence and contribute to price appreciation.

Technological Advancements and Innovation:

The dynamic nature of cryptocurrency technology and the emergence of new projects and innovations can impact market volatility. Technological advancements, such as the introduction of new consensus mechanisms or scalability solutions, can create price movements as investors assess the potential impact on the market and the adoption of cryptocurrencies.

Market Liquidity and Trading Volume:

Cryptocurrency market liquidity and trading volume also contribute to market volatility. Lower liquidity and lower trading volumes make it easier for large buy or sell orders to have a significant impact on prices. As the cryptocurrency market matures and attracts more participants, liquidity and trading volume are expected to increase, potentially leading to a more stable market environment.

Psychological Factors:

Psychological factors, such as fear, greed, and market sentiment, can exacerbate cryptocurrency market volatility. FOMO (Fear of Missing Out) can lead to irrational buying behavior, driving prices higher, while panic selling during market downturns can intensify price declines. Emotional decision-making based on short-term market movements can contribute to increased volatility.

Impact on Investors:

Cryptocurrency market volatility poses both opportunities and challenges for investors. On one hand, volatility provides the potential for significant returns, attracting risk-tolerant investors seeking to capitalize on price fluctuations. On the other hand, sudden and sharp price movements can result in substantial losses if investors are not adequately prepared or fail to employ risk management strategies.

Risk Management Strategies:

Managing risk in a volatile market is crucial for cryptocurrency investors. Diversification, spreading investments across multiple cryptocurrencies or asset classes, can help mitigate risk. Setting clear investment goals, establishing stop-loss orders, and adhering to a disciplined investment strategy can provide a structured approach to navigate market volatility. Additionally, staying informed about market developments and conducting thorough research before making investment decisions can reduce exposure to unnecessary risks.

Long-Term Perspective:

Taking a long-term perspective is essential when investing in cryptocurrencies. While short-term volatility can be unnerving, focusing on the long-term potential and fundamentals of cryptocurrencies can help investors ride out market fluctuations. Understanding the underlying technology, adoption trends, and the broader impact of cryptocurrencies on various industries can provide a foundation for informed investment decisions.

Market Maturity and Stability:

As the cryptocurrency market matures, it is expected to exhibit greater stability and reduced volatility. The entry of institutional investors, the development of robust regulatory frameworks, and increased market liquidity can contribute to a more stable market environment. However, it is important to recognize that cryptocurrency markets may continue to experience periods of volatility even as they evolve and mature.

Evolution of Risk Management Tools:

With increased market participation, risk management tools and strategies are evolving to address cryptocurrency market volatility. Options contracts, futures markets, and cryptocurrency derivatives provide investors with additional tools to hedge against price volatility and manage risk. These instruments can contribute to market stability by offering mechanisms for risk transfer and price discovery.

Educating and Informing Investors:

To navigate cryptocurrency market volatility successfully, education and information play a vital role. Investors should stay informed about market trends, regulatory developments, and technological advancements. Engaging with reputable sources, conducting thorough due diligence, and seeking advice from financial professionals can help investors make informed decisions and mitigate risks.

So, cryptocurrency market volatility is a defining characteristic of the industry. While it presents opportunities for substantial returns, it also poses challenges for investors. Understanding the factors contributing to market volatility, employing risk management strategies, and maintaining a long-term perspective can help investors navigate the dynamic cryptocurrency market. As the market continues to evolve and mature, increased market liquidity, regulatory clarity, and the development of risk management tools are expected to contribute to a more stable and resilient cryptocurrency ecosystem.

Type This URL in Your Browser → *https://bit.ly/Guess_What_This*

Chapter 58: Satoshi's Influence on Privacy Coins

Satoshi Nakamoto's creation of Bitcoin revolutionized the world of finance, and their influence extended beyond the development of the first decentralized cryptocurrency. In this chapter, we explore Satoshi's influence on privacy coins, a subset of cryptocurrencies designed to enhance user privacy and transactional anonymity. We delve into the principles behind privacy coins, their technological features, and the broader implications of Satoshi's vision on privacy in the digital age.

Privacy as a Fundamental Principle:

Privacy was a fundamental principle underlying Satoshi's vision for Bitcoin. While Bitcoin transactions are pseudonymous, meaning that transaction details are recorded on the public blockchain without directly revealing the identities of users, privacy coins build upon this foundation to provide enhanced privacy features. Satoshi's focus on privacy laid the groundwork for the development of privacy-centric cryptocurrencies.

Satoshi's Anonymity:

Satoshi Nakamoto's decision to remain anonymous throughout the creation and development of Bitcoin set a precedent for the importance of privacy in the cryptocurrency space. Satoshi's anonymity demonstrated the value of pseudonymity and the need for individuals to have control over their personal information. This influenced the development of privacy coins that aim to provide stronger privacy protections.

Enhancing Transactional Privacy:

Privacy coins aim to enhance transactional privacy by obfuscating the details of transactions, including sender and recipient identities, transaction amounts, and transaction history. This is achieved through various techniques, such as ring signatures, zero-knowledge proofs, and stealth addresses, which enable users to transact with a higher degree of privacy and anonymity.

Ring Signatures and Confidential Transactions:

Privacy coins often utilize ring signatures, a cryptographic technique that allows a user to sign a transaction on behalf of a group of participants without revealing their specific identity. This makes it difficult to link a specific user to a transaction. Confidential transactions, another privacy-enhancing feature, hide the transaction amounts, further enhancing privacy.

Stealth Addresses and Payment Codes:

Privacy coins employ stealth addresses and payment codes to obscure the recipient's identity. Stealth addresses generate unique addresses for each transaction, making it challenging to link a transaction to a specific recipient. Payment codes, such as the Hierarchical Deterministic (HD) protocol, enable users to generate multiple addresses from a single master key, enhancing privacy by preventing address reuse.

Fungibility and Privacy:

Privacy coins emphasize fungibility, the idea that each unit of a currency is interchangeable and indistinguishable from another. By providing strong privacy features, privacy coins aim to enhance fungibility by making all units of the cryptocurrency equal in value and eliminating the possibility of tainted coins that may be associated with illicit activities.

Balancing Privacy and Regulatory Compliance:

The development of privacy coins has raised concerns about their potential misuse in facilitating illicit activities, such as money laundering or illegal transactions. However, it is important to recognize that privacy and regulatory compliance are not mutually exclusive. Privacy coins can implement features that balance user privacy with the need for transparency and adherence to regulatory requirements.

Evolving Privacy Technologies:

The influence of Satoshi's vision on privacy coins is evident in the continuous evolution of privacy-enhancing technologies. Privacy coins are constantly exploring new cryptographic techniques, zero-knowledge proofs, and advanced privacy protocols to improve privacy while ensuring the security and scalability of their respective networks. This ongoing innovation reflects the commitment to preserving user privacy in the ever-evolving digital landscape.

Broader Implications of Privacy Coins:

Privacy coins have broader implications beyond transactional privacy. They contribute to the ongoing conversation surrounding digital privacy rights, surveillance concerns, and the individual's right to control their personal data. Privacy coins challenge the traditional notion of financial transparency and highlight the need for privacy protections in the digital age.

Regulatory Considerations:

The development and adoption of privacy coins have prompted regulatory scrutiny. Regulatory bodies around the world are grappling with the balance between privacy and the prevention of illicit activities. Striking a balance that allows for privacy while mitigating risks associated with money laundering, terrorist financing, and other illicit activities is an ongoing challenge for regulators.

User Adoption and Privacy Consciousness:

Satoshi's influence on privacy coins extends to the users and the broader cryptocurrency community. Privacy-conscious individuals and those concerned about data privacy are drawn to the principles and technology behind privacy coins. The growing adoption of privacy coins demonstrates the demand for enhanced privacy features in the cryptocurrency ecosystem.

Privacy as a Human Right:

The development of privacy coins aligns with the broader recognition of privacy as a fundamental human right. Satoshi's vision and the subsequent development of privacy coins empower individuals to exercise greater control over their financial transactions and personal data, enabling them to protect their privacy in an increasingly interconnected and digital world.

So, Satoshi Nakamoto's influence on privacy coins is evident in their emphasis on privacy, anonymity, and control over personal information. Privacy coins build upon Satoshi's vision for Bitcoin, providing enhanced privacy features that allow users to transact with increased anonymity. These privacy-centric cryptocurrencies reflect the ongoing conversation surrounding privacy rights, digital surveillance, and the need for user empowerment in the digital age.

Chapter 59: The Future of Bitcoin Governance

Bitcoin, as a decentralized digital currency, operates under a unique governance model that sets it apart from traditional centralized systems. In this chapter, we explore the future of Bitcoin governance, examining the challenges, opportunities, and potential paths forward for the governance of this groundbreaking cryptocurrency.

Decentralized Governance:

Bitcoin's governance is fundamentally decentralized, meaning that decision-making power is distributed among its participants rather than concentrated in a central authority. This decentralized governance model aligns with the ethos of Bitcoin, emphasizing trustlessness, transparency, and community involvement.

Consensus-Based Decision Making:

Bitcoin's governance relies on a consensus-based decision-making process. Participants, often referred to as miners and node operators, come to a consensus through the process of mining and validating transactions. Changes to the Bitcoin protocol, including upgrades and improvements, require broad consensus among the network participants.

Community Engagement:

The Bitcoin community plays a vital role in shaping the future of Bitcoin governance. Discussions, debates, and proposals take place on various online forums, social media platforms, and developer mailing lists. Community engagement allows for the exchange of ideas, the exploration of new technologies, and the resolution of governance-related challenges.

Technical Roadmap and Development:

Bitcoin's governance is closely tied to its technical roadmap and development process. Improvements to the Bitcoin protocol are proposed, reviewed, and implemented by a community of developers. The Bitcoin Improvement Proposal (BIP) process allows individuals to submit proposals for protocol changes, fostering an open and collaborative approach to governance.

Scaling and Capacity:

One of the key challenges facing Bitcoin governance is scaling and capacity. As the number of transactions on the Bitcoin network grows, there is a need for increased scalability to accommodate higher throughput. Finding consensus on scaling solutions, such as the implementation of the Lightning Network or block size adjustments, is an ongoing governance consideration.

Network Security and Consensus Rules:

Maintaining the security and integrity of the Bitcoin network is a critical aspect of governance. Consensus rules, which define the behavior and operation of the network, must be carefully considered, and agreed upon by the community. Changes to consensus rules require widespread consensus to ensure the network's security and prevent potential vulnerabilities.

Governance Models and Experiments:

The future of Bitcoin governance may see the exploration and experimentation of alternative governance models. Some proposals suggest the introduction of formal governance structures, such as on-chain voting or the use of decentralized autonomous organizations (DAOs), to facilitate decision-making processes. These models aim to provide more efficient and inclusive governance mechanisms.

Regulatory and Legal Considerations:

Bitcoin's governance is not limited to technical and community-driven aspects but also involves regulatory and legal considerations. Governments and regulatory bodies worldwide are developing frameworks and guidelines for cryptocurrencies, which may impact the governance of Bitcoin. Balancing regulatory compliance with the decentralized nature of Bitcoin is an ongoing challenge.

Institutional Involvement:

The increasing interest and involvement of institutional players in the Bitcoin ecosystem raise questions about the future of Bitcoin governance. Institutional investors, custodians, and financial institutions bring their own governance frameworks and requirements. Striking a balance between the interests of individual participants and the needs of institutional stakeholders is an important consideration.

Education and User Empowerment:

The future of Bitcoin governance lies in educating and empowering users to make informed decisions. Understanding the principles, technology, and governance processes of Bitcoin is crucial for individuals to actively participate in shaping the network's future. Education initiatives, user-friendly interfaces, and accessible resources contribute to a more empowered and engaged user base.

Interoperability and Collaboration:

Bitcoin's governance is not isolated from other blockchain projects and cryptocurrencies. Interoperability and collaboration between different blockchain networks may influence the future of Bitcoin governance. Sharing insights, learnings, and best practices across projects can lead to collective advancements in governance models and practices.

Evolving Governance Challenges:

As Bitcoin continues to grow and evolve, new governance challenges will emerge. These challenges may include addressing issues related to privacy, environmental sustainability, regulatory compliance, and global coordination. Adaptive governance frameworks that are responsive to emerging challenges will be essential for the sustainable development of Bitcoin.

Chapter 60: The Rise of Central Bank Digital Currencies

In recent years, there has been a growing interest in central bank digital currencies (CBDCs) as an evolution of traditional fiat currencies in a digital era. In this chapter, we delve into the rise of CBDCs, exploring their potential benefits, challenges, and implications for the financial landscape.

Defining Central Bank Digital Currencies:

CBDCs are digital representations of national currencies issued and regulated by central banks. Unlike cryptocurrencies such as Bitcoin, CBDCs are backed by the full faith and credit of the respective governments and aim to retain the stability and control associated with traditional fiat currencies while leveraging the advantages of digital technology.

Enhancing Payment Systems:

One of the primary motivations for the development of CBDCs is to enhance payment systems. CBDCs can potentially facilitate faster, more efficient, and more secure transactions, reducing the reliance on cash and legacy payment methods. By leveraging digital technology, CBDCs aim to improve financial inclusion, reduce costs, and provide a convenient means of payment for individuals and businesses.

Promoting Financial Inclusion:

CBDCs have the potential to promote financial inclusion by providing access to digital financial services for individuals who are unbanked or underbanked. The ease of use and accessibility of CBDCs can enable individuals to participate in the formal financial system, fostering economic empowerment and reducing the reliance on cash-based transactions.

Mitigating Risks and Enhancing Oversight:

CBDCs can also help central banks mitigate certain risks associated with cash-based transactions, such as money laundering, illicit activities, and tax evasion. The traceability and transparency offered by CBDCs enable central banks to enhance regulatory oversight and ensure compliance with existing anti-money laundering (AML) and know-your-customer (KYC) requirements.

Impact on Monetary Policy:

CBDCs have the potential to impact the implementation of monetary policy. The introduction of CBDCs can provide central banks with more direct control over the money supply, enabling more efficient transmission of monetary policy decisions and potentially reducing reliance on intermediaries. However, the design of CBDCs must carefully balance the need for monetary control with privacy and individual autonomy.

Privacy and Data Protection:

The issue of privacy is a significant consideration in the development of CBDCs. Central banks must strike a balance between the benefits of transactional transparency and individual privacy rights. Ensuring robust data protection measures and implementing privacy-enhancing technologies are critical to address concerns related to the collection and use of personal financial data.

Interoperability and Cross-Border Transactions:

CBDCs have the potential to facilitate cross-border transactions, simplifying and accelerating the settlement process. Interoperability between different CBDC systems could enable seamless and cost-effective transactions, reducing reliance on correspondent banking networks and potentially improving financial inclusion globally.

Collaboration and Standardization:

The rise of CBDCs necessitates collaboration and standardization efforts among central banks and international organizations. Standardizing technical protocols, regulatory frameworks, and interoperability mechanisms can facilitate the adoption and integration of CBDCs on a global scale, promoting efficiency, stability, and trust in the digital financial ecosystem.

Coexistence with Existing Financial Systems:

CBDCs are not intended to replace existing financial systems or cash entirely. Instead, they are designed to complement existing forms of money. The coexistence of CBDCs with cash, commercial bank money, and digital payment systems requires careful consideration of interoperability, regulatory frameworks, and public education.

Cybersecurity and Resilience:

The digital nature of CBDCs raises concerns about cybersecurity and resilience. Central banks must prioritize robust security measures to safeguard against cyber threats and ensure the integrity of CBDC systems. Collaboration with cybersecurity experts, rigorous testing, and ongoing monitoring are crucial to maintain public trust in the security and resilience of CBDCs.

Technological Considerations:

The development and implementation of CBDCs require careful consideration of technological aspects. Factors such as scalability, transaction speed, and energy efficiency should be addressed to ensure that CBDC systems can handle large transaction volumes and meet the evolving needs of digital economies.

Public Trust and User Adoption:

The success of CBDCs ultimately relies on public trust and user adoption. Central banks need to communicate the benefits, risks, and security measures associated with CBDCs effectively. Building public trust, fostering financial literacy, and addressing concerns about privacy and data protection are essential for widespread acceptance and adoption of CBDCs.

So, the rise of central bank digital currencies represents an important evolution in the financial landscape. CBDCs have the potential to enhance payment systems, promote financial inclusion, mitigate risks, and improve the efficiency of monetary policy implementation. However, careful considerations must be given to privacy, cybersecurity, interoperability, and regulatory frameworks to ensure the successful implementation and adoption of CBDCs. The ongoing collaboration among central banks, governments, and international organizations will shape the future of CBDCs and their role in the digital economy.

Chapter 61: Satoshi's Cultural Impact

Satoshi Nakamoto's creation of Bitcoin not only revolutionized the world of finance and technology but also had a profound cultural impact. In this chapter, we explore the cultural influence of Satoshi and Bitcoin, examining their impact on various aspects of society, including economics, technology, art, and popular culture.

Redefining Trust and Decentralization:

Satoshi's invention of Bitcoin challenged traditional notions of trust and centralization. The decentralized nature of Bitcoin, powered by blockchain technology, offered an alternative to centralized financial systems, where trust is placed in intermediaries. This redefinition of trust and the emphasis on decentralization inspired a broader cultural shift towards decentralized systems and the exploration of trustless interactions.

Empowering Individuals:

Bitcoin's creation empowered individuals to take control of their financial affairs and be their own bank. The concept of self-sovereignty resonated with those seeking autonomy and independence from traditional financial institutions. This empowerment of individuals to transact directly, without intermediaries, aligned with broader movements advocating for individual sovereignty and empowerment.

Financial Inclusion and Economic Empowerment:

Bitcoin and cryptocurrencies, influenced by Satoshi's vision, have the potential to promote financial inclusion and economic empowerment. By providing access to financial services for the unbanked and underbanked, cryptocurrencies offer opportunities for individuals in regions with limited access to traditional banking systems. This cultural impact extends to enabling microtransactions, supporting freelance economies, and fostering economic opportunities in underserved communities.

Technological Innovation and Open Source Culture:

Satoshi's release of the Bitcoin white paper and the subsequent development of the Bitcoin protocol embraced the principles of open source culture. This cultural impact extends beyond cryptocurrencies, as open source principles became widely adopted in various technological domains. The spirit of collaboration, transparency, and shared knowledge influenced the growth of open source software and the democratization of technology.

Art and Creativity:

Bitcoin's cultural impact can be seen in the world of art and creativity. Cryptocurrencies and blockchain technology have inspired artists to explore new ways of expression, such as creating crypto-inspired artworks, integrating blockchain-based digital ownership, and utilizing cryptocurrencies as a medium of exchange. The fusion of art and technology, fueled by the cultural impact of Bitcoin, has led to innovative art forms and new avenues for artistic expression.

Pop Culture References:

Bitcoin and Satoshi Nakamoto have become cultural touchstones referenced in various forms of popular culture. From movies and TV shows to music lyrics and mainstream media, Bitcoin has found its way into the collective consciousness. Its cultural impact is evident in the emergence of Bitcoin-themed merchandise, conferences, and even Bitcoin-themed restaurants and cafes.

Cryptocurrency Communities and Subcultures:

The cultural impact of Bitcoin is reflected in the formation of vibrant cryptocurrency communities and subcultures. Online forums, social media groups, and meetups bring together enthusiasts, developers, and investors, fostering a sense of camaraderie and shared interests. These communities contribute to the exchange of ideas, knowledge sharing, and the promotion of cryptocurrency adoption.

Challenges to Traditional Financial Systems:

Satoshi's creation of Bitcoin challenged the status quo of traditional financial systems. The cultural impact of this challenge can be seen in the growing interest and exploration of alternative financial systems, such as decentralized finance (DeFi) and the emergence of peer-to-peer lending platforms. Bitcoin's cultural impact fueled the exploration of new models for financial transactions, asset ownership, and wealth distribution.

Academic Discourse and Research:

Bitcoin's cultural impact is evident in the academic community, where research and discourse surrounding cryptocurrencies have flourished. Satoshi's white paper sparked a new field of study, with researchers exploring the economics, cryptography, computer science, and social implications of cryptocurrencies. Academic institutions now offer courses and programs dedicated to blockchain technology and cryptocurrencies, further validating their cultural significance.

Ethical and Philosophical Discussions:

Bitcoin's cultural impact extended to ethical and philosophical discussions surrounding money, economics, and technology. Satoshi's vision challenged conventional economic models and prompted discussions about the nature of money, the role of central banks, and the ethics of financial systems. These conversations influenced broader societal debates about the distribution of wealth, economic inequality, and the potential for democratizing finance.

Social Activism and Humanitarian Efforts:

Bitcoin's cultural impact is evident in its role in social activism and humanitarian efforts. Cryptocurrencies have been used to facilitate charitable donations, support humanitarian initiatives, and provide financial assistance to individuals in need. The transparency and traceability offered by blockchain technology have enabled greater accountability and trust in philanthropic endeavors.

Legacy and Inspiration:

Satoshi Nakamoto's cultural impact lies in their legacy as an influential figure in the development of cryptocurrencies and blockchain technology. Satoshi's vision and the cultural impact of Bitcoin continue to inspire innovators, technologists, and entrepreneurs to explore new possibilities, challenge established norms, and create disruptive solutions across various industries.

So, Satoshi Nakamoto's creation of Bitcoin has had a profound cultural impact that extends beyond the realms of finance and technology. Satoshi's vision redefined trust, empowered individuals, and inspired cultural shifts in areas such as economics, technology, art, and popular culture. The cultural impact of Bitcoin continues to shape our society, influencing how we perceive money, trust, and the potential for decentralized systems in a rapidly evolving digital world.

Chapter 62: Bitcoin's Relationship with Traditional Banking

Bitcoin's emergence as a decentralized digital currency has disrupted traditional financial systems and challenged the role of traditional banking. In this chapter, we explore the complex relationship between Bitcoin and traditional banking, examining the interactions, challenges, and potential collaborations between these two domains.

Initial Hostility and Skepticism:

When Bitcoin first entered the scene, traditional banks viewed it with skepticism and, in some cases, hostility. Bitcoin's decentralized nature and the potential for anonymity raised concerns about illicit activities and regulatory compliance. As a result, many banks initially hesitated to engage with Bitcoin and its associated businesses.

Regulatory Frameworks and Compliance:

The regulatory landscape surrounding Bitcoin has gradually evolved, leading to the establishment of regulatory frameworks and guidelines for cryptocurrencies. As regulatory clarity emerged, traditional banks began to develop compliance measures to address the risks associated with cryptocurrencies, such as anti-money laundering (AML) and know-your-customer (KYC) requirements.

Cryptocurrency Exchanges and Banking Relationships:

Cryptocurrency exchanges, platforms where users can buy, sell, and trade Bitcoin and other cryptocurrencies, have faced challenges in establishing banking relationships. Due to concerns about regulatory compliance and risk mitigation, many banks have been hesitant to provide banking services to cryptocurrency exchanges. This has resulted in difficulties for exchanges to secure traditional banking partnerships, leading to alternative banking solutions.

Collaborations and Partnerships:

Despite the initial hesitation, collaborations and partnerships between traditional banks and the cryptocurrency industry have emerged. Some banks have started exploring ways to integrate Bitcoin into their services, recognizing the potential benefits of cryptocurrencies and blockchain technology. Partnerships between banks and cryptocurrency custody providers have also emerged, allowing for the secure storage of cryptocurrencies on behalf of clients.

Custodial Services:

Traditional banks have recognized the need for secure custodial services for cryptocurrencies. They have started offering institutional-grade custody solutions, leveraging their expertise in security and risk management. These services cater to institutional investors and high-net-worth individuals seeking secure storage solutions for their Bitcoin holdings.

Institutional Interest and Investment:

The growing interest from institutional investors in Bitcoin has prompted traditional banks to explore investment opportunities in cryptocurrencies. Some banks have established divisions dedicated to digital asset management or have started offering Bitcoin-related investment products to their clients. This institutional interest has contributed to the mainstream acceptance and legitimization of Bitcoin.

Central Bank Digital Currencies (CBDCs):

The rise of central bank digital currencies (CBDCs) has further blurred the line between Bitcoin and traditional banking. CBDCs, issued and regulated by central banks, aim to digitize traditional fiat currencies. While CBDCs differ from Bitcoin in terms of decentralization and underlying technology, they represent a digital evolution within the traditional banking system.

Education and Research:

Traditional banks have started investing in education and research initiatives focused on cryptocurrencies and blockchain technology. They have recognized the importance of understanding these emerging technologies to better serve their clients and navigate the evolving financial landscape. Research partnerships with academic institutions and participation in industry conferences and events are becoming more common.

Challenges in Integration:

Integrating Bitcoin into the traditional banking system poses challenges. The scalability of Bitcoin's network, transaction speed, and regulatory considerations are among the key hurdles to overcome. Developing efficient and secure infrastructure for Bitcoin transactions within the existing banking infrastructure requires collaboration between banks, technology providers, and regulatory bodies.

Changing Customer Expectations:

The rise of Bitcoin has influenced customer expectations regarding financial services. As individuals become more familiar with the capabilities of cryptocurrencies, they may seek banking solutions that offer seamless integration with their Bitcoin holdings. Traditional banks are under pressure to adapt to changing customer expectations and offer innovative solutions that bridge the gap between traditional banking and Bitcoin.

Financial Innovation and Competition:

Bitcoin's disruptive potential has spurred financial innovation and competition within the banking industry. Traditional banks are exploring blockchain technology, smart contracts, and digital assets as they recognize the need to adapt to the changing financial landscape. This innovation benefits customers as they gain access to a wider range of financial products and services.

Coexistence and Synergy:

Ultimately, the relationship between Bitcoin and traditional banking is evolving towards coexistence and potential synergy. While Bitcoin challenges traditional banking models, the expertise and infrastructure offered by traditional banks can support the growth and integration of Bitcoin into mainstream financial systems. Collaborations, partnerships, and regulatory frameworks are shaping a path towards a harmonious relationship between Bitcoin and traditional banking.

So, the relationship between Bitcoin and traditional banking has evolved from initial skepticism to collaboration and exploration of potential synergies. Traditional banks have gradually recognized the significance of Bitcoin and cryptocurrencies, leading to the establishment of regulatory frameworks, custodial services, and investment products. While challenges remain in terms of integration and scalability, the changing financial landscape and customer expectations are driving traditional banks to embrace financial innovation and adapt to the disruptive influence of Bitcoin.

Chapter 63: Satoshi's Ideals and Libertarian Philosophy

Satoshi Nakamoto's creation of Bitcoin was not just a technological innovation but also reflected a set of ideals rooted in libertarian philosophy. In this chapter, we explore the ideals and libertarian principles that influenced Satoshi's vision for Bitcoin and its impact on the broader cryptocurrency ecosystem.

Decentralization and Individual Liberty:

At the core of Satoshi's ideals is the concept of decentralization, which aligns with libertarian principles of minimizing centralized control and empowering individuals. By designing Bitcoin as a decentralized currency, Satoshi aimed to create a system where individuals could have control over their financial transactions, free from the influence of intermediaries and government control.

Personal Privacy and Freedom:

Satoshi's vision for Bitcoin emphasized the importance of personal privacy and freedom. Bitcoin transactions, based on pseudonymous addresses, offered a level of privacy that traditional financial systems could not provide. This focus on privacy resonated with libertarian ideals of personal freedom and autonomy, where individuals have the right to conduct financial transactions without intrusive surveillance.

Trustlessness and Distrust of Institutions:

Bitcoin's design aimed to eliminate the need for trust in centralized institutions. Instead, trust was placed in the cryptographic protocols and the decentralized network of participants. This distrust of institutions reflects a core tenet of libertarian philosophy, which emphasizes the potential for corruption and abuse of power within centralized authorities.

Free Market Principles:

Bitcoin's economic model aligns with free market principles, another pillar of libertarian philosophy. The fixed supply of Bitcoin and its decentralized nature allow market forces to determine its value and facilitate free and voluntary exchange. Satoshi's vision embraced the idea of a currency that operates without the interference of central banks or government manipulation.

Opposition to Fiat Currency and Central Banking:

Bitcoin's creation challenged the monopoly of fiat currencies and the role of central banks. Satoshi's writings and the timing of Bitcoin's release, during the aftermath of the 2008 financial crisis, reflect a critique of the traditional financial system. Bitcoin represented an alternative to the inflationary nature of fiat currencies and the potential for abuse of monetary policy by central banks.

Self-Sovereign Individualism:

Satoshi's ideals encompassed the concept of self-sovereign individualism, wherein individuals have the right to control their own financial destiny. By enabling individuals to be their own bank, Bitcoin empowered users with a level of control and autonomy over their funds that was previously unavailable in traditional financial systems. This notion resonates with libertarian ideals of individual sovereignty and self-determination.

Technological Empowerment and Disruption:

Bitcoin's emergence represented a disruptive force in the financial landscape, driven by the power of technology. Satoshi's ideals embraced the transformative potential of technology to challenge established norms and empower individuals. This aligns with libertarian philosophy, which values technological innovation as a catalyst for individual freedom and societal progress.

Voluntary Participation and Consensus:

Bitcoin's governance model, based on voluntary participation and consensus, reflects libertarian ideals of voluntary associations and the rejection of coercive authority. The decentralized nature of Bitcoin allows individuals to choose whether to participate in the network and to reach consensus on changes through a decentralized decision-making process.

Limitations and Critiques:

While Bitcoin embodies several libertarian principles, it is important to recognize that the cryptocurrency ecosystem is diverse, and not all participants or projects share the same ideological perspective. Critics argue that Bitcoin's mining concentration, environmental impact, and potential for wealth inequality can undermine its alignment with libertarian ideals.

Impact on Libertarian Thought and Activism:

Bitcoin's emergence has had a significant impact on libertarian thought and activism. It has provided a tangible example of how decentralized systems can challenge centralized control and has spurred discussions on the role of cryptocurrencies in achieving libertarian ideals. Bitcoin's influence on libertarian circles has led to increased engagement, research, and advocacy surrounding the intersection of technology, economics, and individual freedom.

Evolution and Adaptation:

As the cryptocurrency ecosystem evolves, it is important to recognize that Satoshi's ideals and the broader libertarian philosophy may continue to shape the development of decentralized technologies. However, the practical implementation of these ideals requires ongoing discussion, experimentation, and adaptation to address challenges and ensure the responsible growth of the ecosystem.

Broader Societal Impact:

Satoshi's ideals and Bitcoin's embodiment of libertarian principles have had a broader impact beyond the cryptocurrency space. They have sparked discussions about the nature of money, trust, and the role of technology in society. The exploration of decentralized systems, blockchain applications, and the reimagining of traditional institutions has been influenced by the libertarian philosophy underlying Bitcoin's creation.

So, Satoshi Nakamoto's ideals and libertarian philosophy played a significant role in shaping the vision for Bitcoin and its impact on the cryptocurrency ecosystem. The emphasis on decentralization, individual liberty, free markets, and self-sovereign individualism reflects a broader movement challenging centralized authority and envisioning a more inclusive and technologically empowered society. While the practical implementation of these ideals continues to be debated, the cultural and ideological impact of Satoshi's ideals extends far beyond the realm of cryptocurrencies.

Chapter 64: The Decentralized Finance (DeFi) Movement

The rise of blockchain technology and cryptocurrencies has brought about a revolutionary movement known as decentralized finance, or DeFi. In this chapter, we explore the intricacies of the DeFi movement, its goals, its impact on traditional finance, and the potential it holds for reshaping the financial landscape.

Understanding Decentralized Finance (DeFi):

Decentralized finance refers to a paradigm shift in the financial industry, leveraging blockchain technology to create an open and permissionless ecosystem of financial applications. DeFi aims to provide inclusive, transparent, and autonomous financial services, eliminating the need for intermediaries and allowing users to maintain control over their funds and data.

Key Principles of DeFi:

The DeFi movement is guided by a set of key principles. These include decentralization, open access, transparency, composability, and interoperability. By adhering to these principles, DeFi projects strive to create a more equitable and efficient financial system that empowers individuals and fosters innovation.

Smart Contracts and Programmable Money:

At the heart of the DeFi movement are smart contracts, self-executing agreements stored on a blockchain. Smart contracts enable the automation of financial transactions and the creation of programmable money. They eliminate the need for intermediaries, reducing costs and increasing efficiency in financial operations.

Decentralized Exchanges (DEXs):

Decentralized exchanges are a key component of the DeFi ecosystem. Unlike traditional exchanges that rely on centralized intermediaries, DEXs operate on blockchain networks, allowing users to trade cryptocurrencies directly from their wallets. DEXs promote financial inclusion, enhance privacy, and reduce counterparty risks.

Lending and Borrowing Protocols:

DeFi lending and borrowing protocols enable individuals to lend or borrow cryptocurrencies without the need for traditional financial intermediaries. These protocols operate on blockchain networks and utilize smart contracts to facilitate peer-to-peer lending and borrowing, eliminating geographic restrictions, and offering competitive interest rates.

Stablecoins:

Stablecoins play a vital role in DeFi by providing a price-stable digital asset that can be used for transactions and as a store of value. Stablecoins are often pegged to a fiat currency or collateralized by other assets. They provide stability in a volatile cryptocurrency market and serve as a bridge between traditional finance and the DeFi ecosystem.

Decentralized Asset Management:

DeFi has revolutionized asset management by introducing decentralized asset management protocols. These protocols enable users to invest in a range of digital assets, participate in liquidity mining, and earn rewards without relying on traditional fund managers. The transparency and accessibility of DeFi asset management have attracted a growing number of users seeking greater control over their investments.

Governance and DAOs:

Decentralized Autonomous Organizations (DAOs) are entities governed by smart contracts and blockchain technology. In the DeFi ecosystem, DAOs play a crucial role in decision-making and governance of projects. Token holders participate in voting and propose changes, fostering a more democratic and community-driven approach to project management.

Challenges and Risks:

While DeFi holds immense potential, it also faces challenges and risks. Smart contract vulnerabilities, scalability limitations, regulatory uncertainties, and market volatility are some of the challenges that DeFi projects must address. Moreover, as DeFi attracts more attention and value, the risk of hacking and security breaches increases, necessitating robust security measures.

Potential Impact on Traditional Finance:

Type This URL in Your Browser ⤳ **https://bit.ly/Guess_What_This**

The DeFi movement has the potential to disrupt and transform traditional finance in several ways. By eliminating intermediaries, reducing costs, and increasing accessibility, DeFi can provide financial services to unbanked populations and create new opportunities for small businesses. It also enables individuals to control their financial data and participate in global markets with ease.

Regulatory Considerations:

As DeFi gains prominence, regulators worldwide are grappling with how to approach this novel financial ecosystem. Balancing the need to protect consumers, prevent illicit activities, and foster innovation poses a challenge. Regulatory frameworks are evolving to address the unique characteristics of DeFi while promoting responsible growth and protecting market participants.

Future Trends and Adoption:

The DeFi movement is still in its early stages, but it has gained significant traction. Innovation in DeFi continues to drive new protocols and financial instruments. Integration with traditional finance, institutional participation, and the development of user-friendly interfaces are key factors that can contribute to wider adoption of DeFi. So, the decentralized finance (DeFi) movement represents a paradigm shift in the financial industry, leveraging blockchain technology to create an open and inclusive financial ecosystem. By promoting decentralization, transparency, and user control, DeFi has the potential to revolutionize traditional finance, empowering individuals, and fostering financial innovation. While challenges and regulatory considerations persist, the future of DeFi holds immense promise in reshaping the financial landscape towards a more accessible, efficient, and inclusive global financial system.

Chapter 65: The Ethereum and Bitcoin Connection

Bitcoin and Ethereum are two prominent names in the world of cryptocurrencies, often seen as pioneers in the industry. In this chapter, we delve into the connection between Bitcoin and Ethereum, exploring their similarities, differences, and the significant impact they have had on the cryptocurrency ecosystem.

Shared Origins and Blockchain Technology:

Bitcoin and Ethereum share a common foundation in blockchain technology. Bitcoin, introduced in 2008 by the pseudonymous Satoshi Nakamoto, was the first decentralized cryptocurrency, utilizing blockchain as a distributed ledger to record and verify transactions. Ethereum, created by Vitalik Buterin and launched in 2015, expanded upon the concept by introducing smart contracts, enabling the execution of programmable agreements on the blockchain.

Cryptocurrency vs. Platform:

Bitcoin and Ethereum serve different purposes within the cryptocurrency ecosystem. Bitcoin primarily operates as a digital currency, enabling peer-to-peer transactions and store of value. In contrast, Ethereum functions as a platform for building decentralized applications (DApps) and executing smart contracts. While Bitcoin's primary focus is on financial transactions, Ethereum offers a broader range of functionalities beyond just currency.

Blockchain Consensus Mechanisms:

Bitcoin and Ethereum differ in their consensus mechanisms. Bitcoin utilizes the Proof of Work (PoW) consensus algorithm, where miners compete to solve complex mathematical puzzles to validate transactions and add blocks to the blockchain. Ethereum, on the other hand, is transitioning from PoW to Proof of Stake (PoS) with the Ethereum 2.0 upgrade, which relies on validators with a stake in the network to secure the blockchain.

Programmability and Smart Contracts:

One of the defining features of Ethereum is its ability to execute smart contracts. Smart contracts are self-executing agreements that automatically execute when predefined conditions are met. They enable developers to build decentralized applications, token economies, and complex financial instruments on the Ethereum platform. Bitcoin, while limited in programmability, has seen the development of Layer 2 solutions, such as the Lightning Network, to enhance its functionality.

Tokenization and Token Standards:

Ethereum introduced the concept of tokenization, which allows the creation of digital assets or tokens on the blockchain. Ethereum's token standards, notably ERC-20 and ERC-721, have facilitated the creation of fungible and non-fungible tokens (NFTs). Bitcoin, on the other hand, does not have native support for tokenization, although projects like Counterparty and Omni have enabled token creation on the Bitcoin blockchain.

Decentralized Finance (DeFi) and Smart Contract Platforms:

Ethereum has emerged as a dominant platform for decentralized finance (DeFi) applications. DeFi protocols built on Ethereum enable lending, borrowing, decentralized exchanges, and other financial services. Bitcoin, while primarily focused on being a digital currency, has seen the development of DeFi projects and protocols that aim to bring decentralized financial services to the Bitcoin ecosystem.

Cross-Chain Interoperability:

Both Bitcoin and Ethereum have explored cross-chain interoperability solutions. Various projects and protocols, such as Wrapped Bitcoin (WBTC) and the Ren Protocol, have allowed users to move Bitcoin onto the Ethereum network, enabling the use of Bitcoin in Ethereum-based applications. Additionally, projects like the Lightning Network and decentralized exchanges facilitate interoperability between Bitcoin and other cryptocurrencies.

Market Influence and Liquidity:

Bitcoin has established itself as the most widely recognized and valued cryptocurrency, often referred to as digital gold. Its market dominance and liquidity make it a popular choice for individuals and institutional investors seeking exposure to the cryptocurrency market. Ethereum, with its broader range of functionalities, has seen significant growth in terms of market capitalization and adoption, fueled by the proliferation of decentralized applications and the rise of the DeFi ecosystem.

Complementary Roles and Synergies:

Bitcoin and Ethereum play complementary roles in the cryptocurrency ecosystem. Bitcoin serves as a decentralized digital currency and a store of value, while Ethereum provides a platform for the development of decentralized applications, including DeFi, NFTs, and token economies. Their coexistence and collaboration contribute to the growth and maturity of the broader blockchain and cryptocurrency industry.

Shared Challenges and Future Development:

Bitcoin and Ethereum face common challenges such as scalability, energy consumption, and regulatory considerations. Both networks are actively exploring solutions to improve scalability, such as layer 2 scaling solutions, sharding (in the case of Ethereum), and network upgrades. Additionally, regulatory frameworks are evolving to address the unique characteristics of cryptocurrencies and blockchain technology, shaping their future development.

Interactions and Collaborations:

Bitcoin and Ethereum have witnessed interactions and collaborations over the years. Bitcoin's presence on the Ethereum network through tokenization and cross-chain solutions creates opportunities for integration and synergy between the two ecosystems. Additionally, developers and projects from both communities often collaborate, contributing to the cross-pollination of ideas and the advancement of the overall cryptocurrency space.

Influence on the Cryptocurrency Ecosystem:

Bitcoin and Ethereum, as the two most prominent cryptocurrencies, have had a profound impact on the broader cryptocurrency ecosystem. Their innovations, market influence, and development of new use cases have inspired countless projects and paved the way for the growth of decentralized finance, NFTs, and the exploration of blockchain technology beyond financial applications.

So, Bitcoin and Ethereum represent two significant pillars in the world of cryptocurrencies. While Bitcoin excels as a digital currency and store of value, Ethereum expands the possibilities of blockchain technology

Type This URL in Your Browser ⟶ *https://bit.ly/Guess_What_This*

through its platform for decentralized applications and smart contracts. Their shared origins in blockchain technology, along with their distinctive features and functionalities, have contributed to the growth and diversification of the cryptocurrency ecosystem. The interconnectedness between Bitcoin and Ethereum through cross-chain interoperability and collaborative efforts further strengthens their roles as catalysts for innovation and adoption. As the cryptocurrency landscape continues to evolve, the influence of Bitcoin and Ethereum will undoubtedly shape the future of blockchain technology and its impact on various industries.

Chapter 66: Satoshi's Stance on Smart Contracts

Satoshi Nakamoto, the enigmatic creator of Bitcoin, laid the foundation for blockchain technology and the concept of decentralized digital currency. While Satoshi's primary focus was on Bitcoin as a peer-to-peer electronic cash system, his stance on smart contracts, a fundamental feature of blockchain platforms like Ethereum, remains a topic of discussion and speculation. In this chapter, we delve into Satoshi's views on smart contracts, examining his writings and the implications they hold for the development of decentralized applications.

Early Discussions of Smart Contracts:

Although Satoshi Nakamoto did not explicitly coin the term "smart contract," he hinted at its potential in some of his writings. In a Bitcoin talk forum post from 2010, Satoshi mentioned the possibility of using Bitcoin's scripting language for more than just simple transactions, suggesting that it could be used for more advanced functions like escrow arrangements. This indicates an early recognition of the broader capabilities that smart contracts could offer.

Focus on Simplicity and Security:

Satoshi emphasized the importance of simplicity and security in the design of Bitcoin. His writings reflect a cautious approach to complexity, as he believed that simpler systems were easier to analyze and less prone to vulnerabilities. Smart contracts, with their programmable nature and potential for intricate logic, introduce complexities that Satoshi may have viewed as potentially compromising the security and stability of the system.

Limitations of Bitcoin's Scripting Language:

Bitcoin's scripting language, although Turing-complete to a certain extent, is intentionally limited in functionality. This limitation serves as a design choice to enhance security and mitigate potential risks. Satoshi's focus on creating a reliable and robust digital currency system might have led him to prioritize the development and refinement of Bitcoin's core features, rather than delving into the complexities and potential vulnerabilities associated with expansive smart contract capabilities.

Decentralization and Trustless Transactions:

Satoshi's vision for Bitcoin revolved around decentralization and trustless transactions. The primary goal was to eliminate the need for intermediaries and establish a peer-to-peer network where participants could engage in direct transactions with full control over their funds. Smart contracts, while enabling new possibilities, introduce a level of complexity and dependence on the correct execution of code that may compromise the trustless nature of transactions.

Practical Use Cases and Prioritization:

Satoshi was a pragmatic thinker, often focused on real-world use cases and practical applications of Bitcoin. His writings highlight his interest in building a digital currency that could be widely adopted and used for everyday transactions. While smart contracts offer exciting possibilities, Satoshi may have prioritized the development of a robust and scalable digital currency system that could meet the immediate needs of users.

Influence on Ethereum and Smart Contract Platforms:

Despite Satoshi's reservations or limited emphasis on smart contracts within the Bitcoin ecosystem, his pioneering work undoubtedly paved the way for the development of platforms like Ethereum. Ethereum expanded upon the concept of smart contracts, enabling the execution of programmable agreements and the development of decentralized applications. Satoshi's innovations in blockchain technology provided a foundation for the evolution of smart contracts within the broader cryptocurrency ecosystem.

Evolving Perspectives and Interpretations:

It is important to note that Satoshi's views on smart contracts are open to interpretation and may have evolved over time. Satoshi's disappearance from the public eye and lack of direct communication leave room for speculation and analysis of his intentions. As the blockchain industry progresses, new insights and perspectives may emerge, shedding further light on Satoshi's stance on smart contracts and their potential applications.

Lessons from Bitcoin's Development:

The cautious approach that Satoshi took toward smart contracts provides valuable lessons for the blockchain community. It highlights the importance of carefully considering the security implications and potential risks associated with complex code execution on a decentralized network. Bitcoin's focus on simplicity, security, and the core functionality of a digital currency system has set a strong foundation for the broader blockchain ecosystem.

Building on Satoshi's Vision:

While Satoshi's views on smart contracts might have been less pronounced or explored within the context of Bitcoin, his contributions to blockchain technology have laid the groundwork for the continued development of decentralized applications and smart contract platforms. Satoshi's vision for a peer-to-peer electronic cash system has inspired countless innovators and developers to explore new frontiers in programmable agreements, paving the way for advancements in decentralized finance, tokenization, and various other use cases.

The Evolution of Smart Contracts:

Since Satoshi's time, the concept of smart contracts has evolved significantly, with platforms like Ethereum demonstrating the transformative potential of programmable agreements. The ongoing research and development in the field of smart contracts continue to refine the security, scalability, and usability of decentralized application platforms, addressing some of the concerns that Satoshi might have had during the early stages of blockchain technology.

So, Satoshi Nakamoto's views on smart contracts remain somewhat elusive, with his primary focus on Bitcoin's core functionality as a decentralized digital currency system. While his writings hint at the potential for advanced functionalities, the emphasis on simplicity, security, and the practicality of everyday transactions influenced his approach. Nevertheless, the impact of Bitcoin and Satoshi's pioneering work on the development of smart contract platforms cannot be understated, as they have laid the foundation for the evolution of decentralized applications and programmable agreements within the broader cryptocurrency ecosystem.

Chapter 67: Bitcoin and the Internet of Things (IoT)

The Internet of Things (IoT) is a rapidly growing network of interconnected devices that communicate and exchange data without human intervention. As the world becomes increasingly interconnected, the intersection of Bitcoin and the IoT presents unique opportunities and challenges. In this chapter, we explore the potential impact of Bitcoin on the IoT ecosystem and how these technologies can complement each other.

The IoT Revolution:

The IoT revolution is transforming various industries, from healthcare and transportation to manufacturing and agriculture. Billions of devices, ranging from sensors and wearables to home appliances and industrial machinery, are being connected to the internet, enabling them to collect and share data in real-time. This vast network of interconnected devices has the potential to revolutionize the way we live and work.

The Role of Bitcoin in the IoT:

Bitcoin, as a decentralized digital currency, can play a significant role in the IoT ecosystem. Its properties, such as decentralization, security, and immutability, can address critical challenges faced by IoT devices, including data integrity, trust, and secure transactions. Bitcoin's underlying technology, the blockchain, provides a transparent and tamper-resistant ledger that can be utilized for various IoT applications.

Secure and Efficient Microtransactions:

The IoT involves a multitude of microtransactions, where devices need to exchange value in a secure and efficient manner. Bitcoin's design enables micropayments without the need for intermediaries, allowing devices to transact directly with each other. This can facilitate machine-to-machine (M2M) payments, incentivize data sharing, and enable new business models within the IoT ecosystem.

Data Integrity and Provenance:

Data integrity and provenance are critical concerns in the IoT space. Bitcoin's blockchain can serve as a tamper-resistant and decentralized database for storing and verifying the authenticity of IoT-generated data. By anchoring IoT data onto the blockchain, a transparent and auditable trail can be established, ensuring the integrity and traceability of the information.

Smart Contracts and Autonomous Devices:

Smart contracts, programmable agreements executed on the blockchain, can enhance the functionality of IoT devices. With the integration of smart contracts, IoT devices can autonomously execute predefined actions based on predefined conditions. For example, a smart contract could enable a device to automatically order and pay for maintenance services when certain performance thresholds are met.

Decentralized Identity and Access Management:

In the IoT ecosystem, managing the identities of devices and ensuring secure access is paramount. Bitcoin's decentralized nature can offer solutions for identity and access management challenges. Through the use of cryptographic keys and digital signatures, devices can establish their identity on the blockchain, enabling secure and decentralized access control.

Energy Efficiency and Proof of Stake:

Bitcoin's proof-of-work (PoW) consensus mechanism has faced criticism for its energy consumption. However, emerging solutions, such as the development of the Ethereum 2.0 upgrade and the shift to a proof-of-stake (PoS) consensus mechanism, aim to significantly reduce energy consumption. This transition to PoS can make Bitcoin and other blockchain-based solutions more environmentally friendly and suitable for IoT devices with limited power resources.

Challenges and Considerations:

While the integration of Bitcoin and the IoT holds immense potential, several challenges and considerations need to be addressed. Scalability, interoperability, data privacy, and network security are critical aspects that require attention. Additionally, the resource constraints of IoT devices, such as limited computational power and storage capacity, must be taken into account when designing Bitcoin-based solutions for the IoT.

Use Cases and Applications:

Bitcoin and the IoT can revolutionize various industries by enabling new use cases and applications. For example, in supply chain management, Bitcoin's transparency and immutability can help ensure the traceability and authenticity of goods throughout the entire supply chain. In energy grids, IoT devices can use Bitcoin's micropayment capabilities to autonomously buy and sell energy in a peer-to-peer manner.

Collaborations and Synergies:

The convergence of Bitcoin and the IoT is a collaborative effort involving multiple stakeholders, including blockchain developers, IoT device manufacturers, and industry leaders. Collaborations and partnerships are essential to explore and capitalize on the synergies between these technologies, fostering innovation, and driving adoption in real-world scenarios.

Regulatory Considerations:

As Bitcoin and the IoT continue to evolve, regulatory frameworks need to adapt to address the unique challenges and opportunities presented by their integration. Regulatory clarity regarding data privacy, security, and digital asset transactions is crucial to foster the growth of the IoT ecosystem powered by Bitcoin and blockchain technology.

The Future of Bitcoin and the IoT:

The future of Bitcoin and the IoT holds immense promise. As both technologies mature, we can expect to witness increased integration, innovation, and adoption. Advancements in blockchain scalability, interoperability solutions, and IoT device capabilities will further enable the seamless integration of Bitcoin into the IoT ecosystem, unlocking new possibilities and transforming industries.

So, the integration of Bitcoin and the Internet of Things (IoT) has the potential to revolutionize the way devices interact, transact, and share data in a secure and decentralized manner. Bitcoin's properties, such as decentralization, security, and programmability, address critical challenges faced by IoT devices, while the IoT ecosystem presents unique opportunities for Bitcoin to enable micropayments, enhance data integrity, and facilitate autonomous interactions. Collaboration, regulatory considerations, and technological advancements will shape the future of this exciting intersection, driving innovation and unlocking the full potential of the IoT powered by Bitcoin and blockchain technology.

Chapter 68: The Global Reach of Bitcoin

Bitcoin, the pioneering cryptocurrency introduced by Satoshi Nakamoto, has made a remarkable impact on a global scale. With its decentralized nature and borderless transactions, Bitcoin has transcended geographical boundaries, attracting users, investors, and enthusiasts from all corners of the world. In this chapter, we explore the global reach of Bitcoin, examining its adoption, influence, and challenges in different regions.

Global Adoption:

Bitcoin has achieved widespread adoption in various countries around the world. While its popularity varies from region to region, Bitcoin's decentralized nature and potential for financial inclusion have attracted users seeking an alternative to traditional banking systems. Countries such as the United States, Japan, South Korea, Germany, and Nigeria have emerged as significant hubs for Bitcoin adoption, with a growing number of individuals, businesses, and even governments recognizing its potential.

Financial Inclusion:

One of the key aspects of Bitcoin's global reach is its potential to promote financial inclusion. In many developing countries where traditional banking services are limited, Bitcoin offers a secure and accessible means of storing and transferring value. For the unbanked and underbanked populations, Bitcoin provides an opportunity to participate in the global economy, access financial services, and potentially improve their economic circumstances.

Remittances and Cross-Border Transactions:

Bitcoin's global reach is particularly evident in the realm of remittances and cross-border transactions. Migrant workers and individuals living abroad often face high fees and lengthy processing times when sending money back home. Bitcoin's borderless nature and lower transaction costs provide a more efficient and cost-effective alternative for cross-border transfers, potentially saving billions of dollars in remittance fees each year.

Economic and Political Instability:

Bitcoin's global reach is also influenced by economic and political factors. In countries experiencing economic instability, high inflation rates, or capital controls, Bitcoin can serve as a hedge against inflation and a store of value. Venezuelans, for example, have turned to Bitcoin as a means of preserving their wealth amid hyperinflations. Similarly, citizens in countries with restrictive financial regulations have found refuge in Bitcoin's decentralized and censorship-resistant nature.

Government Attitudes and Regulatory Challenges:

Bitcoin's global reach is not without its challenges. Governments around the world have varied attitudes towards cryptocurrencies, leading to a diverse regulatory landscape. Some countries have embraced Bitcoin and established clear regulatory frameworks to foster its growth, while others have taken a more cautious or restrictive approach. Regulatory challenges and uncertainties can impact Bitcoin's adoption and influence in different regions.

Cultural and Technological Factors:

Cultural and technological factors also influence Bitcoin's global reach. In regions with a high level of technological adoption and digital literacy, Bitcoin has gained traction more rapidly. Additionally, cultural attitudes towards financial systems and innovation play a role in Bitcoin's acceptance and adoption. For example, countries with a strong history of mistrust in centralized institutions may be more open to exploring decentralized alternatives like Bitcoin.

Bitcoin Mining and Energy Consumption:

Bitcoin's global reach is interconnected with its mining network, which spans across different countries. Mining operations are typically concentrated in regions with cheap electricity and favorable regulatory environments. China, for instance, has been a dominant player in Bitcoin mining due to its abundant coal-powered energy and low electricity costs. However, recent efforts to promote greener mining practices have resulted in the decentralization of mining operations to more environmentally friendly regions.

Cultural Exchanges and Local Communities:

Bitcoin's global reach has fostered cultural exchanges and the formation of local Bitcoin communities. Bitcoin enthusiasts and experts come together through meetups, conferences, and online forums to share knowledge, discuss developments, and advocate for the adoption of Bitcoin. These communities play a vital role in spreading awareness, educating newcomers, and contributing to the overall growth and resilience of the Bitcoin network.

Geopolitical Implications:

Bitcoin's global reach also has geopolitical implications. As a decentralized and non-sovereign form of currency, Bitcoin challenges traditional notions of monetary control and influences global discussions on financial sovereignty. It has prompted governments to consider their own digital currency initiatives and explore the potential benefits of blockchain technology for their economies.

Future Perspectives:

The global reach of Bitcoin is ever-evolving. As technological advancements, regulatory frameworks, and financial infrastructure continue to develop, Bitcoin's adoption and influence are likely to expand further. The integration of Bitcoin into existing financial systems, the emergence of institutional investment, and the continued innovation in areas like decentralized finance (DeFi) will shape Bitcoin's future and its impact on the global economy.

So, Bitcoin's global reach is a testament to its disruptive potential and the desire for financial sovereignty in an increasingly interconnected world. From facilitating cross-border transactions and promoting financial inclusion to challenging traditional monetary systems, Bitcoin has transcended geographical boundaries, offering individuals and communities a decentralized and inclusive alternative. While regional differences, regulatory challenges, and cultural nuances exist, the global reach of Bitcoin continues to expand, leaving an indelible mark on the financial landscape of countries worldwide.

Chapter 69: Satoshi's Influence on Cryptocurrency Regulations

The emergence of Bitcoin, created by the pseudonymous figure known as Satoshi Nakamoto, has not only revolutionized the world of finance but has also posed significant challenges for governments and regulatory bodies worldwide. In this chapter, we explore Satoshi's influence on cryptocurrency regulations, examining the impact of Bitcoin's decentralized nature and the underlying blockchain technology on the development of regulatory frameworks.

Decentralization and Regulatory Dilemma:

Bitcoin's decentralized nature presents a unique challenge for regulators. Traditional financial systems rely on centralized authorities to oversee and control monetary transactions. Satoshi's creation of a decentralized digital currency bypasses the need for intermediaries, disrupting established regulatory frameworks. This has forced governments to grapple with new approaches to regulating cryptocurrencies while balancing the need for consumer protection and financial stability.

Global Regulatory Landscape:

The global regulatory landscape for cryptocurrencies is diverse and continuously evolving. In the early days of Bitcoin, regulatory responses varied greatly, with some countries banning or severely restricting cryptocurrencies, while others embraced the technology and established regulatory frameworks. Over time, governments have recognized the importance of striking a balance between fostering innovation and protecting investors, leading to more nuanced regulatory approaches.

Regulatory Challenges and Considerations:

Satoshi's creation of Bitcoin has highlighted several regulatory challenges. These challenges include identifying the appropriate regulatory authority, combating money laundering and illicit activities, addressing consumer protection concerns, and ensuring the stability and integrity of financial systems. Regulators have had to adapt to the unique characteristics of cryptocurrencies, such as their borderless nature, pseudonymous transactions, and decentralized governance.

Early Regulatory Responses:

Initially, regulatory responses to Bitcoin were often reactive and focused on addressing immediate concerns. Money laundering and illicit activities were among the primary concerns, prompting regulators to implement Know Your Customer (KYC) and Anti-Money Laundering (AML) requirements. As the understanding of cryptocurrencies grew, regulators began exploring more comprehensive approaches to regulate this new asset class.

The Emergence of Regulatory Frameworks:

As the popularity of cryptocurrencies increased, governments started developing regulatory frameworks to provide clarity and guidance for businesses and individuals operating within the cryptocurrency space. These frameworks typically address issues such as licensing requirements, taxation, investor protection, and security standards. Countries like the United States, Japan, Switzerland, and Singapore have been at the forefront of creating comprehensive regulatory frameworks.

Regulatory Experimentation and Sandboxes:

Innovation-friendly jurisdictions have embraced regulatory experimentation and established regulatory sandboxes. These sandboxes allow startups and businesses to test new products and services within a controlled environment, providing regulators with valuable insights into the challenges and opportunities presented by cryptocurrencies. This approach encourages collaboration between regulators and industry participants, fostering a better understanding of the technology and its implications.

Global Coordination and Standardization Efforts:

Recognizing the global nature of cryptocurrencies, regulatory bodies have initiated efforts to coordinate and standardize regulations across jurisdictions. Organizations such as the Financial Action Task Force (FATF) and the International Organization of Securities Commissions (IOSCO) have worked towards establishing consistent regulatory standards and enhancing cross-border cooperation to address the challenges posed by cryptocurrencies.

Impact on Financial Innovation:

Satoshi's creation of Bitcoin and the subsequent regulatory responses have had a significant impact on financial innovation. While regulatory frameworks aim to provide clarity and mitigate risks, they can also stifle innovation if too restrictive. Striking the right balance between regulation and innovation is essential to foster the growth of cryptocurrency-related technologies, such as decentralized finance (DeFi), non-fungible tokens (NFTs), and blockchain-based applications.

Evolving Regulatory Approaches:

Regulatory approaches to cryptocurrencies continue to evolve as regulators gain a better understanding of the technology and its implications. Some jurisdictions have adopted a progressive approach, promoting innovation and providing regulatory clarity, while others remain cautious and prefer a wait-and-see approach. The dynamic nature of cryptocurrencies necessitates continuous evaluation and adaptation of regulatory frameworks.

Satoshi's Influence on Regulatory Discourse:

Satoshi Nakamoto's vision for a decentralized digital currency challenges the very foundation of centralized financial systems. The creation of Bitcoin has sparked a global dialogue on the role of governments, central banks, and regulators in a decentralized world. Satoshi's influence on regulatory discourse extends beyond the development of specific regulations and has stimulated discussions on the future of money, financial sovereignty, and the potential benefits of blockchain technology.

Striking a Balance:

Regulating cryptocurrencies requires striking a balance between protecting consumers and investors, mitigating risks, and fostering innovation. Regulators must adapt to the evolving landscape, collaborating with industry participants, and leveraging technological advancements to develop effective regulatory frameworks. A balanced approach that encourages innovation, safeguards against illicit activities, and provides regulatory clarity is crucial for the long-term sustainability of the cryptocurrency ecosystem.

Collaborative Efforts:

The regulation of cryptocurrencies requires collaborative efforts between governments, regulatory bodies, industry participants, and the broader community. Industry self-regulation, industry standards, and engagement with stakeholders can complement regulatory frameworks and contribute to a more transparent and resilient ecosystem. Dialogue and collaboration foster a better understanding of the technology, leading to more informed and effective regulation.

So, Satoshi Nakamoto's creation of Bitcoin has had a profound impact on the regulatory landscape for cryptocurrencies. The decentralized nature of Bitcoin challenges traditional regulatory frameworks and necessitates new approaches to address emerging risks and opportunities. Regulators around the world have grappled with striking a balance between protecting consumers, mitigating risks, and fostering innovation. Satoshi's influence on cryptocurrency regulations extends beyond specific rules and has shaped the global discourse on the future of finance, technology, and the role of governments in a decentralized world.

Chapter 70: Bitcoin's Role in Wealth Inequality

Bitcoin, as a decentralized digital currency, has sparked both enthusiasm and criticism regarding its potential impact on wealth inequality. In this chapter, we delve into the complex relationship between Bitcoin and wealth inequality, exploring the factors that contribute to this dynamic and the various perspectives surrounding the issue.

Understanding Wealth Inequality:

Wealth inequality refers to the unequal distribution of wealth among individuals or groups within a society. It is often measured by indicators such as the Gini coefficient, which quantifies the disparity of wealth distribution. Wealth inequality has long been a subject of societal concern, as it can have profound implications for social mobility, economic stability, and overall well-being.

Bitcoin's Decentralized Nature:

Bitcoin's decentralized nature is one of its defining features. It operates outside the traditional financial system, enabling individuals to have direct control over their funds without relying on intermediaries such as banks. This decentralization can be seen as a potential equalizer, providing access to financial services and opportunities for individuals who are underserved or excluded by the traditional banking system.

Early Adopters and Accumulation of Wealth:

Bitcoin's early adopters, often referred to as "whales," have accumulated substantial wealth as a result of their early investments and mining activities. These individuals have benefited from the significant appreciation of Bitcoin's value over time, leading to a concentration of wealth within a relatively small group. This accumulation has fueled concerns about wealth inequality within the Bitcoin ecosystem.

Volatility and Risk:

Bitcoin's price volatility is another factor that contributes to wealth inequality. While the potential for high returns exists, the inherent volatility of the cryptocurrency market means that investments in Bitcoin can be subject to significant fluctuations in value. Individuals with higher risk tolerance and greater financial resources are more likely to invest in Bitcoin, potentially widening the wealth gap between those who can afford to take risks and those who cannot.

Financial Inclusion and Empowerment:
Bitcoin has the potential to promote financial inclusion and empower individuals who have limited access to traditional banking services. Through Bitcoin, individuals can transact, store value, and engage in economic activities without relying on traditional financial institutions. This can provide opportunities for individuals in economically disadvantaged regions or those who lack identification documents to participate in the global economy.

Technological Barriers and Access:
While Bitcoin's decentralization can offer financial empowerment, it is important to recognize that access to technology and internet connectivity remains a significant barrier for many individuals. Limited access to smartphones, internet infrastructure, and technological literacy can prevent certain segments of the population from benefiting from Bitcoin's potential to address wealth inequality. Bridging the digital divide is crucial to ensuring equal opportunities for all.

Redistribution of Wealth:
Bitcoin's design does not inherently address the issue of wealth redistribution. Unlike traditional economic systems where governments can implement policies to redistribute wealth through taxation and social programs, Bitcoin's decentralized nature makes it challenging to implement similar mechanisms. However, the technology that underpins Bitcoin, such as blockchain, has the potential to enable innovative solutions for wealth redistribution through tokenization, decentralized finance, and peer-to-peer lending platforms.

Social and Economic Implications:
The impact of Bitcoin on wealth inequality extends beyond its immediate ecosystem. The growth of the cryptocurrency market has attracted a significant amount of capital, with wealth being concentrated in the hands of a few individuals and institutions. This concentration of wealth can have broader societal and economic implications, affecting market dynamics, investment patterns, and the overall distribution of resources.

Educational and Awareness Initiatives:

Addressing wealth inequality requires not only technological solutions but also educational initiatives to promote financial literacy and awareness. By providing individuals with the necessary knowledge and tools to navigate the cryptocurrency landscape, they can make informed decisions and mitigate risks. Empowering individuals with financial education can help bridge the gap and ensure that wealth-building opportunities are accessible to a wider range of people.

Ethical Considerations and Social Responsibility:

Bitcoin's role in wealth inequality raises important ethical considerations. While individuals have the freedom to invest in Bitcoin and reap the benefits of its value appreciation, it is crucial to consider the broader social responsibility that comes with accumulating significant wealth. Philanthropy, impact investing, and responsible wealth management are avenues for those who have benefited from Bitcoin's success to contribute to addressing wealth inequality and social challenges.

Regulatory Measures and Public Policy:

Regulatory measures and public policy play a crucial role in addressing wealth inequality related to Bitcoin and other cryptocurrencies. Governments can implement policies that promote financial inclusion, protect consumer interests, and ensure fair market practices. Striking the right balance between fostering innovation and mitigating risks is essential in creating an environment that promotes equality and social well-being.

Collaboration and Industry Initiatives:

Tackling wealth inequality requires collaboration between various stakeholders, including governments, regulatory bodies, industry participants, and civil society organizations. Industry initiatives such as impact investing, decentralized finance, and philanthropic efforts can contribute to addressing wealth inequality and promoting more equitable economic systems. By working together, we can harness the potential of Bitcoin and blockchain technology to create a more inclusive and fair society.

So, the relationship between Bitcoin and wealth inequality is complex and multifaceted. While Bitcoin's decentralized nature has the potential to promote financial inclusion and empower individuals, factors such as early adoption, volatility, and technological barriers can contribute to wealth concentration. Addressing wealth inequality within the Bitcoin ecosystem requires a multi-pronged approach, including educational initiatives, responsible wealth management, regulatory measures, and collaborative efforts to ensure that the benefits of Bitcoin are accessible to a broader segment of society. By leveraging the transformative potential of Bitcoin and blockchain technology while addressing the challenges it presents, we can strive for a more equitable and inclusive future.

Chapter 71: Satoshi's Educational Contributions

Satoshi Nakamoto, the mysterious creator of Bitcoin, not only revolutionized the world of finance but also made significant educational contributions. In this chapter, we explore Satoshi's educational impact, examining how the creation of Bitcoin and the underlying blockchain technology have spurred educational initiatives, fostered knowledge-sharing, and inspired a new generation of learners.

The Birth of Bitcoin and Educational Resources:

When Satoshi Nakamoto introduced Bitcoin to the world in the white paper titled "Bitcoin: A Peer-to-Peer Electronic Cash System," it marked the beginning of a new era in decentralized finance. This groundbreaking document served as an educational resource that laid the foundation for understanding Bitcoin's concepts, mechanisms, and potential applications. Satoshi's clear and concise writing style enabled individuals from diverse backgrounds to grasp the intricacies of the technology.

Online Communities and Forums:

Bitcoin's inception led to the formation of vibrant online communities and forums where enthusiasts, developers, and curious individuals could gather to learn, discuss, and collaborate. Forums like Bitcointalk.org, established by Satoshi himself, became virtual hubs for education and information exchange. These platforms allowed individuals to ask questions, share knowledge, and engage in debates, fostering a collective learning experience.

Open-Source Development and Collaboration:

Bitcoin's open-source nature has played a crucial role in educational endeavors. By making the source code accessible to the public, Satoshi enabled developers and researchers to delve into the technology, examine its inner workings, and contribute to its improvement. This collaborative approach not only promoted a deeper understanding of Bitcoin but also facilitated the sharing of educational resources, research papers, and technical insights.

Blockchain Education Initiatives:

The advent of blockchain technology, the underlying innovation behind Bitcoin, spurred the creation of dedicated educational initiatives. Universities, research institutions, and online platforms began offering courses, workshops, and certifications focused on blockchain and cryptocurrencies. These educational programs catered to a wide range of learners, from beginners seeking a foundational understanding to professionals looking to specialize in blockchain development or business applications.

Academic Research and Publications:

Satoshi's creation of Bitcoin also sparked an explosion of academic research and publications. Scholars from various disciplines, including computer science, economics, and law, delved into the implications and potential of decentralized digital currencies. Their work has contributed to a growing body of knowledge, providing valuable insights into the technical, economic, and social aspects of cryptocurrencies.

Educational Content Platforms:

Numerous online platforms emerged to provide educational content on Bitcoin and blockchain technology. Websites, blogs, and YouTube channels dedicated to explaining the fundamentals of Bitcoin, discussing its potential impact, and sharing tutorials on wallet management and security practices have flourished. These platforms have made learning about Bitcoin accessible to a broad audience, fostering self-paced education and empowering individuals to explore the technology at their own pace.

Satoshi's Teaching Philosophy:

Satoshi's influence extended beyond the creation of Bitcoin and the technical aspects of blockchain. His emphasis on decentralized governance, privacy, and personal responsibility resonated with a philosophy of empowerment and individual agency. Satoshi's teachings encouraged learners to question traditional financial systems, explore new possibilities, and take control of their financial destinies. This educational philosophy has inspired a generation of learners to challenge existing paradigms and embrace the potential of decentralized technologies.

Grassroots Adoption and Education:

Bitcoin's grassroots adoption has also played a significant role in education. Individuals who recognized the transformative potential of

Bitcoin took it upon themselves to educate others within their communities. Meetups, workshops, and grassroots educational initiatives sprouted in cities worldwide, fostering a sense of community and knowledge-sharing. These efforts helped spread awareness and understanding of Bitcoin at a grassroots level, reaching individuals who may not have encountered formal educational resources.

Economic and Financial Literacy:

Bitcoin's emergence has prompted a renewed interest in economic and financial literacy. Understanding Bitcoin requires familiarity with concepts such as monetary policy, cryptography, and digital assets. As a result, individuals have sought to expand their knowledge in these areas, cultivating a deeper understanding of the economic underpinnings of Bitcoin and the broader financial landscape.

Inspiration for Innovation and Entrepreneurship:

Satoshi's creation of Bitcoin has inspired innovation and entrepreneurship in the blockchain space. The educational resources and opportunities surrounding Bitcoin have sparked creativity and driven individuals to explore new applications and business models. Entrepreneurs have built startups, developed blockchain-based solutions, and embarked on research and development projects, contributing to the growing ecosystem of blockchain innovation.

Continued Learning and Adaptation:

Bitcoin's educational impact continues to evolve alongside the technology itself. As blockchain technology expands into new domains, such as decentralized finance (DeFi), non-fungible tokens (NFTs), and smart contract platforms, educational resources have adapted to provide insights into these emerging trends. Ongoing learning and adaptation are essential to staying abreast of the rapid developments in the Bitcoin and blockchain space.

Social Impact and Empowerment:

Beyond its technical aspects, Bitcoin's educational contributions have had a profound social impact. By fostering a deeper understanding of financial systems, decentralization, and personal autonomy, Bitcoin has empowered individuals to take control of their financial lives. It has given them the tools and knowledge to navigate the rapidly changing landscape of digital finance and participate in the global economy on their own terms.

So, Satoshi Nakamoto's creation of Bitcoin and the underlying blockchain technology has had a profound educational impact. Through the publication of the white paper and the establishment of online communities, Satoshi laid the groundwork for understanding Bitcoin's concepts and mechanisms. Educational initiatives, academic research, and grassroots adoption have further fueled the growth of educational resources, fostering a vibrant and inclusive learning ecosystem. Bitcoin's educational impact extends beyond technical knowledge, inspiring individuals to question traditional financial systems, embrace decentralization, and explore new possibilities. As the technology continues to evolve, education remains a crucial aspect of Bitcoin's transformative journey.

Chapter 72: The Psychology of Bitcoin Adoption

Bitcoin's rise as a global phenomenon cannot be attributed solely to its technological advancements. The psychology of human behavior plays a significant role in the adoption and acceptance of Bitcoin. In this chapter, we explore the psychological factors that influence Bitcoin adoption, examining the motivations, biases, and cognitive processes that shape individuals' decisions to embrace this revolutionary digital currency.

Trust and Perception:

Trust is a fundamental aspect of human behavior and a crucial factor in the adoption of new technologies. Bitcoin's decentralized nature challenges traditional trust models, relying instead on cryptographic algorithms and consensus mechanisms. Individuals' perception of Bitcoin's trustworthiness, influenced by factors such as media coverage, personal experiences, and social influence, plays a critical role in their decision to adopt the technology.

Fear of Missing Out (FOMO):

The fear of missing out (FOMO) is a psychological phenomenon that drives individuals to take action based on the fear of missing out on potential gains or opportunities. In the context of Bitcoin, FOMO can lead individuals to invest in the cryptocurrency, driven by the fear of missing out on its increasing value. FOMO can create a sense of urgency and social pressure, influencing individuals to join the Bitcoin bandwagon.

Behavioral Biases:

Various behavioral biases can impact individuals' decision-making processes when it comes to Bitcoin adoption. Confirmation bias, for example, leads individuals to seek information that confirms their existing beliefs or biases about Bitcoin, while the availability bias causes people to overestimate the likelihood of events based on their ease of recall. Understanding these biases is essential to objectively evaluate the risks and benefits of Bitcoin.

Anchoring and Reference Points:

Anchoring refers to the tendency of individuals to rely heavily on initial information when making subsequent judgments or decisions.

In the context of Bitcoin, individuals may anchor their perception of its value based on its price at a particular point in time, leading to biased judgments about its future potential. Additionally, individuals may use established financial reference points, such as gold or fiat currencies, to evaluate Bitcoin's legitimacy and value.

Social Influence and Herd Mentality:

Human beings are inherently social creatures, and social influence plays a significant role in Bitcoin adoption. When individuals observe others adopting or discussing Bitcoin positively, they may be more inclined to follow suit, driven by a sense of belonging or the fear of being left behind. This herd mentality can lead to rapid adoption and, in some cases, speculative bubbles driven by social contagion.

Loss Aversion and Risk Perception:

Loss aversion refers to the tendency of individuals to feel the pain of losses more acutely than the pleasure of gains. When it comes to Bitcoin, the perception of risk is a key consideration. Individuals may be hesitant to adopt Bitcoin due to fears of potential financial losses or security breaches. Understanding and addressing these concerns through education, security measures, and regulatory frameworks is crucial for widespread adoption.

Cognitive Dissonance:

Cognitive dissonance occurs when individuals experience psychological discomfort due to conflicting beliefs or inconsistent behavior. In the context of Bitcoin, individuals who have previously expressed skepticism about cryptocurrencies may experience cognitive dissonance if they begin to recognize the potential benefits and opportunities associated with Bitcoin. Resolving cognitive dissonance often requires individuals to adjust their beliefs or rationalize their decisions.

Innovators, Early Adopters, and the Diffusion of Innovation:

The adoption of new technologies follows a diffusion process, with different segments of the population adopting at different stages. Innovators and early adopters, who tend to be more technologically savvy and open to innovation, play a crucial role in driving initial Bitcoin adoption. As more individuals witness the success and benefits of early adopters, the adoption curve widens, leading to mainstream acceptance.

Perceived Utility and Value Proposition:

Perceived utility refers to individuals' assessment of the usefulness or value they expect to derive from a product or service. Bitcoin's value proposition lies in its potential to provide secure, borderless, and decentralized transactions. Individuals' perception of Bitcoin's utility, whether as a medium of exchange, store of value, or investment opportunity, influences their decision to adopt and hold the cryptocurrency.

Psychological Ownership and Identity:

Psychological ownership refers to the feeling of possessing or having a stake in something, even if it is intangible. Bitcoin ownership can create a sense of psychological ownership and identity, as individuals associate themselves with the technology and its community. This sense of ownership can strengthen the motivation to promote and advocate for Bitcoin, fostering a self-reinforcing cycle of adoption and engagement.

Cognitive Complexity and Education:

Bitcoin's underlying technology and the concepts surrounding it can be complex for individuals unfamiliar with the field of cryptography, economics, or computer science. Cognitive complexity refers to the mental effort required to understand and grasp these complex concepts. Education and accessible resources that simplify and explain Bitcoin in a user-friendly manner can lower cognitive barriers and facilitate adoption.

Emotional Factors:

Emotions play a significant role in decision-making, and Bitcoin adoption is no exception. Excitement, hope, and the thrill of potential financial gains can be powerful motivators for individuals to embrace Bitcoin. Conversely, fear, uncertainty, and anxiety about the risks associated with Bitcoin can deter adoption. Recognizing and addressing the emotional dimensions of Bitcoin adoption can help individuals make more informed and balanced decisions.

So, the psychology of Bitcoin adoption is a multifaceted and dynamic process influenced by a range of psychological factors. Trust, perception, social influence, biases, and cognitive processes all shape individuals' decisions to embrace Bitcoin. Understanding the psychological drivers behind Bitcoin adoption can help regulators, educators, and industry participants develop strategies to address concerns, enhance education, and foster responsible adoption. By combining technological advancements with a deep understanding of human behavior, we can navigate the complex landscape of Bitcoin adoption and build a sustainable and inclusive digital economy.

Chapter 73: Bitcoin's Impact on Developing Economies

Bitcoin, as a decentralized digital currency, has the potential to bring significant benefits to developing economies. In this chapter, we explore the impact of Bitcoin on developing economies, examining how it can foster financial inclusion, promote economic growth, empower individuals, and address challenges faced by traditional financial systems.

Financial Inclusion:

One of the most significant impacts of Bitcoin on developing economies is its potential to foster financial inclusion. Traditional banking systems often fail to reach remote or underserved areas, leaving a significant portion of the population without access to basic financial services. Bitcoin's decentralized nature allows individuals to participate in the global economy without the need for traditional financial intermediaries, providing them with a means to transact, store value, and access financial services.

Cross-Border Remittances:

Cross-border remittances play a vital role in many developing economies, as migrant workers send money back to their home countries to support their families. However, traditional remittance services can be expensive, slow, and subject to intermediaries. Bitcoin offers a more efficient and cost-effective alternative for remittances, enabling faster and cheaper transactions across borders. This can have a significant positive impact on the livelihoods of individuals and families in developing economies, allowing them to receive funds more quickly and at a lower cost.

Protection against Inflation:

Developing economies often face challenges related to inflation and currency devaluation. Bitcoin can serve as a hedge against these economic risks. By diversifying their wealth into Bitcoin, individuals in developing economies can protect their savings from the devaluation of their local currencies. This provides a measure of stability and financial security in environments where traditional fiat currencies may be subject to volatility or economic instability.

Entrepreneurship and Access to Capital:

Access to capital is a crucial factor for entrepreneurship and economic growth. However, traditional banking systems in developing economies may have limited lending capabilities, strict eligibility criteria, or high interest rates. Bitcoin and blockchain technology have given rise to innovative crowdfunding platforms, peer-to-peer lending networks, and decentralized finance (DeFi) applications that enable entrepreneurs in developing economies to access capital directly from global sources without the need for intermediaries. This opens up new avenues for economic empowerment and growth.

Microtransactions and Micropayments:

Bitcoin's divisibility allows for microtransactions and micropayments, which can be particularly beneficial in developing economies where small-value transactions are prevalent. For example, individuals can use Bitcoin to pay for mobile phone top-ups, utility bills, or small purchases online. This facilitates greater efficiency and convenience, especially in regions where traditional payment systems may be costly, inefficient, or inaccessible.

Protection of Property Rights:

In some developing economies, the lack of secure property rights can hinder economic development and individual empowerment. Bitcoin's underlying technology, blockchain, offers the potential for secure and immutable record-keeping. By leveraging blockchain technology, individuals in developing economies can establish verifiable ownership records for land, assets, and intellectual property. This can help protect property rights, reduce corruption, and foster economic development.

Access to Global Markets:

Bitcoin provides individuals in developing economies with access to global markets, enabling them to participate in international trade and e-commerce. Through Bitcoin, entrepreneurs and small businesses can transact with international partners, expand their customer base, and access a broader range of goods and services. This opens up opportunities for economic growth and diversification beyond local markets.

Education and Skill Development:

Bitcoin's impact goes beyond financial transactions. It also presents opportunities for education and skill development in developing economies. As individuals embrace Bitcoin, they gain exposure to new technologies, financial concepts, and digital literacy. This can lead to the development of skills in areas such as blockchain development, cryptocurrency trading, and digital entrepreneurship. Building a workforce with these skills can contribute to economic growth and empower individuals in the digital economy.

Transparency and Accountability:

Corruption and lack of transparency can hinder economic development and social progress in many developing economies. Bitcoin's transparency, enabled by its decentralized and immutable nature, can help address these challenges. By leveraging blockchain technology, governments and organizations can create transparent systems for tracking funds, ensuring accountability, and reducing corruption. This can enhance public trust, attract investment, and promote economic stability.

Challenges and Considerations:

While Bitcoin offers significant potential benefits to developing economies, several challenges and considerations should be addressed. These include technological infrastructure limitations, access to reliable internet connectivity, regulatory frameworks, cybersecurity concerns, and financial literacy. Collaborative efforts between governments, organizations, and the private sector are crucial to creating an enabling environment for Bitcoin adoption and maximizing its positive impact.

Empowering the Unbanked:

A significant portion of the population in developing economies remains unbanked or underbanked, lacking access to basic financial services. Bitcoin can provide an alternative financial system that operates outside traditional banking structures, empowering individuals who have been excluded from the formal financial sector. By offering a secure and accessible platform for financial transactions, Bitcoin has the potential to bridge the gap and bring financial services to the unbanked and underbanked populations.

Partnerships and Knowledge Sharing:

The successful adoption of Bitcoin in developing economies relies on partnerships and knowledge sharing between stakeholders. Collaborative efforts between governments, educational institutions, non-governmental organizations, and the private sector can provide the necessary infrastructure, regulatory frameworks, and educational resources to facilitate Bitcoin adoption and maximize its positive impact. So, Bitcoin's impact on developing economies extends beyond financial transactions. It has the potential to foster financial inclusion, promote economic growth, empower individuals, and address challenges faced by traditional financial systems. By leveraging Bitcoin's decentralized nature, individuals in developing economies can access financial services, protect against inflation, engage in cross-border transactions, and participate in the global economy. However, addressing challenges such as infrastructure limitations, regulatory frameworks, and financial literacy is crucial to realizing Bitcoin's full potential in driving sustainable development and creating opportunities for individuals and communities in developing economies.

Chapter 74: Satoshi's Potential Identity Revealed?

The identity of Satoshi Nakamoto, the elusive creator of Bitcoin, has remained a mystery since the publication of the Bitcoin white paper in 2008. Over the years, numerous speculations and theories have emerged regarding the true identity of Satoshi. In this chapter, we explore some of the potential identities that have been put forward and the evidence supporting these claims, delving into the captivating world of Satoshi Nakamoto's potential identity.

Dorian Nakamoto:

In 2014, a Newsweek article claimed that Dorian Nakamoto, a Japanese-American physicist, was the creator of Bitcoin. The article sparked a media frenzy and led to intense scrutiny of Dorian's life and background. However, Dorian denied any involvement in Bitcoin and stated that he misunderstood the journalist's question. The evidence linking Dorian to Satoshi remains circumstantial, and the mystery persists.

Hal Finney:

Hal Finney, a cryptographic pioneer and one of the earliest Bitcoin users, has been a subject of speculation regarding his potential role as Satoshi. Hal's technical expertise, involvement in the early development of Bitcoin, and close correspondence with Satoshi have fueled these claims. Furthermore, similarities in writing style between Hal and Satoshi have been noted. However, Hal always maintained that he was not Satoshi and was simply an early enthusiast and contributor to the Bitcoin project.

Nick Szabo:

Nick Szabo, a computer scientist, and legal scholar, has also been suggested as a potential candidate for Satoshi Nakamoto. Szabo's work on digital currencies, smart contracts, and his involvement in the cypherpunk movement align with Satoshi's vision and expertise. Additionally, linguistic and coding analysis has highlighted similarities between Szabo's writings and Satoshi's early posts. However, Nick

Szabo has consistently denied being Satoshi and has maintained that he is solely a Bitcoin enthusiast.

Craig Wright:

In 2016, an Australian computer scientist named Craig Wright claimed to be Satoshi Nakamoto. This controversial announcement sparked a heated debate within the cryptocurrency community. However, Wright's claim has been met with skepticism due to the lack of substantial evidence and his failure to provide verifiable cryptographic proof. The dispute over Craig Wright's claim to be Satoshi continues to this day, with many in the community rejecting his assertion.

Group Effort or Pseudonym:

Another theory suggests that Satoshi Nakamoto is not an individual but a group of people or a pseudonym representing multiple contributors to the development of Bitcoin. This theory is supported by the complexity and depth of knowledge displayed in the Bitcoin white paper and the subsequent codebase. The idea of Satoshi being a collective effort aligns with the open-source nature of Bitcoin, where multiple contributors collaborate to advance the technology.

Purposeful Anonymity:

One compelling explanation for the mystery surrounding Satoshi's identity is that it was a deliberate choice to remain anonymous. Satoshi's decision to maintain anonymity can be seen as a strategic move to protect themselves from potential legal or regulatory scrutiny, maintain the decentralized nature of Bitcoin, and allow the technology to speak for itself. Satoshi's anonymity has also helped to cultivate a sense of mystery and intrigue around Bitcoin, fueling its rise as a global phenomenon.

Regardless of the various theories and claims surrounding Satoshi's identity, it is important to note that the true identity of Satoshi Nakamoto remains unknown. Satoshi's decision to remain anonymous has allowed Bitcoin to flourish as a decentralized digital currency, detached from any single individual or authority. The focus should remain on the technological advancements and the transformative potential of Bitcoin rather than the speculative hunt for Satoshi's true identity.

Ultimately, the identity of Satoshi Nakamoto may never be definitively revealed, adding to the allure and mystique of Bitcoin's origins. Satoshi's anonymity has allowed Bitcoin to transcend any single individual and become a symbol of the potential for decentralized and borderless financial systems. Whether Satoshi's true identity is ever uncovered or not, the impact of Bitcoin on the world of finance and technology is undeniable, and its legacy will continue to shape the future of digital currencies and decentralized technologies.

Chapter 75: The Role of Whales in Bitcoin's Ecosystem

In the world of cryptocurrency, the term "whale" refers to individuals or entities who hold a significant amount of a particular cryptocurrency. In the context of Bitcoin, whales are those who possess a substantial number of bitcoins. These whales play a unique and influential role in the Bitcoin ecosystem, impacting market dynamics, price movements, and overall market sentiment. In this chapter, we explore the role of whales in the Bitcoin ecosystem and delve into their behaviors, motivations, and potential implications.

Understanding Whale Behavior:

Whales in the Bitcoin ecosystem are often characterized by their large holdings of bitcoins, sometimes ranging into thousands or even tens of thousands. Their actions, such as buying or selling large volumes of bitcoins, can have a profound impact on the market. Whales may accumulate bitcoins over time, often during periods of low prices, and may strategically liquidate their holdings when they believe the market has reached a favorable price point. Understanding the behavior of whales is crucial for market participants and investors to navigate the volatile cryptocurrency market.

Market Influence:

The sheer size of a whale's holdings gives them significant influence over market dynamics. When a whale buys or sells a large volume of bitcoins, it can trigger price movements and create market volatility. Their actions can create waves of buying or selling pressure, impacting the sentiment and behavior of other market participants. Consequently, the actions of whales can be closely monitored and analyzed to gain insights into potential market trends and sentiment shifts.

Liquidity Provision:

Whales also serve as a source of liquidity in the Bitcoin market. When other market participants want to buy or sell large volumes of bitcoins, they often rely on the liquidity provided by whales to execute their trades. Whales with significant holdings can facilitate these large trades, improving market efficiency and reducing slippage. The presence of whales in the market ensures that there is sufficient liquidity to accommodate the trading needs of various participants.

Price Manipulation Concerns:

The influence of whales has raised concerns about potential price manipulation. With their ability to buy or sell large volumes of bitcoins, whales can create artificial price movements or engage in manipulative trading strategies, such as "pump and dump" schemes. These activities can have a negative impact on market integrity and the confidence of retail investors. Regulators and market surveillance entities have been working to identify and deter such manipulative practices to ensure fair and orderly markets.

Long-Term Investment Strategies:

Not all whale activities are driven by short-term trading or manipulation. Many whales adopt long-term investment strategies, holding onto their bitcoins with the belief in its long-term value and potential as a store of value or digital gold. These long-term investors contribute to the overall stability of the Bitcoin ecosystem by providing a foundation of strong hands who are less likely to panic sell during periods of market volatility.

Market Sentiment and Psychological Impact:

Whale activities and their publicized movements can have a psychological impact on the broader market. The buying or selling actions of whales can create a sense of FOMO (fear of missing out) or FUD (fear, uncertainty, and doubt) among retail investors and traders. The perception of whales' actions can influence market sentiment, leading to reactionary buying or selling behaviors from smaller investors. Understanding and interpreting whale movements require a nuanced analysis that considers both their trading patterns and the broader market context.

Diversification and Risk Management:

Whales often diversify their holdings across various cryptocurrencies and assets beyond Bitcoin. This diversification strategy helps them manage risk and mitigate potential losses. By spreading their holdings across different cryptocurrencies, assets, or investment vehicles, whales aim to protect their wealth from the inherent volatility and risks associated with individual cryptocurrencies.

Stewardship and Responsibility:

As influential participants in the Bitcoin ecosystem, whales also bear a sense of stewardship and responsibility. Their actions can impact the wider adoption and acceptance of Bitcoin. Some whales actively engage in philanthropic efforts, supporting projects and initiatives that promote the development and adoption of cryptocurrencies. By using their wealth to drive positive change and innovation, these whales contribute to the overall growth and maturity of the cryptocurrency ecosystem.

Regulatory Considerations:

The influence of whales in the cryptocurrency market has drawn attention from regulators and policymakers. Concerns about market manipulation, insider trading, and unfair practices have prompted regulatory discussions and potential interventions to ensure market integrity and protect retail investors. Balancing the need for regulation while maintaining the decentralized and innovative nature of cryptocurrencies remains a complex challenge.

Evolving Landscape:

As the cryptocurrency landscape evolves, the influence and behaviors of whales may change. The increasing institutional participation and the emergence of regulated financial products, such as Bitcoin exchange-traded funds (ETFs), can potentially reshape the dynamics of whale activities. Institutional investors may bring a different perspective and set of behaviors to the market, influencing the actions and behaviors of existing whales.

So, whales play a significant role in the Bitcoin ecosystem, exerting influence over market dynamics, liquidity provision, and overall market sentiment. Their behaviors and actions can impact price movements and market volatility, necessitating a deeper understanding of their motivations and activities. While concerns about market manipulation exist, whales also contribute to market liquidity and provide a foundation of long-term investors. As the cryptocurrency landscape continues to evolve, finding the right balance between market regulation, investor protection, and fostering innovation will be crucial in ensuring the continued growth and sustainability of the Bitcoin ecosystem.

Chapter 76: The Environmental Debate Surrounding Bitcoin

Bitcoin, as a decentralized digital currency, has been at the center of a heated environmental debate. Critics argue that the energy consumption associated with Bitcoin mining is excessive and harmful to the environment, while proponents maintain that the benefits of a decentralized financial system outweigh the environmental concerns. In this chapter, we delve into the environmental debate surrounding Bitcoin, exploring the energy consumption of mining, the sustainability of Bitcoin, and potential solutions to mitigate its environmental impact.

Understanding Bitcoin Mining:

Bitcoin mining is the process by which new bitcoins are created and transactions are verified and added to the blockchain. It involves solving complex mathematical problems using powerful computers, which requires significant computational power and, consequently, energy consumption. Miners compete to solve these mathematical puzzles, and the first one to find the solution is rewarded with newly minted bitcoins.

Energy Consumption:

Bitcoin mining is often criticized for its high energy consumption. The energy-intensive process of mining, coupled with the increasing difficulty of mining new bitcoins, has led to a significant amount of computational power being deployed worldwide. This requires a substantial amount of electricity, contributing to the carbon footprint associated with Bitcoin mining.

Proof-of-Work (PoW) Consensus Mechanism:

Bitcoin's PoW consensus mechanism, while robust and secure, is a primary driver of its energy consumption. PoW requires miners to solve complex mathematical problems, which necessitates extensive computational power. As the Bitcoin network grows and attracts more miners, the energy requirements for mining increase.

Renewable Energy Usage:

A common counterargument is that a significant portion of Bitcoin mining relies on renewable energy sources. Some mining operations are located in regions with abundant renewable energy resources, such as hydroelectric power. In these areas, Bitcoin mining can potentially contribute to the utilization of excess renewable energy that would otherwise go to waste. However, it is important to note that the overall energy mix for Bitcoin mining is diverse and varies depending on the location of mining operations.

E-Waste Concerns:

Another environmental concern associated with Bitcoin mining is the disposal of electronic waste (e-waste). The constant need for more powerful mining equipment leads to a rapid turnover of hardware, contributing to the accumulation of e-waste. Proper recycling and responsible e-waste management practices are crucial to minimize the environmental impact of mining hardware disposal.

Sustainability Initiatives:

The Bitcoin community and industry players have recognized the need to address the environmental impact of Bitcoin mining. Various initiatives and projects are underway to promote sustainability and reduce the carbon footprint of Bitcoin. Some miners are actively seeking ways to increase their use of renewable energy sources and adopt energy-efficient mining practices. Additionally, research and development efforts are focused on developing alternative consensus mechanisms that require less energy, such as Proof-of-Stake (PoS) or other consensus algorithms.

Offsetting Carbon Emissions:

Another approach to mitigating the environmental impact of Bitcoin mining is through carbon offsetting. Some mining operations and industry participants are voluntarily offsetting their carbon emissions by investing in renewable energy projects or purchasing carbon credits. These initiatives aim to balance out the carbon emissions associated with Bitcoin mining, effectively neutralizing its environmental impact.

Innovations in Mining Efficiency:

Technological advancements in mining hardware and efficiency improvements can also contribute to reducing the energy consumption of Bitcoin mining. Manufacturers are continually developing more energy-efficient mining equipment, which can lead to a more sustainable mining industry. Additionally, advancements in cooling systems and mining facility design can help optimize energy usage and reduce waste heat.

Scalability and Layer 2 Solutions:

Scalability solutions, such as the Lightning Network, aim to reduce the burden on the main Bitcoin blockchain, making transactions faster and more efficient. These Layer 2 solutions have the potential to alleviate some of the energy consumption associated with the processing and verification of large volumes of transactions on the main blockchain.

Public Awareness and Education:

Increasing public awareness and education about the environmental impact of Bitcoin mining is essential. By understanding the energy consumption of Bitcoin and its environmental implications, individuals can make informed decisions regarding their participation in the Bitcoin ecosystem. Encouraging responsible mining practices and supporting sustainable initiatives can help shape a more environmentally conscious Bitcoin industry.

Collaboration with Renewable Energy Providers:

Partnerships and collaborations between the Bitcoin industry and renewable energy providers can further promote the use of clean energy in mining operations. By establishing relationships with renewable energy companies, mining operations can prioritize the use of renewable energy sources, driving the transition towards a greener mining industry.

Regulatory Considerations:

Regulatory frameworks and policies related to energy consumption and environmental impact can play a role in shaping the sustainability of Bitcoin mining. Governments and regulatory bodies can incentivize or enforce sustainable practices, encourage the use of renewable energy, and establish guidelines for responsible e-waste management within the Bitcoin mining industry.

So, the environmental debate surrounding Bitcoin's energy consumption is multifaceted and complex. While Bitcoin mining does consume a significant amount of energy, efforts are being made to mitigate its environmental impact. The industry is exploring various solutions, including increased use of renewable energy, carbon offsetting, technological innovations, and scalability improvements. Public awareness, education, and responsible mining practices are crucial in addressing the environmental concerns associated with Bitcoin. By fostering collaboration, innovation, and sustainable practices, the Bitcoin community can strive towards a more environmentally conscious and sustainable future for the cryptocurrency ecosystem.

Type This URL in Your Browser ⟶ ***https://bit.ly/Guess_What_This***

Chapter 77: Satoshi's View on Digital Privacy

Satoshi Nakamoto, the enigmatic creator of Bitcoin, not only revolutionized the world of finance but also had a profound impact on the concept of digital privacy. In this chapter, we explore Satoshi's views on digital privacy, examining how Bitcoin embodies principles of privacy and anonymity, and the implications this has for individuals and society.

Pseudonymity and Anonymity:

From the outset, Satoshi Nakamoto recognized the importance of privacy in the digital age. By choosing to operate under a pseudonym, Satoshi maintained a level of anonymity, allowing the focus to remain on the technology rather than on a central figure. This decision set the tone for the privacy-centric nature of Bitcoin.

Decentralization and Privacy:

One of Satoshi's core motivations was to create a decentralized digital currency that would not be subject to centralized control or surveillance. By using a peer-to-peer network and cryptographic principles, Bitcoin enables individuals to transact directly with each other, without the need for intermediaries. This decentralized approach inherently promotes privacy by removing the need to trust third parties with personal and financial information.

User Control:

Satoshi emphasized the importance of users having full control over their funds and personal data. Traditional financial systems often require individuals to entrust their financial information to banks or other intermediaries. In contrast, Bitcoin empowers users to be their own custodians, giving them control over their private keys and the ability to transact pseudonymously. This control over personal information enhances privacy and reduces the risk of data breaches or unauthorized access.

Pseudonymous Transactions:

Bitcoin transactions are pseudonymous, meaning that while the transaction details are publicly recorded on the blockchain, the real-world identities of the participants are not directly linked to those transactions. Instead, participants are identified by cryptographic addresses. This pseudonymity offers a level of privacy by allowing users to transact without revealing personal information.

Address Reuse and Privacy Concerns:

While Bitcoin transactions are pseudonymous, address reuse can compromise privacy. Reusing the same Bitcoin address for multiple transactions can potentially allow third parties to link those transactions together and create a profile of an individual's activity. Satoshi acknowledged this concern and recommended the use of new addresses for each transaction to enhance privacy.

Privacy-Enhancing Techniques:

Satoshi recognized the need for additional privacy-enhancing techniques beyond the basic pseudonymity provided by Bitcoin. Although these techniques were not explicitly implemented by Satoshi, concepts such as CoinJoin and the use of privacy-focused cryptocurrencies have emerged to enhance transaction privacy. CoinJoin allows multiple users to combine their transactions, making it more challenging to trace individual transactions on the blockchain.

Balancing Privacy and Regulatory Compliance:

Satoshi acknowledged the need to balance privacy with the necessity of regulatory compliance. While privacy is an essential aspect of Bitcoin, Satoshi recognized that illicit activities could exploit this privacy. Satoshi believed that the benefits of privacy in empowering individuals and promoting financial freedom outweighed the risks associated with potential misuse.

Transparent and Auditable:

Bitcoin's transparency and auditable nature should not be overlooked when considering privacy. While individual transactions may be pseudonymous, the entire transaction history is publicly recorded on the blockchain, allowing anyone to verify the integrity and validity of transactions. This transparency fosters trust in the system and reduces the reliance on intermediaries for auditing and verification purposes.

Privacy as a Fundamental Right:

Satoshi's vision extended beyond the technical aspects of Bitcoin. He understood that privacy is a fundamental human right. In an era marked by increasing surveillance and data breaches, Satoshi's creation provided a means for individuals to reclaim their privacy and exercise control over their personal information.

Privacy in the Digital Age:

Satoshi's perspective on digital privacy resonates even more strongly today as our lives become increasingly intertwined with digital technologies. From social media platforms to financial institutions, our personal data is constantly collected, analyzed, and shared. Bitcoin represents an alternative, where individuals can transact privately and securely, reducing their exposure to data breaches and surveillance.

Evolving Privacy Landscape:

While Satoshi laid the foundation for privacy in Bitcoin, the privacy landscape has continued to evolve. Various advancements and technologies, such as privacy-focused cryptocurrencies and privacy-preserving protocols, have emerged to enhance privacy within the broader cryptocurrency ecosystem. These developments aim to address the limitations and challenges associated with privacy in Bitcoin and improve the overall privacy experience for users.

Privacy vs. Transparency Debate:

The tension between privacy and transparency remains an ongoing discussion within the cryptocurrency community and society at large. Striking the right balance between individual privacy and the need for transparency to prevent illicit activities and maintain regulatory compliance is a complex challenge. It requires ongoing dialogue, technological advancements, and thoughtful policy frameworks to ensure that privacy is protected without compromising important societal interests.

So, Satoshi Nakamoto recognized the importance of digital privacy and designed Bitcoin to embody principles of privacy, pseudonymity, and user control. By creating a decentralized and pseudonymous digital currency, Satoshi aimed to empower individuals and protect their privacy in an increasingly digital world. While challenges and debates persist, Satoshi's vision has inspired ongoing efforts to enhance privacy within the cryptocurrency ecosystem and redefine the boundaries of digital privacy for the betterment of individuals and society as a whole.

Chapter 78: Bitcoin's Influence on Traditional Investments

Bitcoin, the world's first decentralized cryptocurrency, has not only disrupted the financial industry but also exerted a significant influence on traditional investments. In this chapter, we explore how Bitcoin has impacted various aspects of traditional investments, including diversification, risk management, institutional adoption, and the emergence of new investment opportunities.

Diversification and Portfolio Allocation:

Bitcoin has emerged as a new asset class, offering investors an alternative avenue for diversification. Traditional portfolios typically consist of stocks, bonds, and real estate, but Bitcoin introduces a non-correlated asset that can potentially enhance portfolio diversification. By adding Bitcoin to their investment portfolios, investors can potentially reduce overall risk and increase the potential for returns, especially during periods of economic uncertainty or market volatility.

Store of Value and Inflation Hedge:

Bitcoin's limited supply and its design as a decentralized digital currency have positioned it as a potential store of value and an inflation hedge. Traditional investments such as fiat currencies and bonds may be subject to inflationary pressures, whereas Bitcoin's scarcity and decentralized nature make it an attractive option for preserving purchasing power over the long term. This unique characteristic of Bitcoin has drawn the attention of investors seeking to protect their wealth from the erosive effects of inflation.

Risk Management and Portfolio Insurance:

Bitcoin's decentralized nature and independence from traditional financial systems make it an attractive option for risk management and portfolio insurance. In times of economic instability or geopolitical turmoil, traditional investments may suffer significant losses. Bitcoin, as a separate and decentralized asset, can act as a hedge against such events, providing a degree of protection for investors' portfolios. By allocating a portion of their investments to Bitcoin, investors can potentially reduce the overall risk exposure of their portfolios.

Institutional Adoption:

In recent years, there has been a notable increase in institutional adoption of Bitcoin and other cryptocurrencies. Institutional investors, including hedge funds, asset managers, and pension funds, have recognized the potential of Bitcoin as a legitimate investment asset. This institutional adoption has contributed to the mainstream acceptance of Bitcoin and has further fueled its growth. The entrance of institutional players has also brought increased liquidity and stability to the Bitcoin market, making it more attractive to traditional investors.

Bitcoin Futures and Derivatives:

The introduction of Bitcoin futures contracts and other derivatives has facilitated the integration of Bitcoin into traditional financial markets. Bitcoin futures allow investors to speculate on the future price of Bitcoin without directly owning the underlying asset. This financial instrument provides an avenue for traditional investors who may be restricted from directly investing in cryptocurrencies to gain exposure to Bitcoin's price movements and participate in the market.

Digital Asset Investment Funds:

The rise of digital asset investment funds has made it easier for traditional investors to gain exposure to Bitcoin and other cryptocurrencies. These funds pool investors' capital and allocate it to a diversified portfolio of digital assets, including Bitcoin. By investing in these funds, traditional investors can benefit from professional management, secure storage solutions, and regulatory compliance, alleviating some of the concerns associated with self-custody and regulatory complexities.

Initial Coin Offerings (ICOs):

Bitcoin's success has paved the way for the emergence of a new fundraising mechanism called Initial Coin Offerings (ICOs). ICOs allow projects to raise funds by issuing their own digital tokens or cryptocurrencies. While ICOs have faced regulatory scrutiny, they have also presented new investment opportunities for traditional investors seeking exposure to early-stage blockchain projects. However, it is crucial for investors to exercise caution and conduct thorough due diligence when considering ICO investments, as they come with unique risks and challenges.

Changing Paradigms of Value:

Bitcoin's rise has challenged traditional notions of value and the role of centralized institutions in financial systems. The concept of decentralized digital currency has sparked discussions about the nature of money, trust, and the role of intermediaries in financial transactions. Traditional investors are increasingly recognizing the importance of understanding and adapting to this changing paradigm, as it has the potential to reshape the future of finance and investments.

Regulatory Considerations:

Bitcoin's influence on traditional investments has also prompted regulatory considerations and discussions. Regulators around the world are grappling with the task of providing a regulatory framework that balances investor protection with innovation. As the regulatory landscape continues to evolve, it is crucial for investors to stay informed about the legal and regulatory developments surrounding Bitcoin and other cryptocurrencies to make informed investment decisions.

Evolving Investment Landscape:

The influence of Bitcoin on traditional investments is part of a broader shift in the investment landscape. As technology advances and digital assets gain more mainstream acceptance, investors are exploring new investment opportunities beyond traditional asset classes. The rise of cryptocurrencies, blockchain technology, and decentralized finance (DeFi) has opened up a new frontier for traditional investors to diversify their portfolios and potentially capitalize on emerging trends and opportunities.

So, Bitcoin's influence on traditional investments is undeniable. It has provided new avenues for diversification, risk management, and portfolio allocation. The increasing institutional adoption of Bitcoin has brought legitimacy and stability to the cryptocurrency market. The emergence of Bitcoin futures, digital asset investment funds, and ICOs has expanded the range of investment opportunities available to traditional investors. However, as with any investment, it is essential for investors to conduct thorough research, understand the risks involved, and seek professional advice when necessary. As the investment landscape continues to evolve, the integration of Bitcoin and other cryptocurrencies into traditional investment strategies will likely continue to shape the future of finance.

Chapter 79: The Quest for Satoshi's Lost Bitcoins

The mystery surrounding Satoshi Nakamoto, the pseudonymous creator of Bitcoin, goes beyond the enigma of his true identity. Another intriguing aspect of Satoshi's story revolves around the bitcoins he mined in the early days of the cryptocurrency. Satoshi's bitcoins hold immense value, both in terms of their monetary worth and the historical significance they carry. In this chapter, we embark on a fascinating journey to explore the quest for Satoshi's lost bitcoins, uncovering the challenges, speculation, and potential outcomes that surround this captivating pursuit.

Satoshi's Bitcoin Stash:

Satoshi Nakamoto, during his active involvement in the Bitcoin project, mined a substantial number of bitcoins. Estimates suggest that Satoshi's holdings amount to approximately 1.1 million bitcoins, which, at the time of writing, is worth a significant sum. However, the mystery lies in the fact that Satoshi has not touched these bitcoins for many years, leading to speculation about their fate.

The Genesis Block and Unspent Coins:

The first block of the Bitcoin blockchain, known as the Genesis Block, holds a special place in Bitcoin's history. It contains a hidden message, signaling Satoshi's intention to launch a decentralized digital currency. Additionally, within this block, Satoshi embedded a reward of 50 bitcoins, known as the "coinbase" transaction. These coins, often referred to as "Satoshi's coins," have never been spent or moved.

The Importance of Satoshi's Coins:

Satoshi's coins carry immense value, not only due to their potential financial worth but also because they hold historical significance. The untouched nature of these coins makes them a symbol of Satoshi's vision and the early days of Bitcoin. They represent the genesis of a revolutionary technology that has reshaped the world of finance.

Satoshi's Intentional Inactivity:

Satoshi's decision to leave his bitcoins untouched has led to speculation about his motivations. Some believe that Satoshi chose to maintain the coins as a testament to his commitment to the principles of decentralization, ensuring that no single entity has control over the Bitcoin network. Others speculate that Satoshi's inactivity may be due to concerns about potential legal and regulatory repercussions.

The Hunt for Satoshi's Private Keys:

The search for Satoshi's private keys, which would grant access to his bitcoins, has become a topic of fascination within the cryptocurrency community. Individuals and organizations have attempted various methods to uncover the private keys, ranging from cryptographic analysis to scouring online forums for clues left by Satoshi. However, to date, no one has been successful in revealing Satoshi's private keys.

Ownership Claims and Speculation:

Over the years, several individuals have come forward claiming to be Satoshi Nakamoto or asserting ownership of Satoshi's bitcoins. These claims have sparked intense debates and skepticism within the community. Each claimant faces scrutiny as they attempt to provide evidence or cryptographic signatures to validate their assertions.

Wallet Security and Cryptographic Complexity:

Satoshi's bitcoins are stored in one or more digital wallets, protected by cryptographic security measures. These security features, such as private keys and multi-signature schemes, ensure that the bitcoins remain secure from unauthorized access. The complex nature of these security measures poses significant challenges for anyone attempting to access the coins without the necessary credentials.

Potential Outcomes:

The fate of Satoshi's bitcoins remains uncertain, and there are several potential outcomes to consider. It is possible that Satoshi intentionally chose never to access or spend the coins, leaving them as a lasting testament to his creation. Alternatively, Satoshi's private keys may have been lost or destroyed, rendering the coins forever inaccessible. Finally, if someone were to successfully uncover the private keys, it would open up a range of possibilities, from benevolent actions such as supporting Bitcoin development to more controversial decisions that could impact the cryptocurrency market.

Impact on Bitcoin's Ecosystem:

The discovery and potential movement of Satoshi's bitcoins could have profound effects on the Bitcoin ecosystem. The sudden influx of such a significant number of bitcoins into the market could impact its price and market dynamics. Furthermore, the actions taken by the individual or entity controlling the coins could influence public perception, confidence, and the direction of the cryptocurrency industry.

The Mystery Endures:

While the quest for Satoshi's lost bitcoins continues, it is important to recognize that the mystery surrounding their fate adds to the allure and intrigue of Bitcoin's origin story. Satoshi Nakamoto's decision to remain anonymous and the enigmatic nature of his coins have become part of Bitcoin's mythology, contributing to its global appeal and ongoing fascination.

So, the quest for Satoshi's lost bitcoins represents a captivating aspect of Bitcoin's history. The value, historical significance, and mysteries surrounding these untouched coins have captivated the imagination of the cryptocurrency community. While the search for Satoshi's private keys continues, the quest serves as a reminder of the profound impact of Bitcoin and the enduring legacy of its creator. As the Bitcoin ecosystem evolves, the fate of Satoshi's bitcoins remains a subject of speculation, anticipation, and ongoing exploration.

Chapter 80: Bitcoin's Integration with Social Media

Bitcoin, the revolutionary digital currency, has not only disrupted traditional financial systems but has also found its way into the realm of social media. The integration of Bitcoin with social media platforms has created new opportunities for individuals to engage with the cryptocurrency, share information, and even transact directly within the social media environment. In this chapter, we delve into the details of Bitcoin's integration with social media, exploring its benefits, challenges, and the potential impact on both the cryptocurrency and social media landscapes.

Bitcoin Tipping and Micropayments:

One of the early manifestations of Bitcoin's integration with social media was the concept of Bitcoin tipping. Tipping allows users to show appreciation for valuable content by sending small amounts of Bitcoin directly to content creators. This feature fosters a sense of community, encourages high-quality contributions, and provides a direct financial incentive for users to engage with content they find valuable. Micropayments through Bitcoin tipping enable users to support creators in a frictionless and decentralized manner.

Crowdfunding and Donations:

Bitcoin's integration with social media platforms has also facilitated the use of the cryptocurrency for crowdfunding and charitable donations. Social media users can create campaigns or fundraising initiatives, allowing their network to contribute to the cause using Bitcoin. This direct and transparent method of fundraising removes the need for intermediaries, reduces transaction costs, and enables individuals to support causes they believe in with ease.

Decentralized Social Media Platforms:

Bitcoin's ethos of decentralization aligns well with the emergence of decentralized social media platforms. These platforms aim to give users more control over their data, eliminate censorship, and provide a more transparent and community-driven experience. Bitcoin can play a role in decentralized social media by enabling users to transact and engage directly without relying on centralized intermediaries. This integration fosters a sense of autonomy and user empowerment.

Social Media Payments and E-Commerce:

Bitcoin's integration with social media platforms also opens up new possibilities for e-commerce and social commerce. Social media users can leverage Bitcoin as a payment option for purchasing goods and services directly within the platform. This integration simplifies the payment process, eliminates the need for traditional financial intermediaries, and provides users with more privacy and control over their financial transactions.

Education and Information Sharing:

Social media platforms serve as powerful channels for information sharing and education. Bitcoin's integration with social media has facilitated the dissemination of knowledge about cryptocurrencies, blockchain technology, and financial literacy. Bitcoin enthusiasts and experts can share educational content, insights, and analysis, helping to spread awareness and understanding of this transformative technology to a broader audience.

Bitcoin Influencers and Social Media Marketing:

Bitcoin's integration with social media has given rise to a new breed of influencers—individuals who have amassed a substantial following and leverage their influence to educate and promote Bitcoin-related content. These influencers play a crucial role in driving adoption, shaping public perception, and expanding the reach of Bitcoin within social media ecosystems. Social media platforms provide an ideal space for Bitcoin enthusiasts to engage with these influencers, share insights, and stay informed about the latest developments.

Challenges and Risks:

While the integration of Bitcoin with social media brings numerous benefits, it also poses challenges and risks. One of the primary concerns is the potential for scams and fraudulent activities. Social media platforms are prone to malicious actors who may attempt to exploit users by promoting fake Bitcoin giveaways or investment schemes. Users must exercise caution, conduct thorough research, and verify information before engaging in any Bitcoin-related activities on social media.

Regulatory Considerations:

The integration of Bitcoin with social media platforms has regulatory implications that must be addressed. Governments and regulatory bodies are increasingly focusing on the regulation of cryptocurrencies, including activities related to social media. Platforms may need to implement Know Your Customer (KYC) and Anti-Money Laundering (AML) measures to ensure compliance and mitigate potential risks associated with Bitcoin transactions.

Social Impact and Financial Inclusion:

Bitcoin's integration with social media has the potential to have a significant social impact, particularly in areas with limited access to traditional financial services. By enabling individuals to transact and engage with Bitcoin directly on social media, the technology can contribute to financial inclusion, empower individuals economically, and foster greater financial literacy and independence.

Future Prospects:

As social media continues to evolve, so does the integration of Bitcoin and other cryptocurrencies. The potential for seamless Bitcoin transactions, decentralized social media platforms, and the integration of blockchain technology for data privacy and security holds promise for a more integrated and user-centric social media experience. Bitcoin's integration with social media will likely continue to evolve and shape the way individuals interact with and perceive digital currencies.

So, the integration of Bitcoin with social media platforms has expanded the reach, adoption, and utility of the cryptocurrency. From tipping content creators to facilitating crowdfunding, Bitcoin has brought new opportunities for financial engagement, information sharing, and community building within the social media landscape. However, users must remain vigilant to navigate the risks associated with scams and fraud. As the integration deepens, Bitcoin's presence in social media has the potential to drive financial inclusion, empower individuals, and reshape the future of both finance and social media.

Chapter 81: Satoshi's Influence on Cryptocurrency Exchanges

Satoshi Nakamoto, the mysterious creator of Bitcoin, not only revolutionized the world of finance with the invention of the first cryptocurrency but also had a significant impact on the development and evolution of cryptocurrency exchanges. These exchanges serve as crucial gateways for individuals to buy, sell, and trade cryptocurrencies, including Bitcoin. In this chapter, we delve into Satoshi's influence on cryptocurrency exchanges, exploring the key advancements, challenges, and the ongoing transformation of these platforms.

Early Pioneering Exchanges:

In the early days of Bitcoin, cryptocurrency exchanges were sparse and often lacked the robust infrastructure and security measures seen today. Nevertheless, they played a pivotal role in facilitating the exchange of Bitcoin for fiat currencies and other cryptocurrencies. Platforms such as Mt. Gox, which was initially a trading platform for Magic: The Gathering cards, became one of the earliest and most influential Bitcoin exchanges. Satoshi's creation of Bitcoin laid the foundation for these early exchanges to emerge and provide a platform for users to transact.

Satoshi's Vision of Decentralization:

Satoshi Nakamoto's vision for Bitcoin emphasized the importance of decentralization, enabling users to have direct control over their funds without the need for intermediaries. This vision aligns with the principles of cryptocurrency exchanges built on blockchain technology, which aim to reduce reliance on centralized authorities and create a more trustless environment for trading. Satoshi's influence on exchanges fostered the development of decentralized exchanges (DEXs), which enable peer-to-peer trading without the need for a centralized authority.

Security Enhancements:

Satoshi's influence extends to the emphasis on security within cryptocurrency exchanges. As Bitcoin gained popularity and the value of cryptocurrencies grew, exchanges faced the challenge of securing users' funds and protecting against hacking attempts. The concepts of cryptographic keys, cold storage, and multi-signature wallets were championed by Satoshi and have become standard practices in ensuring the security of users' assets within exchanges.

Market Liquidity and Trading Pairs:

The concept of market liquidity within cryptocurrency exchanges was greatly influenced by Satoshi's work. Bitcoin's status as the first and most widely recognized cryptocurrency led to its inclusion as a trading pair on most exchanges. The availability of Bitcoin as a base currency facilitated the growth of other cryptocurrencies, as traders could easily exchange their Bitcoin for altcoins and vice versa. Satoshi's influence on the establishment of Bitcoin as the dominant trading pair has shaped the market dynamics and liquidity of cryptocurrencies.

Regulatory Compliance:

The regulatory landscape surrounding cryptocurrency exchanges has evolved significantly since Bitcoin's inception. Governments and regulatory bodies worldwide have sought to establish frameworks to ensure consumer protection, prevent money laundering, and combat illicit activities. Satoshi's commitment to transparency and trustlessness has influenced the efforts of cryptocurrency exchanges to adhere to regulatory standards and implement know-your-customer (KYC) and anti-money laundering (AML) procedures.

User Experience and Interface Design:

Satoshi Nakamoto's creation of Bitcoin laid the foundation for the development of user-friendly interfaces and streamlined user experiences within cryptocurrency exchanges. Early exchanges often had complex and intimidating interfaces, hindering widespread adoption. However, as the industry matured, exchanges began to prioritize user experience, offering intuitive interfaces, easy-to-use trading platforms, and comprehensive charting tools. Satoshi's emphasis on usability and accessibility has influenced the ongoing improvements in user experience across cryptocurrency exchanges.

International Accessibility:

Bitcoin's global nature and decentralized structure have contributed to the international accessibility of cryptocurrency exchanges. Satoshi's vision of a borderless financial system aligns with the ability of users worldwide to access and trade cryptocurrencies on these platforms. The influence of Bitcoin, as the pioneering cryptocurrency, has paved the way for exchanges to cater to users from different countries, offering multi-language support, diverse fiat currency options, and compliance with international regulations.

Innovation and Expansion:

Satoshi Nakamoto's groundbreaking creation of Bitcoin has sparked a wave of innovation and expansion within the cryptocurrency exchange ecosystem. Exchanges have continually evolved to meet the changing needs of users, introducing features such as margin trading, futures contracts, options trading, and decentralized finance (DeFi) integration. Satoshi's influence on the creation of Bitcoin has spurred ongoing developments, leading to a vibrant and diverse landscape of cryptocurrency exchanges.

Challenges and Opportunities:

While Satoshi's influence on cryptocurrency exchanges has been significant, challenges and opportunities persist. Exchanges face ongoing concerns regarding security, regulatory compliance, market manipulation, and transparency. Additionally, scalability and transaction throughput remain areas of exploration and improvement. However, the dynamic nature of the cryptocurrency industry presents numerous opportunities for innovation, collaboration, and the development of new exchange models that align with Satoshi's principles of decentralization and user empowerment.

The Future of Exchanges:

As the cryptocurrency industry continues to mature, the future of cryptocurrency exchanges holds great promise. The influence of Satoshi Nakamoto will continue to shape the development of exchanges, ensuring a focus on security, usability, and decentralization. The integration of emerging technologies such as blockchain, artificial intelligence, and decentralized finance will drive further innovation within the exchange ecosystem, creating new avenues for trading, liquidity provision, and financial inclusion.

So, Satoshi Nakamoto's influence on cryptocurrency exchanges cannot be understated. His creation of Bitcoin laid the foundation for the emergence of these platforms, shaping their principles, security practices, and market dynamics. Satoshi's vision of decentralization and user empowerment has influenced the ongoing development of exchanges, leading to enhanced security measures, improved user experiences, and the expansion of trading options. As the cryptocurrency industry evolves, exchanges will continue to adapt, incorporating new technologies and regulatory standards, while remaining grounded in the principles set forth by Satoshi Nakamoto.

Chapter 82: Bitcoin's Use Cases Beyond Currency

Bitcoin, the world's first decentralized digital currency, has gained significant recognition as a medium of exchange and store of value. However, its potential extends far beyond these traditional financial use cases. Bitcoin's underlying technology, blockchain, has sparked innovation and exploration across various industries. In this chapter, we delve into the diverse use cases of Bitcoin beyond currency, exploring its applications in areas such as remittances, supply chain management, identity verification, and more.

Remittances and Cross-Border Payments:

Bitcoin offers a promising solution for remittances and cross-border payments, particularly in regions where traditional banking systems are inaccessible or expensive. By leveraging Bitcoin's decentralized nature and low transaction fees, individuals can transfer funds internationally quickly and securely. Bitcoin's borderless nature makes it an attractive alternative to traditional remittance services, potentially reducing costs and increasing financial inclusion for underserved populations.

Micropayments and Tipping:

Bitcoin's divisibility allows for micropayments, enabling the transfer of small amounts of value online. This capability opens up possibilities for microtransactions in various industries, such as content monetization, pay-per-use services, and tipping platforms. Bitcoin's integration with social media and content-sharing platforms has made microtipping a viable option for users to show appreciation for valuable content or support creators.

Supply Chain Management and Traceability:

The transparency and immutability of blockchain technology have the potential to transform supply chain management. By utilizing Bitcoin's blockchain, stakeholders can record and verify transactions, ensuring transparency and traceability throughout the supply chain. This can help prevent counterfeiting, improve product authenticity, and enhance accountability, particularly in industries such as food, pharmaceuticals, and luxury goods.

Identity Verification and Authentication:

Bitcoin's blockchain can be leveraged for identity verification and authentication. Traditional methods of identity verification often involve intermediaries and are susceptible to fraud and data breaches. Bitcoin's decentralized nature allows for the creation of self-sovereign identity systems, where individuals control their personal information and share it securely and selectively when necessary. This has the potential to enhance privacy, reduce identity theft, and streamline processes that require identity verification.

Decentralized Internet and Web3.0:

Bitcoin's decentralized nature aligns with the vision of a decentralized internet, often referred to as Web3.0. Bitcoin's blockchain technology can serve as the foundation for decentralized applications (dApps) and decentralized autonomous organizations (DAOs). These applications aim to eliminate reliance on centralized entities, promote data ownership and privacy, and create a more user-centric and democratic internet ecosystem.

Intellectual Property and Copyright Protection:

The blockchain technology behind Bitcoin has the potential to revolutionize intellectual property (IP) protection and copyright enforcement. By timestamping and storing digital assets on the blockchain, creators can establish proof of ownership and protect their intellectual property rights. Smart contracts built on blockchain can facilitate the automated licensing and royalty payments, ensuring fair compensation and reducing infringement issues.

Crowdfunding and Tokenization:

Bitcoin's blockchain technology has paved the way for innovative fundraising models, such as Initial Coin Offerings (ICOs) and tokenization. Startups and projects can issue their own digital tokens or coins, representing ownership or utility, and raise funds from a global pool of investors. This democratizes access to capital and opens up investment opportunities to a broader audience. Tokenization also enables the fractional ownership of assets, such as real estate or artwork, making them more liquid and accessible to a wider range of investors.

Secure Digital Voting:

Bitcoin's blockchain provides the potential for secure and transparent digital voting systems. The immutability and tamper-resistant nature of blockchain technology can ensure the integrity of voting records and prevent fraudulent activities. By leveraging Bitcoin's decentralized architecture, digital voting systems can enhance transparency, reduce the potential for voter fraud, and increase participation in democratic processes.

Financial Inclusion and Banking the Unbanked:

Bitcoin has the potential to promote financial inclusion by providing individuals without access to traditional banking services with a means to participate in the global economy. Bitcoin wallets can be accessed with just a smartphone and an internet connection, enabling the unbanked to store, send, and receive value securely. This can empower individuals in underserved regions, granting them access to basic financial services and the opportunity to participate in economic activities.

Innovation and Exploration:

Bitcoin's influence goes beyond these specific use cases. Its underlying blockchain technology has inspired a wave of innovation and exploration across industries. Developers and entrepreneurs continue to discover new ways to leverage the decentralized, transparent, and secure nature of Bitcoin's blockchain to create innovative solutions that address existing challenges and unlock new possibilities.

So, Bitcoin's potential extends far beyond its use as a currency. From facilitating cross-border payments and supply chain management to enabling decentralized internet and digital identity verification, Bitcoin's underlying blockchain technology has opened doors to countless applications. As the cryptocurrency and blockchain ecosystem evolves, we can expect further exploration and innovation, with Bitcoin serving as a catalyst for transformative change across industries. By embracing Bitcoin's capabilities beyond currency, we can unlock the true potential of this groundbreaking technology and shape a more decentralized, transparent, and inclusive future.

Chapter 83: Satoshi's Intellectual Legacy

Satoshi Nakamoto, the enigmatic creator of Bitcoin, not only introduced the world to a revolutionary digital currency but also left behind a profound intellectual legacy. Satoshi's groundbreaking ideas and innovative solutions have shaped the landscape of cryptocurrencies, blockchain technology, and decentralized systems. In this chapter, we explore the key aspects of Satoshi's intellectual legacy, including his contributions to computer science, cryptography, economics, and governance.

Innovative Use of Blockchain Technology:

Satoshi Nakamoto's most significant intellectual contribution was the introduction of blockchain technology through the Bitcoin white paper. Satoshi's innovative combination of cryptographic techniques, distributed consensus, and decentralized architecture provided a solution to the long-standing double-spending problem in digital currencies. The blockchain, as conceptualized by Satoshi, enables a secure and transparent ledger that eliminates the need for intermediaries and allows for peer-to-peer transactions.

Distributed Consensus and Proof of Work:

Satoshi's intellectual legacy includes the concept of distributed consensus and the introduction of the proof-of-work consensus mechanism. By requiring participants in the Bitcoin network to solve computationally intensive puzzles to validate transactions and add blocks to the blockchain, Satoshi ensured the security and integrity of the network. The proof-of-work consensus mechanism laid the foundation for the decentralized governance of cryptocurrencies and has since been adopted by many other blockchain projects.

Cryptography and Security:

Satoshi's understanding and application of cryptographic principles played a crucial role in the development of Bitcoin. The use of public-key cryptography to secure transactions and wallets, along with the integration of cryptographic hashes to maintain the integrity of the blockchain, demonstrated Satoshi's deep understanding of cryptographic protocols. This intellectual contribution has influenced not only the field of cryptocurrencies but also the broader discipline of computer security.

Economic Theory and Incentive Structures:

Satoshi Nakamoto's intellectual legacy extends beyond technology and cryptography to the realm of economic theory. Bitcoin's design incorporates an innovative incentive structure that aligns the interests of network participants and ensures the security and stability of the network. Satoshi's understanding of economic principles, such as scarcity, game theory, and the role of incentives, laid the groundwork for the emergence of cryptocurrency mining and the economic model behind Bitcoin.

Decentralization and Trustless Systems:

Satoshi's intellectual legacy is rooted in his deep skepticism of centralized institutions and his belief in the power of decentralized, trustless systems. Bitcoin's design embodies these principles, enabling individuals to transact directly with one another without relying on intermediaries or trusted third parties. Satoshi's vision of a decentralized and transparent financial system challenged the conventional wisdom and opened up new possibilities for trust and collaboration in the digital age.

Open-Source Development and Collaboration:

Satoshi's intellectual legacy also encompasses the principles of open-source development and collaborative innovation. By releasing the Bitcoin code as open-source software, Satoshi fostered a culture of transparency, peer review, and community involvement. This approach allowed developers worldwide to contribute to the improvement and evolution of the Bitcoin protocol, leading to the emergence of a vibrant and diverse ecosystem of cryptocurrencies and blockchain projects.

Governance and Consensus Building:

While Satoshi disappeared from the public eye, his intellectual legacy influenced the ongoing discussions around governance and consensus building in decentralized systems. Satoshi's emphasis on consensus through the proof-of-work mechanism inspired further research into alternative consensus algorithms, such as proof-of-stake and delegated proof-of-stake. The question of how to govern and evolve decentralized systems remains a topic of debate and exploration in the cryptocurrency and blockchain communities.

Inspiration for Future Innovators:

Satoshi Nakamoto's intellectual legacy continues to inspire and motivate future innovators, researchers, and entrepreneurs. His creation of Bitcoin and the underlying blockchain technology served as a catalyst for a wave of technological and social transformation. The principles of decentralization, transparency, and trust that Satoshi championed have sparked a global movement toward reimagining traditional systems and exploring the potential of blockchain technology across various industries.

Impact on Society and Finance:

Satoshi's intellectual legacy extends beyond the realm of technology and has profound implications for society and finance. Bitcoin and other cryptocurrencies have challenged traditional financial systems, opening up possibilities for financial inclusion, reducing barriers to entry, and enabling more efficient cross-border transactions. The decentralized nature of blockchain technology has the potential to empower individuals, foster trust, and reshape the balance of power in various aspects of society.

Unveiling Satoshi's True Identity:

One aspect of Satoshi's intellectual legacy that remains a subject of fascination and speculation is the mystery surrounding his true identity. While the identity of Satoshi Nakamoto remains unknown, the impact of his creation and ideas continue to shape the world of cryptocurrencies and blockchain technology. The intrigue surrounding Satoshi's identity serves as a testament to his intellectual legacy and the enduring influence of his work.

So, Satoshi Nakamoto's intellectual legacy is far-reaching and multifaceted. His contributions to computer science, cryptography, economics, and governance have laid the foundation for the development of cryptocurrencies and blockchain technology. Satoshi's ideas and innovations continue to drive research, inspire new projects, and challenge traditional paradigms. As the cryptocurrency and blockchain ecosystem evolves, Satoshi's intellectual legacy serves as a guiding light, reminding us of the transformative power of decentralized, transparent, and trustless systems in shaping the future of finance, technology, and society as a whole. While the true identity of Satoshi Nakamoto may remain a mystery, his ideas and intellectual contributions will continue to shape the trajectory of cryptocurrencies and blockchain technology for years to come.

Chapter 84: The Role of Bitcoin in Political Campaigns

In recent years, Bitcoin has made its way into the realm of political campaigns, offering new possibilities for fundraising, transparency, and civic engagement. The decentralized and borderless nature of Bitcoin has attracted the attention of political candidates and activists seeking alternative methods to finance their campaigns, engage with supporters, and promote their political agendas. In this chapter, we explore the role of Bitcoin in political campaigns, examining its impact on fundraising, transparency, and the broader democratic process.

Fundraising and Donations:

Bitcoin has emerged as a unique tool for political fundraising, providing candidates with an additional avenue to receive contributions. Accepting Bitcoin donations allows candidates to tap into a global network of supporters who believe in their political ideologies, regardless of geographical limitations. By leveraging Bitcoin's decentralized infrastructure, candidates can receive donations directly, without the need for intermediaries or traditional banking systems. This offers a level of autonomy and financial inclusivity, particularly for candidates with limited access to traditional fundraising channels.

Transparency and Accountability:

Bitcoin's underlying blockchain technology offers the potential for increased transparency and accountability in political campaigns. Donations made in Bitcoin are recorded on the public blockchain, allowing for greater visibility and traceability. This transparency can help mitigate concerns of illicit campaign financing and foster trust between candidates and their supporters. Furthermore, smart contracts built on blockchain can automate the reporting and disclosure of campaign contributions, ensuring compliance with campaign finance regulations.

Financial Inclusion and Access:

Bitcoin's ability to facilitate cross-border transactions with minimal fees and without relying on traditional financial institutions makes it an attractive option for political campaigns aiming to reach a broader audience. Bitcoin donations can enable individuals from different countries to support candidates and causes they align with, overcoming limitations imposed by national borders and currency exchange barriers. This fosters a sense of inclusivity and allows for greater participation in the political process.

Engagement and Grassroots Movements:

Bitcoin's integration with social media and online platforms has facilitated the growth of grassroots movements and political activism. Cryptocurrency enthusiasts and supporters can easily share information about candidates and their policy positions, promote fundraising efforts, and mobilize communities through various online channels. Bitcoin's ease of use and accessibility contribute to the democratization of political engagement, allowing individuals to participate and support candidates regardless of their location or financial status.

Resistance to Censorship and Interference:

Bitcoin's decentralized nature provides a level of resistance to censorship and interference that can be particularly valuable in politically sensitive environments. In regions where freedom of speech and political activities are restricted, Bitcoin can serve as a tool for individuals to support political causes without fear of reprisal. Cryptocurrency wallets and transactions can be created and conducted pseudonymously, offering a degree of privacy and protection for donors and activists.

Exploring Campaign Financing Alternatives:

Bitcoin's emergence in political campaigns has sparked discussions about alternative campaign financing models. Some candidates and activists are exploring the concept of decentralized autonomous organizations (DAOs) or token-based systems, where supporters hold tokens that represent a stake in the campaign's success. These innovative models can reshape traditional campaign financing and foster a greater sense of ownership and participation among supporters.

Regulatory Challenges and Compliance:

While Bitcoin offers unique opportunities for political campaigns, it also presents regulatory challenges. Campaign finance regulations vary across jurisdictions, and cryptocurrency donations may raise questions regarding disclosure requirements, contribution limits, and the source of funds. Candidates and campaign teams must navigate these complexities and work closely with legal and regulatory experts to ensure compliance with existing laws.

Public Perception and Trust:

The integration of Bitcoin into political campaigns also raises questions of public perception and trust. Cryptocurrencies, including Bitcoin, have often been associated with volatility and criminal activities. Candidates accepting Bitcoin donations must address these concerns by educating the public about the technology, emphasizing transparency, and ensuring robust security measures to protect the integrity of the campaign's financial operations.

Future Implications and Innovation:

As Bitcoin continues to evolve, so too will its role in political campaigns. The integration of additional layers of privacy, scalability, and smart contract functionality may further enhance the potential of Bitcoin in political fundraising and transparency. Additionally, the exploration of decentralized voting systems built on blockchain technology could revolutionize the democratic process by enabling secure, transparent, and tamper-resistant elections.

So, Bitcoin's entry into the realm of political campaigns has introduced new possibilities for fundraising, transparency, and civic engagement. The decentralized nature of Bitcoin and its underlying blockchain technology offer candidates and activists unique opportunities to connect with supporters, engage in fundraising, and promote their political agendas. However, challenges related to regulation, public perception, and trust must be carefully navigated. As Bitcoin and the cryptocurrency ecosystem continue to evolve, the role of Bitcoin in political campaigns will likely continue to expand, reshaping the way campaigns are financed, conducted, and perceived in the democratic process.

Chapter 85: The Battle for Bitcoin's Soul

Bitcoin, as a decentralized digital currency, has captured the imagination of millions worldwide. However, the path forward for Bitcoin is not without its challenges and debates. Over the years, a battle has emerged within the Bitcoin community, centered around differing visions, philosophies, and technical approaches. In this chapter, we delve into the battle for Bitcoin's soul, exploring the key controversies and discussions that have shaped the trajectory of this groundbreaking cryptocurrency.

Scaling Debate:

One of the most significant battles in Bitcoin's history revolved around the issue of scaling the network to accommodate a larger number of transactions. This debate primarily focused on two opposing approaches: increasing the block size versus implementing off-chain scaling solutions like the Lightning Network. Advocates for larger blocks argued for immediate scalability, while proponents of off-chain solutions emphasized the importance of preserving decentralization and security. This debate sparked passionate discussions within the community and led to the creation of alternative cryptocurrencies like Bitcoin Cash.

Governance and Decision-Making:

Another contentious aspect of the battle for Bitcoin's soul revolves around governance and decision-making processes. Bitcoin's decentralized nature poses challenges when it comes to making important decisions about protocol upgrades and changes. Various proposals, such as the implementation of soft forks or hard forks, have generated heated discussions about who should have the power to decide the future direction of Bitcoin. The question of how to achieve consensus and balance the interests of different stakeholders remains a topic of ongoing debate.

Privacy and Anonymity:

Privacy has been a significant point of contention within the Bitcoin community. Some argue that Bitcoin's pseudonymous nature is sufficient to protect user privacy, while others advocate for additional privacy-enhancing technologies. The battle between privacy-focused coins and those emphasizing regulatory compliance highlights differing viewpoints on the balance between privacy and transparency. Solutions like confidential transactions and privacy-oriented wallets have been proposed to address concerns surrounding privacy and anonymity.

Decentralization and Mining Centralization:

The issue of mining centralization has sparked debates regarding the fundamental principles of decentralization. As the mining industry consolidated and large-scale mining operations emerged, concerns were raised about the concentration of power and potential threats to the network's security and decentralization. Discussions around mining algorithms, consensus mechanisms, and the distribution of mining rewards have sought to address these concerns and preserve Bitcoin's core principles.

Altcoins and Competition:

Bitcoin's dominance as the first cryptocurrency has faced challenges from a multitude of alternative coins, commonly referred to as altcoins. The battle between Bitcoin and altcoins revolves around factors such as technological advancements, governance models, and community support. Supporters of Bitcoin argue for its robustness, network effects, and proven track record, while proponents of altcoins highlight their unique features and potential to address specific use cases. This ongoing competition drives innovation and pushes the boundaries of what is possible in the world of digital currencies.

Financialization and Institutional Adoption:

The increasing interest and involvement of financial institutions and large corporations in the Bitcoin ecosystem have sparked debates about the potential impact on decentralization and the soul of Bitcoin. Some argue that institutional adoption brings legitimacy, liquidity, and financial infrastructure to the space, while others express concerns about potential centralization and the loss of the original vision of a peer-to-peer digital currency. Discussions surrounding custody, regulation, and the interaction between traditional finance and Bitcoin continue to shape the narrative and direction of the cryptocurrency.

Environmental Concerns:

The environmental impact of Bitcoin mining has become a topic of intense debate in recent years. Critics argue that Bitcoin's energy consumption contributes to carbon emissions and exacerbates climate change. The battle for Bitcoin's soul includes discussions about the importance of sustainability and the exploration of alternative mining methods and energy sources. Solutions such as renewable energy-powered mining and the development of more energy-efficient consensus algorithms are being explored to address these concerns.

Socioeconomic Impact:

Bitcoin's potential socioeconomic impact has also been a subject of debate. Some argue that Bitcoin has the potential to empower individuals, reduce financial inequalities, and provide financial inclusion for the unbanked. Others express concerns about potential wealth concentration and the impact on traditional financial systems. The battle for Bitcoin's soul encompasses discussions about the social and economic implications of a decentralized digital currency and the responsibility of the community to address these challenges.

So, the battle for Bitcoin's soul is a testament to the vibrant and diverse nature of the cryptocurrency community. The controversies and debates surrounding scaling, governance, privacy, decentralization, competition, financialization, environmental concerns, and socioeconomic impact reflect the ongoing quest to define and shape the future of Bitcoin. While differing perspectives and visions may create tension, they also foster innovation, critical thinking, and the evolution of the cryptocurrency ecosystem. Ultimately, the battle for Bitcoin's soul is a reflection of the community's collective commitment to realizing the full potential of this transformative technology while preserving its fundamental principles of decentralization, security, and user empowerment.

Chapter 86: Satoshi's Impact on Online Fundraising

Satoshi Nakamoto, the mysterious creator of Bitcoin, has had a profound impact on various aspects of the digital world, including online fundraising. Satoshi's invention of Bitcoin and the underlying blockchain technology has revolutionized the way individuals and organizations raise funds, enabling new opportunities for financial inclusivity, transparency, and global participation. In this chapter, we explore Satoshi's impact on online fundraising, examining the key advancements, challenges, and transformative potential brought forth by his creation.

Democratization of Fundraising:

One of the most significant contributions of Satoshi Nakamoto to online fundraising is the democratization of the process. Traditional fundraising often involved complex intermediaries, restrictive regulations, and limited access to financial resources. With Bitcoin, anyone with an internet connection can create a digital wallet and receive direct donations from individuals worldwide. This has empowered individuals, grassroots movements, and charitable organizations to engage in fundraising efforts without the need for costly infrastructure or cumbersome bureaucracy.

Global Reach and Financial Inclusion:

Satoshi's creation of Bitcoin has unlocked new possibilities for online fundraising on a global scale. By removing barriers such as geographical limitations, currency exchange fees, and cross-border transaction delays, Bitcoin enables individuals from different countries to contribute to causes they believe in, regardless of their location or traditional banking access. This has facilitated financial inclusion and expanded the donor pool, enabling individuals with limited resources to participate in fundraising initiatives.

Transparency and Accountability:

Transparency and accountability have long been concerns in traditional fundraising. Satoshi's invention of the blockchain, a transparent and immutable ledger, has introduced a new level of transparency to online fundraising. Every Bitcoin transaction is recorded on the blockchain, allowing donors to verify the movement of funds, and ensuring greater accountability for how funds are utilized. This transparency helps build trust between fundraisers and donors, fostering a culture of openness and responsible stewardship.

Reduced Transaction Costs:

Traditional payment methods often involve significant transaction fees, particularly for cross-border transactions. Bitcoin, on the other hand, offers the potential for significantly lower transaction costs. By bypassing traditional financial intermediaries, Bitcoin eliminates the need for costly banking infrastructure and associated fees. This reduction in transaction costs makes it more economically viable for fundraisers to collect and allocate funds, ensuring that a larger portion of the donated amount goes directly toward the intended cause.

Innovative Fundraising Models:

Satoshi's impact on online fundraising extends beyond the traditional model of soliciting direct donations. The invention of smart contracts on blockchain platforms has opened up new avenues for innovative fundraising models, such as Initial Coin Offerings (ICOs) and token-based crowdfunding. These models enable projects and organizations to issue their own tokens, representing a stake in the project, and raise funds by selling these tokens to interested supporters. This approach allows for greater flexibility, participation, and potential return on investment for contributors.

Microtransactions and Micropayments:

Bitcoin's divisibility into smaller units, such as satoshis (the smallest unit of Bitcoin), has facilitated microtransactions and micropayments. This has implications for online fundraising, as it allows for the collection of small donations that would otherwise be impractical using traditional payment methods. Microtransactions enable individuals to contribute even the smallest amounts to causes they care about, fostering a sense of collective impact and participation.

Decentralized Autonomous Organizations (DAOs):

Satoshi's impact on online fundraising can also be seen in the emergence of Decentralized Autonomous Organizations (DAOs). DAOs are organizations governed by smart contracts and operate on blockchain platforms. They enable participants to pool their resources and make collective decisions on fund allocation and project governance. This decentralized approach to fundraising and decision-making has the potential to disrupt traditional organizational structures and empower communities to support causes directly.

Regulatory and Compliance Challenges:

While Satoshi's creation of Bitcoin has opened up new possibilities for online fundraising, it has also raised regulatory and compliance challenges. The decentralized and pseudonymous nature of Bitcoin transactions has prompted regulatory bodies to develop guidelines to address concerns related to money laundering, terrorist financing, and fraud. Fundraisers must navigate these evolving regulatory landscapes and work in collaboration with legal experts to ensure compliance while maximizing the potential of Bitcoin for fundraising efforts.

Security and Trust:

One of the critical considerations in online fundraising is ensuring the security of donated funds and maintaining trust between fundraisers and donors. Satoshi's impact on online fundraising includes advancements in security measures, such as multi-signature wallets, cold storage solutions, and the use of cryptographic techniques. These measures enhance the security of donated funds, protect against theft or unauthorized access, and instill confidence in donors, further strengthening the online fundraising ecosystem.

Future Potential and Innovation:

Satoshi Nakamoto's impact on online fundraising is still unfolding, with the potential for further innovation and transformative advancements. As blockchain technology evolves, new layers of privacy, scalability, and smart contract functionality can be integrated into online fundraising platforms. Additionally, advancements in decentralized identity solutions and reputation systems may further enhance trust and enable more personalized donor experiences.

So, Satoshi Nakamoto's creation of Bitcoin has had a significant impact on online fundraising, revolutionizing the way individuals and organizations engage in fundraising initiatives. His vision of a decentralized, transparent, and inclusive financial system has opened up new avenues for financial empowerment, global participation, and innovative fundraising models. While challenges related to regulation, security, and trust persist, Satoshi's legacy continues to inspire individuals and organizations to explore the transformative potential of online fundraising. As the technology evolves and the ecosystem matures, the battle for Satoshi's soul will continue to shape the future of online fundraising, paving the way for a more accessible, transparent, and inclusive financial landscape. With each donation made, each cause supported, and each innovative project funded, Satoshi's impact on online fundraising grows, leaving a lasting legacy that transcends boundaries and empowers individuals to make a positive impact in the world.

Chapter 87: The Connection Between Bitcoin and Cybercrime

Bitcoin, the pioneering cryptocurrency created by Satoshi Nakamoto, has been both celebrated for its innovative technology and criticized for its association with cybercrime. While Bitcoin itself is a neutral and decentralized digital currency, its characteristics have made it attractive to cybercriminals seeking anonymity, financial gain, and illicit activities. In this chapter, we explore the connection between Bitcoin and cybercrime, shedding light on the challenges, misconceptions, and efforts to mitigate illicit use within the cryptocurrency ecosystem.

Pseudonymity and Anonymity:

Bitcoin's pseudonymous nature, which allows users to transact without revealing their real-world identities, has been one of the key features that attracted cybercriminals. It provides a level of privacy that traditional financial systems often lack. However, it is crucial to note that Bitcoin transactions are recorded on a public ledger called the blockchain, making them traceable and auditable. While pseudonymity can offer some level of privacy, it does not guarantee complete anonymity, as sophisticated forensic techniques can be employed to track and identify suspicious activities.

Darknet Marketplaces:

One of the most prominent associations between Bitcoin and cybercrime is its use in darknet marketplaces. These underground online platforms facilitate the buying and selling of illegal goods and services, including drugs, counterfeit documents, stolen data, and hacking tools. Bitcoin's decentralized nature and relative ease of use make it an appealing choice for conducting illicit transactions within these hidden corners of the internet. However, it is important to highlight that the majority of Bitcoin transactions are conducted for legitimate purposes, and the use of Bitcoin in darknet marketplaces represents only a small fraction of its overall usage.

Ransomware Attacks:

Ransomware attacks, where malicious actors encrypt victims' data and demand a ransom payment in Bitcoin, have become increasingly prevalent in recent years. Bitcoin's decentralized and censorship-resistant nature makes it an ideal choice for ransomware payments, as it allows cybercriminals to receive funds without being easily traced or shut down by authorities. It is important to note that Bitcoin itself is not responsible for ransomware attacks; rather, it is the misuse of the cryptocurrency by criminals that enables these activities. Efforts are being made by law enforcement agencies and cybersecurity experts to combat ransomware attacks and raise awareness about prevention and mitigation strategies.

Money Laundering:

Bitcoin has also been associated with money laundering, where illicit funds are concealed and transformed into seemingly legitimate funds through a series of transactions. Its pseudonymous nature, coupled with the ability to transfer funds globally and quickly, has been exploited by money launderers. However, it is important to recognize that traditional financial systems have long been used for money laundering as well, and regulations and compliance measures are being developed to address these concerns within the cryptocurrency ecosystem.

Regulatory Efforts and Compliance:

Governments and regulatory bodies have recognized the need to address the potential misuse of cryptocurrencies for illicit activities. Various jurisdictions have implemented Know Your Customer (KYC) and Anti-Money Laundering (AML) regulations for cryptocurrency exchanges and service providers. These measures aim to increase transparency and accountability within the ecosystem, making it more challenging for cybercriminals to exploit the system for illicit gains. Compliance with regulatory requirements is increasingly becoming the norm for legitimate cryptocurrency businesses, fostering a more responsible and secure environment.

Blockchain Analytics and Law Enforcement:

Law enforcement agencies and blockchain analytics firms have developed sophisticated tools and techniques to track and analyze Bitcoin transactions for investigative purposes. By leveraging the transparent nature of the blockchain, these tools can help identify patterns, trace funds, and uncover illicit activities. Such efforts have led to successful prosecutions of cybercriminals involved in various forms of cryptocurrency-related crimes. Collaboration between the cryptocurrency community, law enforcement agencies, and regulatory bodies is vital in combating cybercrime and ensuring the integrity of the ecosystem.

Education and Awareness:

Promoting education and awareness about the risks and precautions associated with cryptocurrencies is essential for combating cybercrime. Individuals and organizations should be educated about best practices for securing their Bitcoin wallets, recognizing phishing attempts, and understanding the potential consequences of engaging in illicit activities. By fostering a culture of responsible cryptocurrency use and encouraging ethical practices, the broader community can collectively work towards minimizing the negative impact of cybercrime.

Innovation and Security Solutions:

In response to the challenges posed by cybercrime, the cryptocurrency community is continuously innovating to enhance security and address vulnerabilities. Advanced cryptographic techniques, multi-signature wallets, and hardware wallets are being developed to provide users with more robust protection against hacking and fraud. Additionally, collaborations between industry players, researchers, and cybersecurity experts aim to identify and mitigate potential risks within the ecosystem, strengthening its resilience against cybercriminal activities.

So, while Bitcoin has been associated with cybercrime, it is important to understand that the cryptocurrency itself is not inherently illicit. Rather, it is the misuse and exploitation of its features by cybercriminals that contribute to its connection with illegal activities. Efforts are being made to increase regulation, enhance security measures, and raise awareness to address these challenges. By fostering responsible use, collaboration between stakeholders, and leveraging technological advancements, the cryptocurrency ecosystem can strive towards a safer and more trusted environment, dissociating itself from the negative associations with cybercrime.

Chapter 88: The Rise of Stablecoins and Satoshi's Perspective

In recent years, the cryptocurrency market has witnessed the emergence and growing popularity of stablecoins, a type of digital asset designed to minimize price volatility by pegging their value to external assets such as fiat currencies or commodities. Stablecoins have garnered attention from individuals, businesses, and even governments due to their potential to provide stability, facilitate seamless transactions, and bridge the gap between traditional financial systems and the decentralized world of cryptocurrencies. In this chapter, we explore the rise of stablecoins and reflect on Satoshi Nakamoto's perspective on this innovative development.

Stability in a Volatile Market:

One of the main driving forces behind the rise of stablecoins is the need for stability in the volatile cryptocurrency market. While Bitcoin and other cryptocurrencies have experienced significant price fluctuations, stablecoins aim to provide a reliable store of value by maintaining a stable price. This stability makes stablecoins more appealing for day-to-day transactions, long-term savings, and even as a unit of account.

Satoshi's Vision of a Digital Cash System:

Satoshi Nakamoto's vision, as outlined in the Bitcoin white paper, was to create a decentralized digital cash system that could enable peer-to-peer transactions without the need for intermediaries. While Bitcoin itself does not provide price stability, Satoshi's vision for a frictionless and efficient payment system resonates with the goals of stablecoins. Stablecoins aim to combine the benefits of cryptocurrencies, such as fast and borderless transactions, with the stability of traditional fiat currencies.

Enabling Seamless Transactions:

Stablecoins have the potential to facilitate seamless transactions within the cryptocurrency ecosystem. By pegging their value to a stable external asset, stablecoins provide a familiar and easy-to-understand unit of value. This enables individuals and businesses to transact without worrying about the value fluctuation that is commonly associated with cryptocurrencies. Stablecoins also offer the advantage of fast and inexpensive cross-border transactions, making them an attractive alternative to traditional remittance systems.

Bridging the Gap Between Fiat and Cryptocurrencies:

Stablecoins serve as a bridge between the traditional financial system and the world of cryptocurrencies. By pegging their value to a fiat currency, stablecoins provide a familiar and accessible entry point for individuals who may be hesitant to venture into the volatile cryptocurrency market. This bridge has the potential to increase adoption and acceptance of cryptocurrencies on a global scale, as stablecoins provide a more stable and user-friendly experience.

Transparency and Auditability:

Stablecoins built on blockchain technology inherit the transparency and auditability features of their underlying blockchain. This transparency allows users to verify the supply, collateralization, and transactions associated with stablecoins. In line with Satoshi's vision of a transparent financial system, stablecoins contribute to a more accountable and trustworthy ecosystem.

Potential Regulatory Considerations:

As stablecoins gain popularity, regulators around the world are paying close attention to their development. Regulatory frameworks are being established to ensure compliance, consumer protection, and financial stability. While Satoshi Nakamoto did not directly address stablecoins in his writings, his emphasis on decentralization and individual empowerment may imply support for innovative financial instruments that promote financial inclusion, provided they align with the core principles of transparency and security.

Challenges and Risks:

While stablecoins offer numerous benefits, they also come with challenges and risks. The most significant challenge lies in maintaining the stability of the pegged value. Ensuring that the stablecoin is fully backed by the pegged asset, maintaining proper reserves, and implementing robust governance mechanisms are critical to prevent instability or loss of trust. Additionally, the centralized nature of some stablecoins introduces counterparty risk, as users rely on the stability and integrity of the issuing entity.

Evolution and Diversification:

Stablecoins are evolving rapidly, with various types and models entering the market. While some stablecoins are fully collateralized with traditional assets, others leverage algorithmic mechanisms or a combination of both. This diversification provides users with choices that suit their specific needs and preferences. Satoshi Nakamoto's emphasis on innovation and experimentation aligns with the evolving nature of stablecoins, as they continue to iterate and improve their design.

Integration with Decentralized Finance (DeFi):

The rise of stablecoins has significantly contributed to the growth of the Decentralized Finance (DeFi) ecosystem. Stablecoins serve as a cornerstone of many DeFi protocols, enabling activities such as lending, borrowing, yield farming, and decentralized exchanges. This integration expands the possibilities of decentralized finance, empowering individuals with more control over their financial assets and fostering a permissionless and inclusive financial system.

So, the rise of stablecoins represents a significant development in the cryptocurrency space, aligning with Satoshi Nakamoto's vision of a decentralized and efficient financial system. While Satoshi did not explicitly address stablecoins, the underlying principles of stability, transparency, and empowerment resonate with the goals of stablecoin projects. As stablecoins continue to evolve and gain acceptance, their impact on global finance and the cryptocurrency ecosystem is likely to grow. It will be essential for stakeholders, including regulators, users, and issuers, to navigate the challenges and risks associated with stablecoins while embracing the potential benefits they offer in the pursuit of Satoshi's vision of a more inclusive and decentralized financial future.

Chapter 89: The Socioeconomic Implications of Bitcoin

Bitcoin, the world's first decentralized digital currency, has had a profound impact on the socioeconomic landscape since its inception. Its disruptive nature, unique features, and growing adoption have raised important questions and sparked debates regarding its implications for various aspects of society. In this chapter, we delve into the socioeconomic implications of Bitcoin, exploring both the opportunities and challenges it presents.

Financial Inclusion:

Bitcoin has the potential to promote financial inclusion by providing access to financial services for the unbanked and underbanked populations. With a smartphone and internet connection, individuals can participate in the Bitcoin network, store value, and engage in peer-to-peer transactions. By bypassing traditional banking systems and their associated barriers, Bitcoin offers individuals in underserved regions an opportunity to participate in the global economy.

Empowering Individuals:

Bitcoin's decentralized nature empowers individuals by giving them full control over their funds. Users can manage their own private keys and transact without intermediaries, fostering financial sovereignty and reducing reliance on centralized institutions. This empowerment aligns with Satoshi Nakamoto's vision of a peer-to-peer electronic cash system, where individuals have direct control over their financial transactions.

Remittances:

Bitcoin has the potential to revolutionize cross-border remittances, which are often costly and time-consuming. By enabling fast and low-cost transfers, Bitcoin can significantly reduce transaction fees and facilitate seamless remittances. This has the potential to benefit individuals and families who rely on remittances for their livelihoods, particularly in developing countries.

Economic Stability:

Bitcoin's limited supply and predetermined issuance schedule provide an alternative to traditional monetary systems, which are subject to inflation and government intervention. Bitcoin's deflationary nature can potentially act as a hedge against inflation and provide stability in regions with volatile or unstable currencies. However, it is important to note that Bitcoin's price volatility can also pose risks and challenges in terms of financial planning and economic stability.

Wealth Redistribution:

Bitcoin's decentralized nature challenges traditional models of wealth distribution. As individuals have the ability to accumulate and hold Bitcoin, it can potentially contribute to wealth concentration. However, Bitcoin also provides opportunities for individuals to accumulate wealth through mining, investing, or entrepreneurial activities. The implications for wealth redistribution are complex and can vary depending on individual circumstances and market dynamics.

Privacy and Surveillance:

Bitcoin offers a degree of privacy in transactions, allowing individuals to conduct transactions without revealing their real-world identities. This can provide protection against financial surveillance and censorship. However, concerns have been raised regarding the potential use of Bitcoin for illicit activities. Striking a balance between privacy and compliance with regulations remains a challenge for the cryptocurrency ecosystem.

Environmental Impact:

Bitcoin mining, the process by which new bitcoins are created and transactions are verified, requires significant computational power and energy consumption. The environmental impact of Bitcoin mining has been a subject of debate, particularly in relation to the energy sources used and the carbon footprint associated with the process. Efforts are being made to increase the use of renewable energy and develop more energy-efficient mining technologies to mitigate this impact.

Regulatory Challenges:

Bitcoin's decentralized nature presents regulatory challenges for governments and policymakers. The absence of a central authority makes it difficult to enforce traditional financial regulations. Governments around the world are grappling with the task of striking a balance between protecting consumers, preventing illicit activities, and fostering innovation within the cryptocurrency space. Regulatory frameworks continue to evolve to address these challenges.

Technological Innovation:

Bitcoin's underlying technology, blockchain, has sparked innovation and paved the way for the development of numerous applications beyond digital currency. Blockchain technology has the potential to revolutionize various industries, including supply chain management, voting systems, and identity verification. The socioeconomic implications of this broader blockchain innovation extend beyond Bitcoin itself.

Investor Speculation:

Bitcoin's price volatility has attracted investors seeking high returns. While this has led to significant financial gains for some, it has also raised concerns about market manipulation and the potential for speculative bubbles. The impact of investor speculation on socioeconomic dynamics, wealth inequality, and market stability is an ongoing area of study and discussion.

So, Bitcoin's socioeconomic implications are wide-ranging and multifaceted. It offers opportunities for financial inclusion, empowerment, and innovation, while also presenting challenges related to regulation, wealth distribution, and environmental impact. As Bitcoin and the broader cryptocurrency ecosystem continue to evolve, it is essential for stakeholders, including governments, businesses, and individuals, to actively engage in constructive dialogue, address challenges, and harness the potential benefits for a more inclusive and sustainable socioeconomic future.

Chapter 90: Satoshi's Philosophy on Financial Empowerment

Satoshi Nakamoto, the pseudonymous creator of Bitcoin, has left behind a remarkable legacy that goes beyond the technology itself. Satoshi's writings and actions reflect a philosophy centered around the empowerment of individuals through financial freedom and independence. In this chapter, we delve into Satoshi's philosophy on financial empowerment, exploring the principles and ideas that underpin this vision.

Democratizing Finance:

Satoshi Nakamoto believed in the democratization of finance, challenging the existing centralized financial systems that disproportionately favor a select few. By introducing Bitcoin, Satoshi aimed to create a decentralized and inclusive financial ecosystem that enables anyone with an internet connection to participate, irrespective of their background or geographic location. Satoshi's philosophy embraces the idea that individuals should have direct control over their financial affairs, free from the limitations and gatekeepers of traditional financial institutions.

Peer-to-Peer Transactions:

At the core of Satoshi's philosophy is the concept of peer-to-peer transactions. Satoshi envisioned a system where individuals could transact directly with one another, without the need for intermediaries such as banks or payment processors. This vision aligns with the principles of decentralization, trustlessness, and privacy. By removing intermediaries, Satoshi aimed to reduce transaction costs, increase efficiency, and promote financial autonomy.

Financial Privacy:

Satoshi emphasized the importance of financial privacy as a fundamental right. Traditional financial systems often require individuals to divulge sensitive personal information when conducting transactions, compromising privacy, and exposing individuals to potential risks. Bitcoin, with its pseudonymous nature, offers individuals the ability to transact without revealing their real-world identities. Satoshi's philosophy recognizes the need for privacy as a means of protecting individuals' financial security and autonomy.

Individual Empowerment:

Satoshi's philosophy centers around empowering individuals to take control of their financial destinies. By giving individuals the ability to store and transfer value independently, Satoshi aimed to eliminate the need for reliance on centralized authorities. This empowerment extends to economic decision-making, enabling individuals to determine the fate of their financial assets without external interference. Satoshi's philosophy embraces the idea that financial decisions should be in the hands of the individuals themselves, rather than being dictated by centralized institutions or governments.

Financial Inclusion:

Satoshi recognized the importance of financial inclusion and sought to address the issue of unbanked and underbanked populations. Traditional banking systems often have high barriers to entry, leaving millions of people around the world without access to basic financial services. Bitcoin provides an opportunity for financial inclusion, as individuals can participate in the network with a smartphone and internet connection, without the need for a traditional bank account. Satoshi's philosophy envisions a world where everyone has equal access to financial services and can participate in the global economy on their own terms.

Resistance to Censorship and Control:

Satoshi's philosophy opposes censorship and control over individuals' financial transactions. Traditional financial systems are susceptible to censorship, where transactions can be halted, or funds frozen at the discretion of centralized authorities. Bitcoin, with its decentralized nature and cryptographic security, resists such censorship attempts. Satoshi believed that individuals should have the freedom to engage in financial transactions without fear of external interference or arbitrary restrictions.

Financial Education and Responsibility:

Satoshi's philosophy emphasizes the importance of financial education and responsibility. Bitcoin empowers individuals to take full control over their funds, but with that power comes the responsibility to understand and manage their finances effectively. Satoshi recognized the need for individuals to educate themselves about the technology, security best practices, and the implications of their financial decisions. By promoting financial literacy and personal responsibility, Satoshi's philosophy encourages individuals to make informed choices and protect their financial well-being.

Long-Term Thinking and Stability:

Satoshi's philosophy encourages long-term thinking and stability in the financial realm. By introducing a limited supply and a predictable issuance schedule, Satoshi aimed to create a system that fosters stability and discourages short-term speculation. This long-term perspective aligns with the vision of Bitcoin as a store of value and a medium of exchange that maintains its purchasing power over time.

So, Satoshi Nakamoto's philosophy on financial empowerment is rooted in principles of decentralization, peer-to-peer transactions, privacy, and individual autonomy. Satoshi envisioned a financial system that challenges the status quo, empowers individuals, and promotes financial inclusion. While Bitcoin embodies many of these principles, Satoshi's philosophy extends beyond the technology itself, emphasizing the importance of financial education, privacy, and responsible decision-making. By embracing Satoshi's philosophy, individuals can embark on a journey towards greater financial empowerment, taking control of their financial destinies and participating in a more inclusive and equitable financial future.

Chapter 91: Bitcoin's Intersection with Artificial Intelligence

Bitcoin, the pioneering cryptocurrency, and artificial intelligence (AI), the field of computer science focused on creating intelligent machines, are two groundbreaking technologies that have captured the imagination of the world. While Bitcoin revolutionizes finance and transactions, AI holds the potential to transform various industries. In this chapter, we explore the intersection of Bitcoin and artificial intelligence, examining the potential synergies, challenges, and implications of their convergence.

Enhanced Security and Fraud Detection:

Artificial intelligence techniques can bolster the security of the Bitcoin network by detecting and preventing fraudulent activities. AI algorithms can analyze patterns and anomalies in transaction data, identify suspicious behavior, and help protect against hacking attempts. By leveraging machine learning and data analysis, AI can enhance the security and integrity of the Bitcoin ecosystem, making it more resilient against potential threats.

Trading and Investment Strategies:

The volatility of Bitcoin's price has attracted investors and traders seeking opportunities for profit. Artificial intelligence, with its ability to analyze vast amounts of data and identify patterns, has the potential to enhance trading strategies in the cryptocurrency market. AI algorithms can analyze historical price data, market trends, and other relevant factors to make predictions and inform investment decisions. By leveraging AI's analytical capabilities, traders and investors can potentially gain insights and make more informed choices.

Improved Blockchain Scalability:

As the adoption of Bitcoin grows, scalability becomes an important consideration. Artificial intelligence techniques can be employed to optimize the blockchain's performance and address scalability challenges. AI algorithms can analyze network data, identify bottlenecks, and propose solutions to improve transaction throughput and reduce congestion. Additionally, AI can help enhance consensus mechanisms and optimize the overall efficiency of the blockchain network.

Natural Language Processing for Bitcoin Research:

Bitcoin's decentralized nature has led to a wealth of information and research being generated across various online platforms. Artificial intelligence techniques, specifically natural language processing (NLP), can be used to analyze and understand this vast amount of textual data. NLP algorithms can extract valuable insights from articles, forums, social media, and other sources to help researchers, analysts, and enthusiasts stay informed about Bitcoin-related developments and sentiment.

Smart Contracts and Automation:

Bitcoin's underlying technology, blockchain, has paved the way for the development of smart contracts, self-executing contracts with the terms of the agreement directly written into the code. Artificial intelligence can enhance smart contract functionality by enabling autonomous decision-making based on predefined rules and real-time data. AI-powered smart contracts can streamline processes, automate transactions, and facilitate complex interactions within the Bitcoin ecosystem.

AI-Powered Bitcoin Wallets:

Artificial intelligence can enhance the user experience and security of Bitcoin wallets. AI algorithms can analyze user behavior patterns, detect potential security risks, and provide personalized recommendations for securing funds. Additionally, AI can simplify the user interface and improve usability, making Bitcoin more accessible to a broader audience.

Data Analysis and Market Predictions:

Bitcoin's transaction data, combined with AI's data analysis capabilities, can provide valuable insights into market trends and patterns. AI algorithms can process large volumes of transaction data, identify correlations, and make predictions about market behavior. These insights can be utilized by traders, analysts, and researchers to make more informed decisions and gain a deeper understanding of the dynamics of the Bitcoin market.

Ethical Considerations:

The intersection of Bitcoin and artificial intelligence raises ethical considerations. AI algorithms can potentially be used to manipulate the Bitcoin market or conduct malicious activities. Additionally, the use of AI-powered bots in trading can introduce new challenges related to market fairness and transparency. It is crucial to establish ethical frameworks, regulatory measures, and responsible practices to ensure the ethical and responsible deployment of AI within the Bitcoin ecosystem.

So, the convergence of Bitcoin and artificial intelligence presents a range of exciting possibilities and challenges. AI has the potential to enhance the security, scalability, user experience, and analytical capabilities of the Bitcoin ecosystem. However, it is important to approach this intersection with caution, addressing ethical considerations and ensuring responsible use of AI technologies. The ongoing exploration of Bitcoin's intersection with artificial intelligence holds promise for advancing both fields and shaping the future of finance and technology.

Chapter 92: The Bitcoin Community's Response to Satoshi's Absence

Since Satoshi Nakamoto's mysterious departure from the Bitcoin project in 2010, the absence of the creator has left the Bitcoin community in a state of curiosity, speculation, and reflection. Satoshi's decision to remain anonymous and withdraw from active involvement has raised questions about the implications of their absence and the impact on the development and evolution of Bitcoin. In this chapter, we explore the Bitcoin community's response to Satoshi's absence, examining the various perspectives, theories, and implications surrounding this enigmatic figure.

The Initial Reactions:

When Satoshi Nakamoto disappeared, the Bitcoin community experienced a mix of surprise, curiosity, and uncertainty. Satoshi's departure left behind a groundbreaking technology, but the absence of its creator left the community with many unanswered questions. Some members were concerned about the future direction of Bitcoin, while others saw it as an opportunity for the community to take ownership and further develop the technology independently.

The Cult of Satoshi:

Satoshi Nakamoto's anonymity and the aura of mystery surrounding their identity led to the emergence of a "Cult of Satoshi" within the Bitcoin community. Some enthusiasts idolized Satoshi as a visionary and revered figure, attributing almost mythical status to their contributions. The community drew inspiration from Satoshi's writings, the Bitcoin white paper, and the early forum posts, finding guidance in the vision and principles outlined by the anonymous creator.

Community-driven Development:

Satoshi's absence compelled the Bitcoin community to take on a more active role in the development and governance of the protocol. The decentralized nature of Bitcoin allowed for community-driven initiatives, with developers, miners, and users collaborating to propose and implement improvements. This grassroots approach, characterized by open-source collaboration and consensus-building, became a defining feature of the Bitcoin community's response to Satoshi's absence.

Satoshi's Unclaimed Bitcoins:

One of the ongoing mysteries surrounding Satoshi's absence is the sizeable stash of bitcoins believed to be owned by the creator. Satoshi's early mining efforts are estimated to have accumulated a significant amount of bitcoins, but these remain unclaimed and untouched. Speculation regarding the potential impact of Satoshi's bitcoins entering the market has been a topic of discussion within the community, with debates about their potential sale or redistribution.

Debates on Satoshi's Motivations:

Satoshi Nakamoto's motivations for creating Bitcoin continue to be a subject of debate within the community. Some believe that Satoshi's primary objective was to challenge the existing financial system and empower individuals with a decentralized currency. Others speculate about potential personal motives or ideological principles that drove Satoshi's involvement. The community's response to Satoshi's absence reflects a desire to understand and uphold the principles and vision outlined in the Bitcoin white paper.

The Quest for Satoshi's Identity:

Despite Satoshi Nakamoto's intentional anonymity, the Bitcoin community has not ceased its efforts to uncover the creator's true identity. Over the years, numerous individuals have been speculated to be Satoshi, leading to intense media scrutiny and investigations. However, all attempts to definitively reveal Satoshi's identity have been inconclusive, with no individual or group providing concrete evidence to confirm their connection to the creator. The pursuit of Satoshi's identity remains an ongoing curiosity within the Bitcoin community.

Satoshi's Legacy:

While Satoshi Nakamoto's absence has left an undeniable void, their legacy within the Bitcoin community remains profound. Satoshi's contributions provided the foundation for a global decentralized currency and sparked a movement towards financial sovereignty. The Bitcoin community continues to uphold Satoshi's vision of peer-to-peer electronic cash and decentralized governance, carrying forward the principles outlined in the early writings and forum posts. Satoshi's legacy serves as a reminder of the transformative power of ideas and the potential for individuals to reshape the world through technology.

Embracing the Unknown:

Rather than dwelling on the absence of Satoshi, the Bitcoin community has learned to embrace the unknown and move forward. The focus has shifted to the technology itself, community collaboration, and the ongoing evolution of Bitcoin. The absence of a central figure has fostered a sense of collective ownership and responsibility within the community, with individuals and organizations actively contributing to the development, adoption, and advocacy of Bitcoin.

So, the Bitcoin community's response to Satoshi Nakamoto's absence has been marked by curiosity, resilience, and self-governance. Satoshi's enigmatic departure spurred the community to take ownership of the technology and uphold the principles outlined in the early writings. Rather than being hindered by the absence of a known leader, the Bitcoin community has thrived, forging its path, and continuing to shape the future of decentralized finance. Satoshi Nakamoto's legacy lives on through the Bitcoin community's ongoing dedication to the principles of decentralization, financial empowerment, and innovation.

Chapter 93: Satoshi's Influence on Cryptocurrency Education

Cryptocurrencies, spearheaded by Bitcoin, have sparked a global interest in decentralized digital assets and blockchain technology. In this chapter, we explore the significant influence of Satoshi Nakamoto, the mysterious creator of Bitcoin, on cryptocurrency education. Satoshi's groundbreaking work not only introduced a revolutionary financial system but also paved the way for an entirely new field of study and learning. Let's dive into the ways in which Satoshi has shaped cryptocurrency education and its impact on individuals, institutions, and the broader adoption of digital currencies.

Introduction to Blockchain Technology:

Satoshi Nakamoto's white paper, titled "Bitcoin: A Peer-to-Peer Electronic Cash System," served as the foundation for understanding blockchain technology. This seminal document outlined the key principles and mechanisms that underpin Bitcoin and other cryptocurrencies. It introduced concepts such as decentralization, cryptographic security, consensus mechanisms, and transaction verification, providing a comprehensive introduction to blockchain technology and its potential applications.

Decentralized Finance (DeFi) and Smart Contracts:

Satoshi's creation of Bitcoin laid the groundwork for the emergence of decentralized finance (DeFi) and smart contracts. As the cryptocurrency ecosystem expanded, educational resources began to focus on these concepts. Satoshi's influence inspired developers and educators to explore the potential of decentralized financial applications and programmable contracts. Today, individuals can learn about DeFi protocols, decentralized exchanges, and smart contract development, benefiting from Satoshi's initial vision.

Cryptography and Security:

Bitcoin's success relies heavily on the cryptographic principles that ensure the security and integrity of the network. Satoshi Nakamoto's implementation of cryptographic techniques, such as public-key cryptography and hash functions, introduced individuals to the world of digital security and encryption. Cryptocurrency education now encompasses the study of cryptographic protocols, digital signatures, and secure key management, allowing individuals to better understand the principles of secure digital transactions.

Distributed Ledger Technology (DLT):

The concept of a distributed ledger, as proposed by Satoshi Nakamoto, introduced a paradigm shift in record-keeping and transparency. Cryptocurrency education now encompasses the study of distributed ledger technology (DLT) beyond Bitcoin. Individuals can learn about various blockchain implementations, including public and private networks, permissioned ledgers, and consensus algorithms. Satoshi's contribution to DLT has paved the way for innovative applications in finance, supply chain management, and governance.

Economic and Monetary Theory:

Satoshi's creation of a decentralized currency challenged traditional economic and monetary theories. Cryptocurrency education now explores the economic implications of digital currencies, including concepts such as scarcity, inflation resistance, and monetary policy. Satoshi's introduction of a deflationary currency with a capped supply sparked discussions on the potential long-term economic effects of cryptocurrencies, serving as a catalyst for research and academic study in this field.

Online Resources and Communities:

The open-source nature of Bitcoin and the subsequent proliferation of cryptocurrencies has fostered a vibrant online community. Satoshi's influence on cryptocurrency education can be seen in the wealth of online resources, forums, and communities dedicated to learning and discussing digital currencies. These platforms provide a space for individuals to share knowledge, ask questions, and engage in educational discussions about cryptocurrencies and blockchain technology.

Academic Programs and Courses:

Satoshi Nakamoto's influence has extended to the realm of academia, with universities and educational institutions offering courses, programs, and research opportunities related to cryptocurrencies and blockchain technology. Academic disciplines such as computer science, economics, and finance now include coursework and research focused on understanding the underlying principles of cryptocurrencies, blockchain technology, and their potential societal impact.

Awareness and Mass Adoption:

Satoshi's creation of Bitcoin ignited a global interest in cryptocurrencies, leading to increased awareness and mainstream adoption. This surge in popularity has driven the need for cryptocurrency education to cater to a wider audience. Educational initiatives, both online and offline, aim to bridge the knowledge gap and empower individuals with the understanding and skills necessary to participate in the cryptocurrency ecosystem confidently.

Ethical and Regulatory Considerations:

As cryptocurrencies gained traction, issues surrounding ethics, security, and regulatory frameworks arose. Satoshi's absence prompted educational initiatives to address these considerations. Cryptocurrency education now covers topics such as legal and regulatory compliance, cryptocurrency taxation, cybersecurity best practices, and ethical considerations in cryptocurrency use. By promoting responsible practices and compliance, cryptocurrency education aims to ensure the sustainable and ethical growth of the industry.

So, Satoshi Nakamoto's influence on cryptocurrency education cannot be overstated. Their creation of Bitcoin has sparked a global interest in cryptocurrencies, blockchain technology, and the decentralized finance revolution. Satoshi's contributions have laid the foundation for an entire field of study, providing individuals with the tools to explore the technical, economic, and societal implications of digital currencies. As the cryptocurrency ecosystem continues to evolve, Satoshi's influence will remain embedded in the educational resources, institutions, and communities that drive the adoption and understanding of cryptocurrencies worldwide.

Chapter 94: The Dark Web and Bitcoin's Role

The Dark Web, a hidden part of the internet accessible only through specialized software, has long been associated with illicit activities, anonymity, and illicit marketplaces. Bitcoin, the pioneering cryptocurrency created by Satoshi Nakamoto, has often been linked to the Dark Web due to its perceived potential for facilitating anonymous transactions. In this chapter, we will explore the relationship between Bitcoin and the Dark Web, delving into its complexities, challenges, and the broader implications for both technology and society.

Understanding the Dark Web:

The Dark Web is a part of the internet that operates outside the bounds of traditional search engines and standard web browsers. It is accessed through special software, such as Tor (The Onion Router), which anonymizes users' identities and facilitates communication through a network of relays. The Dark Web hosts various websites and marketplaces that are not indexed by search engines and are known for their illicit activities.

Bitcoin's Pseudonymity:

Bitcoin, with its decentralized nature and pseudonymous transactions, has been seen as an ideal currency for individuals seeking anonymity on the Dark Web. While Bitcoin transactions are recorded on a public ledger, called the blockchain, the real-world identities behind these transactions are often difficult to trace. This characteristic has made Bitcoin popular among those engaging in illicit activities on the Dark Web.

Dark Web Marketplaces:

Dark Web marketplaces, such as Silk Road, AlphaBay, and Hansa Market, have gained notoriety for facilitating the sale of illegal goods and services. These marketplaces allow users to buy and sell drugs, counterfeit documents, hacking tools, stolen data, and more. Bitcoin emerged as the preferred currency for these transactions due to its perceived anonymity and ease of use.

Challenges of Anonymity:

While Bitcoin offers a certain level of pseudonymity, it is not entirely anonymous. Transactions on the blockchain are transparent and can be analyzed to uncover patterns and potentially identify users. Law enforcement agencies and cybersecurity experts have developed techniques to trace Bitcoin transactions and link them to individuals involved in illicit activities. The misconception of Bitcoin's complete anonymity has led to the apprehension of many individuals using it on the Dark Web.

Takedown of Dark Web Marketplaces:

Over the years, law enforcement agencies worldwide have made significant efforts to combat illegal activities on the Dark Web. Several high-profile takedowns of major marketplaces have occurred, resulting in the seizure of assets, arrests, and the disruption of illicit operations. These efforts have revealed the vulnerabilities and limitations of Bitcoin's pseudonymity and have led to the emergence of alternative cryptocurrencies designed to enhance privacy and anonymity.

Regulatory Measures:

The association between Bitcoin and the Dark Web has prompted increased scrutiny and regulatory measures aimed at preventing the misuse of cryptocurrencies for illicit activities. Governments and regulatory bodies have implemented Know Your Customer (KYC) and Anti-Money Laundering (AML) policies to impose greater transparency and accountability in the cryptocurrency ecosystem. These measures seek to discourage the use of cryptocurrencies for illegal purposes and enhance cooperation between cryptocurrency exchanges and law enforcement agencies.

Bitcoin's Wider Applications:

While Bitcoin's association with the Dark Web has garnered significant attention, it is crucial to recognize that Bitcoin's use extends far beyond illicit activities. Bitcoin and other cryptocurrencies have emerged as viable alternatives to traditional financial systems, providing opportunities for financial inclusion, cross-border transactions, and decentralized finance. Blockchain technology, which underpins cryptocurrencies like Bitcoin, has found applications in various industries, including supply chain management, healthcare, and voting systems.

Education and Awareness:

As the public becomes more aware of the Dark Web and its association with Bitcoin, education and awareness campaigns play a vital role in promoting responsible cryptocurrency use. Educating individuals about the risks associated with engaging in illegal activities on the Dark Web and emphasizing the importance of complying with legal and regulatory requirements can help foster a more responsible and ethical cryptocurrency ecosystem.

So, while Bitcoin's association with the Dark Web has perpetuated a perception of anonymity and illicit activities, it is essential to distinguish between the technology itself and its potential misuse. Bitcoin's pseudonymity has attracted attention from those seeking anonymity, but it is not a foolproof method for conducting illicit activities. The association between Bitcoin and the Dark Web has prompted regulatory measures, increased transparency, and the development of privacy-enhancing technologies. As the cryptocurrency ecosystem evolves, it is crucial to focus on the broader implications of blockchain technology and Bitcoin's potential to transform industries, promote financial inclusion, and reshape traditional financial systems.

Chapter 95: Bitcoin's Influence on Microtransactions

In the world of digital currencies, Bitcoin has emerged as a transformative force, challenging traditional payment systems, and opening up new possibilities for financial transactions. One area where Bitcoin has made a significant impact is in the realm of microtransactions. In this chapter, we explore the influence of Bitcoin on microtransactions, examining its benefits, challenges, and the potential it holds for the future of small-scale digital transactions.

Defining Microtransactions:

Microtransactions refer to small financial transactions involving tiny amounts of money. They typically involve low-value purchases, donations, or payments for digital content, services, or products. Traditionally, the high fees associated with traditional payment systems have made microtransactions economically unfeasible. Bitcoin, with its low transaction fees and divisibility, has emerged as a viable solution for conducting microtransactions.

Lower Transaction Costs:

One of the key advantages of Bitcoin for microtransactions is its ability to reduce transaction costs. Traditional payment systems often impose fixed fees or a percentage-based fee structure, which can be prohibitive for small-value transactions. Bitcoin's decentralized nature and lack of intermediaries allow for lower transaction fees, making microtransactions more economically viable.

Global Accessibility:

Bitcoin's borderless nature and ability to facilitate cross-border transactions have greatly influenced microtransactions on a global scale. With traditional payment systems, international microtransactions often involve complex procedures, high fees, and lengthy settlement times. Bitcoin, on the other hand, enables individuals from different parts of the world to engage in frictionless microtransactions, bypassing the limitations of traditional financial systems.

Empowering Content Creators:

Microtransactions have the potential to revolutionize the way content creators monetize their work. With Bitcoin, creators can receive direct payments for digital content such as articles, music, videos, and artwork. By eliminating intermediaries, such as publishing platforms or streaming services, content creators can have greater control over their revenue streams and establish direct relationships with their audiences.

Donations and Crowdfunding:

Bitcoin has also played a significant role in enabling micro-donations and crowdfunding initiatives. Non-profit organizations, charities, and independent creators can receive small, individual contributions from a global community of Bitcoin users. This opens up new possibilities for funding social causes, supporting innovative projects, and promoting grassroots initiatives that might otherwise struggle to gain traction through traditional fundraising channels.

Micropayments for Digital Services:

Bitcoin has facilitated the rise of micropayments for digital services that were previously challenging to monetize. For instance, online platforms offering small-value services such as pay-per-view content, in-game purchases, premium features, or data access can seamlessly integrate Bitcoin as a payment option. This enables users to pay only for the specific features or content they require, enhancing the overall user experience.

Challenges and Scalability:

While Bitcoin offers several advantages for microtransactions, it is not without its challenges. Scalability has been a recurring issue, with the Bitcoin network experiencing limitations in processing a high volume of transactions quickly. This has led to delays and increased transaction fees during periods of high network congestion. However, ongoing research and technological developments, such as the Lightning Network, aim to address these scalability challenges and enable faster, more cost-effective microtransactions on the Bitcoin network.

User Experience and Education:

The successful integration of Bitcoin into the microtransaction ecosystem relies on user experience and education. For widespread adoption of Bitcoin microtransactions, user-friendly wallets, intuitive payment interfaces, and seamless integration into existing platforms are crucial. Additionally, educating users about the benefits, security practices, and best use cases of Bitcoin for microtransactions can help build trust and confidence in the technology.

Future Potential:

As Bitcoin continues to evolve, its influence on microtransactions is likely to expand further. Improvements in scalability, user experience, and the development of layer-two solutions like the Lightning Network hold promise for enhancing the efficiency and accessibility of Bitcoin microtransactions. Additionally, the emergence of tokenized assets and non-fungible tokens (NFTs) presents new opportunities for microtransactions, enabling the exchange of unique digital assets in a frictionless manner.

So, Bitcoin has had a profound influence on microtransactions, providing a viable solution for conducting small-value digital transactions. Its low transaction fees, global accessibility, and ability to empower content creators and facilitate crowdfunding have opened up new possibilities for financial interactions in the digital age. While challenges such as scalability and user experience remain, ongoing developments and innovations in the Bitcoin ecosystem hold promise for further enhancing the efficiency and adoption of Bitcoin microtransactions. As the digital economy continues to evolve, Bitcoin's influence on microtransactions is likely to shape the future of digital commerce and financial interactions at a small scale.

Chapter 96: Satoshi's Vision for a Cashless Society

In the realm of cryptocurrencies, one figure stands out as the visionary behind the revolutionary technology of Bitcoin—Satoshi Nakamoto. Satoshi's creation of Bitcoin was driven by a desire to challenge traditional financial systems and empower individuals with a decentralized and peer-to-peer digital currency. One aspect of Satoshi's vision that often sparks intrigue is his perspective on a cashless society. In this chapter, we delve into Satoshi's vision for a cashless society, exploring the motivations behind it, the potential benefits and challenges, and its implications for the future.

The Motivation for a Cashless Society:

Satoshi Nakamoto's vision for a cashless society stemmed from a desire to create a more efficient and inclusive financial system. Traditional cash-based transactions have limitations such as high costs, security risks, and lack of transparency. By replacing physical cash with a digital currency like Bitcoin, Satoshi envisioned a more secure, cost-effective, and accessible means of conducting financial transactions.

Efficiency and Cost Reduction:

A cashless society offers significant efficiency gains compared to a cash-based system. Digital transactions can be processed quickly, reducing waiting times at payment points, and eliminating the need for physical cash handling. Furthermore, a cashless society can reduce costs associated with printing, storing, and transporting physical currency, potentially freeing up resources for other societal needs.

Financial Inclusion:

Satoshi believed that a cashless society could promote financial inclusion by providing access to financial services for the unbanked and underbanked populations. With a digital currency like Bitcoin, individuals without traditional bank accounts can participate in the global economy, send, and receive payments, and store value securely. The elimination of geographical barriers and the need for a centralized intermediary can enhance financial inclusion on a global scale.

Transparency and Accountability:

Bitcoin's underlying technology, the blockchain, offers unprecedented transparency and accountability. Every transaction recorded on the blockchain is verifiable and traceable, creating a permanent and auditable record. In a cashless society built on blockchain technology, financial transactions can be more easily monitored, reducing opportunities for corruption, money laundering, and illicit activities.

Privacy Concerns:

While Satoshi's vision emphasized transparency, he also recognized the importance of privacy. Bitcoin transactions are pseudonymous, with wallet addresses representing users rather than real-world identities. This allows for a certain level of privacy, but it also raises concerns about the potential for surveillance and the balance between privacy and transparency in a cashless society.

Technological Challenges:

Realizing Satoshi's vision for a cashless society requires overcoming technological challenges. Scaling Bitcoin to handle a large volume of transactions quickly and efficiently remains a significant hurdle. Additionally, ensuring the security and integrity of digital wallets and payment systems is crucial to prevent unauthorized access and protect users' funds.

Cultural and Societal Adoption:

Transitioning to a cashless society involves not only technological advancements but also changes in cultural and societal norms. Cash has deep-rooted cultural significance and is ingrained in many societies' everyday transactions. Overcoming this cultural attachment and fostering trust in digital currencies is a gradual process that requires education, awareness, and the development of user-friendly interfaces and infrastructure.

Collaboration with Traditional Systems:

Satoshi's vision for a cashless society does not necessarily imply the complete elimination of traditional financial systems. Rather, it envisions a symbiotic relationship where digital currencies coexist with traditional fiat currencies. Collaboration between digital currencies and established financial institutions can bridge the gap between the old and new systems, facilitating a smooth transition to a cashless society.

The Future of Cashless Societies:

Satoshi's vision for a cashless society extends beyond Bitcoin. As the cryptocurrency landscape evolves, other digital currencies and central bank digital currencies (CBDCs) may play significant roles in shaping cashless societies. CBDCs, backed by central banks, have the potential to combine the benefits of digital currencies with the stability and trust associated with government-backed fiat currencies.

So, Satoshi Nakamoto's vision for a cashless society with Bitcoin as a decentralized digital currency reflects his desire to create a more efficient, inclusive, and transparent financial system. While realizing this vision comes with challenges, advancements in technology, increased awareness, and collaboration between traditional financial systems and digital currencies are paving the way for a potential cashless future. As societies evolve, the realization of Satoshi's vision for a cashless society could revolutionize how we transact, promote financial inclusion, and reshape the global financial landscape.

Chapter 97: The Bitcoin Patent Controversy

In the world of cryptocurrencies, Bitcoin has achieved remarkable success as a decentralized digital currency that operates without a central authority. Satoshi Nakamoto, the enigmatic creator of Bitcoin, released the software as open-source, allowing anyone to use, modify, and build upon it. This openness has fostered innovation and collaboration within the Bitcoin community. However, the concept of patenting Bitcoin-related technologies has generated controversy and debate. In this chapter, we explore the Bitcoin patent controversy, examining the arguments for and against patenting in the Bitcoin ecosystem, and the potential implications for innovation and the future of Bitcoin.

The Open-Source Ethos of Bitcoin:

Bitcoin's success can be attributed, in part, to its open-source nature. Satoshi Nakamoto's decision to release the Bitcoin software under an open-source license fostered transparency, collaboration, and innovation within the Bitcoin community. Open-source software allows developers to freely access, modify, and distribute the code, promoting community-driven development and ensuring that the technology remains accessible to all.

The Argument for Bitcoin Patents:

Some proponents argue that patents can incentivize innovation and provide legal protection for individuals or companies investing resources into developing Bitcoin-related technologies. Patents can serve as a means of recouping research and development costs, as well as attracting investment and partnerships. Additionally, patents can help establish standards and prevent the misappropriation of inventions by other parties.

Challenges with Patenting Bitcoin:

Critics of Bitcoin patents argue that patents are incompatible with the open-source ethos of Bitcoin. Patenting key technologies or protocols could stifle innovation, limit collaboration, and create barriers to entry for new developers and startups. Patents could lead to fragmentation and the emergence of competing standards, hindering the interoperability and progress of the Bitcoin ecosystem.

Patent Trolls and Litigation Risks:

Another concern surrounding Bitcoin patents is the potential for patent trolls, entities that acquire patents solely for the purpose of extracting licensing fees or suing other individuals or companies. The existence of patent trolls and the risk of litigation could create a hostile environment for innovation and deter developers from contributing to the Bitcoin ecosystem.

Patentable Bitcoin-related Technologies:

Despite the controversy surrounding Bitcoin patents, there are areas where patenting can be relevant and beneficial. For instance, specific hardware components or novel applications built on top of the Bitcoin protocol may be eligible for patent protection. However, many argue that the core protocols and fundamental aspects of Bitcoin should remain open-source and free from patents.

Collaborative Approaches:

In response to the patent controversy, some companies and organizations within the Bitcoin ecosystem have adopted collaborative approaches to intellectual property. Initiatives such as the Open Invention Network and the Defensive Patent License aim to create a defensive patent pool and promote the sharing of patents among members. These collaborative efforts seek to protect innovation while avoiding the potential negative impacts of aggressive patent enforcement.

Regulatory Considerations:

The regulation of patents within the Bitcoin ecosystem varies across jurisdictions. Some countries, such as the United States, have more lenient patent laws, while others have stricter requirements for patentability. The absence of clear regulations specifically tailored to digital currencies and blockchain technology has led to uncertainty and inconsistencies in patent enforcement.

Balancing Innovation and Protection:

Finding the right balance between encouraging innovation and protecting intellectual property is a complex challenge. The Bitcoin community continues to explore alternative mechanisms for incentivizing innovation, such as open patents or defensive patent strategies that discourage aggressive enforcement. These approaches aim to strike a balance between protecting inventors' rights and maintaining the collaborative and open nature of the Bitcoin ecosystem.

The Future of Bitcoin Patents:

As the Bitcoin ecosystem evolves and matures, the debate surrounding Bitcoin patents is likely to continue. The community's ability to navigate the patent landscape and find creative solutions that foster innovation while protecting inventors' rights will play a significant role in shaping the future of Bitcoin. Regulatory developments and legal precedents regarding patentability in the blockchain space will also influence the landscape of Bitcoin patents.

So, the Bitcoin patent controversy raises important questions about the balance between innovation, collaboration, and intellectual property protection within the Bitcoin ecosystem. While patents can provide incentives and protections for inventors, they also have the potential to stifle innovation and create barriers to entry. The Bitcoin community must navigate these challenges carefully to ensure that the spirit of openness and collaboration that has driven Bitcoin's success is preserved. Ultimately, the future of Bitcoin patents will depend on the collective efforts of the community to find creative solutions that promote innovation while maintaining the principles of decentralization and accessibility that underpin the Bitcoin revolution.

Chapter 98: The Cultural Impact of "Satoshi Nakamoto"

In the world of cryptocurrencies, few names carry as much weight as Satoshi Nakamoto. As the mysterious creator of Bitcoin, Satoshi Nakamoto's influence extends far beyond the realm of technology and finance. Satoshi's creation of Bitcoin, combined with the enigma surrounding their true identity, has sparked curiosity, speculation, and debate among enthusiasts, researchers, and the general public alike. In this chapter, we delve into the cultural impact of "Satoshi Nakamoto," exploring the fascination surrounding the name, the implications of the pseudonymous nature of Bitcoin's creator, and the lasting legacy of Satoshi in popular culture.

The Enigma of Satoshi Nakamoto:

One of the defining aspects of Satoshi Nakamoto is the unknown identity behind the name. While several individuals have been speculated to be Satoshi, the true identity remains elusive. This air of mystery has captured the imagination of people worldwide, turning Satoshi Nakamoto into a figure of intrigue and speculation. The quest to uncover the true identity of Satoshi has become a subject of documentaries, books, and even academic research.

Pseudonymity and Decentralization:

Satoshi Nakamoto's choice to operate under a pseudonym aligns with the principles of decentralization that underpin Bitcoin. By stepping away from the traditional model of a centralized authority figure, Satoshi allowed Bitcoin to thrive as a decentralized digital currency. The pseudonymous nature of Satoshi has contributed to the idea that Bitcoin is not controlled by any single individual or institution, but rather by a community of users working collectively to maintain the network.

Cult of Personality:

The concept of Satoshi Nakamoto has taken on a life of its own, developing a cult-like following within the cryptocurrency community. The persona of Satoshi has become synonymous with innovation, revolution, and the vision of a decentralized future. Satoshi's ideas and philosophy have inspired countless individuals to explore blockchain technology, create their own cryptocurrencies, and challenge traditional financial systems.

Satoshi's White Paper:

Satoshi Nakamoto's publication of the Bitcoin white paper in 2008 marked a pivotal moment in the history of cryptocurrencies. The white paper, titled "Bitcoin: A Peer-to-Peer Electronic Cash System," outlined the principles and technical details of Bitcoin, laying the foundation for its development and adoption. Today, the white paper stands as a testament to Satoshi's intellectual prowess and has become a revered document within the cryptocurrency community.

Satoshi as an Iconic Figure:

Satoshi Nakamoto's influence has transcended the boundaries of the cryptocurrency space, permeating popular culture and mainstream media. Satoshi has been portrayed in various forms, from artistic interpretations to caricatures in cartoons. The image of Satoshi has become synonymous with the idea of a revolutionary figure who challenged the status quo and introduced a new era of digital currency.

Satoshi's Influence on Art and Literature:

The enigmatic nature of Satoshi Nakamoto has inspired artists, writers, and filmmakers to explore the concept of the mysterious creator in their work. Art exhibits, novels, and films have all been created around the theme of Satoshi and the impact of Bitcoin on society. Satoshi's story has become part of the collective cultural consciousness, serving as a source of inspiration for creative minds around the world.

Satoshi's Influence on Trust and Authority:

The concept of trust and authority has been redefined by the emergence of Satoshi Nakamoto and Bitcoin. Satoshi's decision to release Bitcoin as open-source software, without claiming ownership or authority, challenged traditional notions of trust and centralization. The trust in Bitcoin now lies in the technology itself, its consensus mechanisms, and the collective efforts of the community. Satoshi's approach has inspired discussions on the nature of trust, authority, and decentralization in various domains beyond cryptocurrencies.

Satoshi's Intellectual Legacy:

Beyond the enigma of their identity, Satoshi Nakamoto's intellectual contributions to the fields of cryptography, computer science, and economics cannot be understated. The concepts of blockchain, decentralized consensus, and the proof-of-work mechanism introduced in the Bitcoin white paper have shaped the development of cryptocurrencies and influenced broader discussions on distributed systems and trustless networks.

Satoshi's Enduring Influence:

Although Satoshi Nakamoto has remained absent from the public eye since 2010, their influence continues to be felt in the world of cryptocurrencies and beyond. The principles and concepts introduced by Satoshi have inspired a new wave of innovation, with countless individuals and organizations building upon the foundation laid by Bitcoin. The idea of a decentralized, transparent, and secure financial system has gained traction and has the potential to reshape the global economy.

So, the cultural impact of "Satoshi Nakamoto" extends far beyond the realm of technology and finance. The mystery surrounding Satoshi's true identity, combined with their contributions to the world of cryptocurrencies, has elevated Satoshi to the status of an iconic figure. Satoshi's vision for a decentralized future, embodied in the creation of Bitcoin, has inspired individuals, artists, and thinkers to reimagine the possibilities of trust, authority, and financial systems. The legacy of Satoshi Nakamoto serves as a reminder of the power of ideas, the potential for disruptive innovation, and the enduring impact of a single individual on the course of history.

Chapter 99: Bitcoin's Potential in Peer-to-Peer Lending

In the realm of finance, peer-to-peer lending has emerged as an alternative to traditional banking systems, allowing individuals to lend and borrow directly from one another without intermediaries. Bitcoin, the pioneering cryptocurrency, holds the potential to revolutionize the peer-to-peer lending landscape even further. In this chapter, we explore the potential of Bitcoin in peer-to-peer lending, discussing its advantages, challenges, and the transformative impact it could have on the borrowing and lending experience.

Understanding Peer-to-Peer Lending:

Peer-to-peer lending, also known as P2P lending or marketplace lending, enables individuals to lend and borrow money directly without involving traditional financial institutions. Through online platforms, borrowers can access loans from a pool of willing lenders who fund the loans in exchange for interest payments. This model offers borrowers more accessible loan options and potentially lower interest rates, while lenders have the opportunity to earn higher returns compared to traditional savings accounts.

Advantages of Bitcoin in Peer-to-Peer Lending:

Bitcoin brings several unique advantages to the realm of peer-to-peer lending: a. Global Accessibility: Bitcoin operates on a decentralized network, enabling transactions to occur across borders without the need for intermediaries. This global accessibility expands the potential borrower and lender pool, facilitating cross-border lending opportunities. b. Lower Transaction Costs: Bitcoin transactions typically involve lower fees compared to traditional payment systems, reducing the cost of transferring funds between lenders and borrowers. This cost-effectiveness can result in more favorable loan terms for borrowers and increased returns for lenders. c. Faster Transactions: Bitcoin transactions occur quickly, often within minutes, compared to traditional bank transfers, which may take days to complete. The speed of Bitcoin transactions enables borrowers to access funds promptly and allows lenders to reinvest their returns more efficiently.

Mitigating Risk and Enhancing Security:

Bitcoin's underlying technology, blockchain, provides enhanced security and transparency, addressing some of the risks associated with peer-to-peer lending: a. Smart Contracts: Bitcoin's blockchain can facilitate the implementation of smart contracts, which are self-executing contracts with predefined conditions. Smart contracts can automate loan agreements, ensuring that funds are released to borrowers only when predefined conditions are met, reducing the risk of default, and increasing trust between parties. b. Immutable Transaction Records: Every Bitcoin transaction is recorded on the blockchain, creating an immutable audit trail. This transparency can enhance the credibility of borrower and lender profiles, allowing participants to evaluate the creditworthiness of potential counterparties more effectively. c. Decentralized Verification: Bitcoin's decentralized nature eliminates the need for a central authority to verify and authenticate transactions. Instead, the verification process relies on the consensus mechanism of the blockchain, making it difficult for fraudulent activities to go unnoticed.

Challenges and Limitations:

While Bitcoin holds promise in peer-to-peer lending, several challenges and limitations need to be considered: a. Volatility: Bitcoin's value is subject to significant price fluctuations, which can introduce uncertainty for lenders and borrowers. This volatility may affect the loan terms, interest rates, and the overall stability of the lending platform. Implementing measures to mitigate this risk, such as using stablecoins or creating loan products tied to fiat currencies, may be necessary. b. Regulatory Environment: Peer-to-peer lending platforms, whether traditional or Bitcoin-based, operate within a regulatory framework that may vary from country to country. Compliance with financial regulations and anti-money laundering laws is crucial to ensure a secure and legally compliant lending environment. c. Limited Adoption: Despite the growing popularity of Bitcoin, its mainstream adoption as a currency is still limited. This factor can affect the pool of potential lenders and borrowers within the Bitcoin ecosystem, limiting the scalability and reach of peer-to-peer lending platforms.

Innovations and Future Possibilities:

As the Bitcoin ecosystem evolves, several innovations and developments hold the potential to overcome existing challenges and expand the capabilities of Bitcoin in peer-to-peer lending: a. Stablecoin Integration: Stablecoins, cryptocurrencies pegged to stable assets such as fiat currencies, can address the issue of Bitcoin's volatility. Integrating stablecoins into peer-to-peer lending platforms can provide stability in loan terms and create a more predictable borrowing and lending environment. b. Decentralized Lending Platforms: The principles of decentralization inherent in Bitcoin can be further extended to peer-to-peer lending platforms. Decentralized lending platforms built on blockchain technology eliminate the need for intermediaries altogether, fostering a more efficient and inclusive lending ecosystem. c. Automated Lending Protocols: Smart contract platforms built on Bitcoin, such as the Lightning Network, can facilitate the development of automated lending protocols. These protocols would enable lenders to pool their funds, automatically distribute loans, and handle repayments, creating a more streamlined and autonomous lending experience.

So, Bitcoin's potential in peer-to-peer lending is undeniable. Its global accessibility, lower transaction costs, and enhanced security offer unique advantages for borrowers and lenders. However, challenges such as volatility and regulatory considerations must be addressed for Bitcoin-based peer-to-peer lending to reach its full potential. As the Bitcoin ecosystem continues to evolve and innovative solutions emerge, the transformative impact of Bitcoin in peer-to-peer lending holds the promise of revolutionizing the borrowing and lending landscape, making financial services more accessible, efficient, and inclusive for individuals worldwide.

Chapter 100: The Enduring Mystery of Satoshi Nakamoto

In the world of cryptocurrencies, few mysteries are as captivating as the identity of Satoshi Nakamoto, the enigmatic creator of Bitcoin. Over a decade since the publication of the Bitcoin white paper, the true identity of Satoshi remains unknown, giving rise to endless speculation and curiosity. In this chapter, we delve deep into the enduring mystery of Satoshi Nakamoto, exploring the various theories, the impact of their anonymity, and the fascination that continues to surround this elusive figure.

The Birth of Bitcoin and the Pseudonym:

Satoshi Nakamoto burst onto the scene in October 2008 with the release of the Bitcoin white paper. From the start, Satoshi chose to operate under a pseudonym, raising eyebrows and sparking intrigue. The decision to remain anonymous has added a layer of mystique to the Bitcoin project, leading many to question the reasons behind Satoshi's choice.

Theories on Satoshi's Identity:

Numerous theories have emerged over the years, attempting to unveil the person or group behind the name Satoshi Nakamoto. Some have speculated that Satoshi is an individual with a strong background in cryptography or computer science, while others believe it could be a collective effort or even a pseudonym for a prominent figure. Names like Nick Szabo, Hal Finney, and Dorian Nakamoto have all been suggested as potential candidates, but no definitive proof has emerged.

Satoshi's Disappearance and the Impact:

After launching Bitcoin and contributing to its early development, Satoshi Nakamoto gradually faded from the public eye. In April 2011, Satoshi made their final known communication, leaving the Bitcoin project to the community. This disappearance has only added to the intrigue and speculation surrounding Satoshi's true identity.

Satoshi's Contribution to Cryptocurrency:

Regardless of their identity, there's no denying the immense impact Satoshi Nakamoto has had on the world of cryptocurrencies. The creation of Bitcoin revolutionized the concept of digital currency, introducing the revolutionary blockchain technology that underpins many cryptocurrencies today. Satoshi's innovative ideas, including decentralized consensus and the proof-of-work mechanism, have shaped the development of the entire cryptocurrency ecosystem.

The Symbolism of Satoshi Nakamoto:

Satoshi Nakamoto has become a symbol of resistance against centralized power and traditional financial institutions. The decision to remain anonymous aligns with the ethos of decentralization and freedom from institutional control that Bitcoin represents. Satoshi Nakamoto has become a champion for those seeking financial sovereignty, as well as a source of inspiration for individuals who believe in challenging the status quo.

Satoshi's Impact on Society:

The enigma of Satoshi Nakamoto has transcended the world of cryptocurrencies, leaving a lasting impact on society as a whole. Satoshi's creation has sparked a global conversation about the future of money, the potential of decentralized technologies, and the power of innovation. The idea that an individual or group could challenge the existing financial order and create an alternative monetary system has inspired individuals, entrepreneurs, and even governments to explore the possibilities of blockchain technology.

Satoshi's Philosophy and Vision:

Beyond their technical contributions, Satoshi Nakamoto has left behind a philosophical and ideological legacy. Through the Bitcoin white paper and subsequent communications, Satoshi expressed a vision of financial empowerment, privacy, and trustless transactions. This vision continues to inspire individuals and shape the development of cryptocurrencies and decentralized systems today.

The Cultural Phenomenon:

Satoshi Nakamoto has become a cultural phenomenon, with numerous books, documentaries, and films exploring the mystery and impact of their creation. Satoshi's story has captivated the imaginations of people worldwide, becoming a subject of intrigue and fascination beyond the confines of the cryptocurrency community.

The Legacy of Satoshi Nakamoto:

Regardless of whether Satoshi's true identity is ever revealed, their impact and legacy are undeniable. Satoshi Nakamoto's creation of Bitcoin has revolutionized the way we think about money, trust, and financial systems. The ripple effects of Satoshi's work continue to shape the world, with cryptocurrencies and blockchain technology becoming integral parts of various industries.

So, the enduring mystery of Satoshi Nakamoto and their anonymous role in the creation of Bitcoin has captivated the world. The quest to uncover Satoshi's true identity has become a subject of fascination and speculation, generating countless theories and discussions. Beyond the identity, the impact of Satoshi's creation and the philosophy behind Bitcoin continue to shape the evolution of cryptocurrencies and decentralized technologies. Satoshi Nakamoto's legacy serves as a reminder of the power of ideas and the potential for individuals to challenge and transform existing systems. Whether Satoshi's identity is ever revealed or not, their contribution to the world of cryptocurrencies and the collective imagination will forever be etched in history.

So,

In the pages of this book, we have embarked on a fascinating journey through the world of Bitcoin and the enduring mystery of Satoshi Nakamoto. From the origins of Satoshi's vision to the evolution of Bitcoin's technology, we have unraveled the intricacies and explored the impact of this groundbreaking digital currency.

Throughout our exploration, we have witnessed the birth of Bitcoin and the enigma surrounding Satoshi Nakamoto's identity. We have examined the various theories and speculations, from prominent figures to collective efforts, but the true identity remains shrouded in mystery. And perhaps, that mystery is part of the enduring allure of Bitcoin and its creator.

Satoshi Nakamoto's legacy extends far beyond their anonymity. Their intellectual contributions, economic philosophy, and technical prowess have left an indelible mark on the world of cryptocurrencies and blockchain technology. Satoshi's vision of decentralization, financial empowerment, and trustless transactions has inspired countless individuals and fueled the growth of a vibrant and evolving ecosystem.

Bitcoin's impact on society cannot be overstated. It has sparked global conversations about the future of money, the potential of decentralized technologies, and the power of innovation. The decentralized nature of Bitcoin challenges traditional financial institutions and provides individuals with new avenues for financial sovereignty and inclusion. It has opened doors to alternative financial systems and inspired the exploration of blockchain applications in various industries.

The enduring mystery surrounding Satoshi Nakamoto has turned them into a cultural icon, symbolizing resistance against centralized power and traditional financial structures. Their creation of Bitcoin has captured the collective imagination, leading to a global movement for financial autonomy and a quest to challenge the status quo.

As we conclude our journey, we are left with a profound appreciation for the impact of Bitcoin and the enigmatic presence of Satoshi Nakamoto. While the quest to unveil Satoshi's true identity may continue, their contributions and influence on the world of cryptocurrencies will forever be etched in history.

Bitcoin Unveiled has provided us with a glimpse into the technological marvel that is Bitcoin and the human fascination that surrounds it. From its early days to the present, Bitcoin has demonstrated its resilience, adaptability, and potential to reshape our financial systems. Satoshi Nakamoto's creation has inspired a new wave of innovation, fueled by the principles of decentralization, transparency, and trustlessness.

As we venture forth into the future, let us carry with us the lessons learned from Bitcoin and the mystery of Satoshi Nakamoto. Let us embrace the potential of decentralized technologies to empower individuals, promote financial inclusion, and challenge existing power structures. And let us never forget the transformative power of an idea and the enduring legacy of Satoshi Nakamoto.

In the realm of Bitcoin and beyond, the journey continues. New chapters are being written, and the impact of Satoshi Nakamoto's creation continues to unfold. We invite you to be part of this ongoing story, to embrace the possibilities, and to contribute to the shaping of a future where financial systems are transparent, inclusive, and built on the principles of decentralization.

Thank you for joining us on this captivating journey through the world of Bitcoin Unveiled. May it inspire you to explore, question, and reimagine the possibilities that lie ahead.

Type This URL in Your Browser → ***https://bit.ly/Guess_What_This***

Thanks *for going through all of the book chapters until the end! Your review is **Valuable** to us as publishers.*

Please consider leaving your honest feedback on this book and help others benefit from it.

Made with the help of: chat.openai.com

www.ingramcontent.com/pod-product-compliance
Lightning Source LLC
Chambersburg PA
CBHW052140220526
45471CB00004B/1461